This book may be kept

A fine   charged
for

THE CLOSED SHOP IN BRITAIN

THE CLOSED SHOP

IN BRITAIN

By

W. E. J. McCARTHY

UNIVERSITY OF CALIFORNIA PRESS

BERKELEY AND LOS ANGELES

1964

PRINTED IN GREAT BRITAIN

In Memoriam

E. M.

PREFACE

IT is a pleasure to be able to thank some of those who have made it possible for me to write this book. It is based on my doctorial thesis and my first debt is to my supervisors: Allan Flanders, Senior Lecturer in Industrial Relations in Oxford University, who was my university supervisor, and Hugh Clegg, Official Fellow of Nuffield College, who was my college supervisor. They have given me every possible assistance, and have peppered each successive draft with invaluable criticism and advice.

I should also like to thank my examiners, K. G. J. C. Knowles, of the Oxford Institute of Statistics, and Cyril Grunfeld, of the London School of Economics, who performed similar services with the final version of the thesis. Mr. Grunfeld also read a separate draft of the legal chapters. Professor Kahn-Freund, also of the London School of Economics, read the first draft of the second part of the study, and I am grateful to him for a penetrating analysis of the gaps in my knowledge of the law which prevented me from perpetuating many errors. Mr. K. W. Wedderburn, of Clare College, Cambridge, corrected any legal errors that had crept into the final draft of this book, and made numerous useful suggestions. I should like to thank him especially for his help in understanding the significance of Rookes v. Barnard—a case which came at a most unfortunate time, for me at least. I must also thank my colleague, Mr. Alan Fox, for reading an early draft, and making valuable comments and suggestions. Mrs. Lynn Yates typed all the many drafts with great accuracy and patience.

Unfortunately, it is not possible to name all those who gave so freely of their time and knowledge on both sides of industry, and enabled me to gather the information on which this study depends. In the course of more than three years' field work I contacted over three hundred representatives of trade unions and employers, many of whom stressed that they preferred to remain anonymous. At conferences and schools I have spoken on the subject of the closed shop to many more. I am always surprised at the willingness of busy people to spend time and trouble answering academic inquiries, frankly and confidentially. I can only hope that those who disagree with my conclusions will not feel that I have failed to appreciate how it looks from their point of view.

Fortunately, there are three exceptions which I feel I can and must make to this rule of anonymity. Firstly, I should like to thank the Executive Council and Officers of the Amalgamated Society of Woodworkers, for agreeing to distribute a questionnaire to their branches, and for the assistance of their Research Officer, Mr. Tom Connolly, in interpreting the replies, and helping me in my inquiries generally. Secondly, I should like to thank the Executive Council and Officers of the Amalgamated Engineering Union, for distributing a similar questionnaire, and for the assistance of their Research Officer, Mr. George Aitken. Thirdly, I am particularly grateful to Mr. A. I. Marsh, of the Oxford Extra-Mural Delegacy, whose unique knowledge of the engineering industry has always been at my disposal. He was kind enough to let me benefit from his own very considerable contacts on both sides of the industry, and he assisted in the circulation of a questionnaire to a representative cross-section of firms.

I should also like to thank Dr. R.W. Rideout, of London University, for allowing me to read his Ph.D. thesis, 'The Right to Membership of Trade Unions', and Mr. F. P. Graham, for access to his thesis, 'A Legal Analysis of Trade Union Discipline', presented for the Diploma in Law at Oxford University. I found both works of considerable use to a layman trying to fight his way through to an understanding of trade union law. I am also indebted to the Warden and Fellows of Nuffield College, for electing me first to a studentship, and then to a Research Fellowship, and to the Leverhulme Trustees, since the latter stages of this study were financed out of a grant from the Trust to Nuffield College for research in industrial relations.

Finally, I thank my wife for unfailing encouragement, innumerable improvements and a unique knowledge of my shortcomings. All fallacies, errors and omissions are my fault.

W. E. J. McCarthy

Nuffield College

CONTENTS

PART ONE

DESCRIPTION AND FUNCTIONS

CHAP.   PAGE

1. THE NATURE OF THE CLOSED SHOP . . . 3
   (1) The Factual Vacuum 3
   (2) Objections to the term 'The Closed Shop' . . 7
   (3) Variations Within the Practice . . . 16
       (a) Variations in Form 16
       (b) Variations in Enforcement . . . 20
       (c) Variations in Scope 22
       (d) Minor Variations 23
   (4) The Semi-Closed Shop 24

2. THE CLOSED SHOP PATTERN 27
   (1) Sources of Information 27
   (2) The Extent of the Practice . . . 28
       (a) Comprehensively Closed Trades . . . 30
       (b) Mainly Closed Trades 30
       (c) Mainly Open Trades 30
       (d) Comprehensively Open Trades . . . 30
   (3) Variations in Form 37
       (a) The Labour Supply Shop . . . 38
       (b) The Labour Pool Shop 42
       (c) The Craft Qualification Shop . . . 45
       (d) The Promotion Veto Shop . . . 49
       (e) Post-Entry Shops 52
   (4) Variations in Enforcement . . . 52
       (a) Coal Miners 53
       (b) Dockers 55
       (c) Scottish Bakers 56
       (d) London Transport Workers . . . 56
       (e) Entertainment Workers . . . 57
       (f) Co-operative Workers . . . 58
       (g) The Limits of Informal Recognition . . 62
       (h) Closed Shop Strikes 64

CHAP.   PAGE

(5) Variations in Scope 67
   (a) Craftsmen 67
   (b) Non-Craftsmen 68
   (c) Regional Variations 72
(6) Minor Variations 74
(7) Analogous Practices in the Professions . . 75
(8) General Summary 78

3. SOME EXPLANATIONS FOR THE CLOSED SHOP . . 80
(1) The Demand for Trade Union Solidarity . . 81
(2) The Effect of the Closed Shop on Solidarity . . 84
(3) The Employers' Role 88
(4) The Questions to be Answered . . . 93

4. THE FUNCTIONS OF THE CLOSED SHOP . . . 95
(1) Job Regulation and Union Sanction . . . 95
(2) The Functions of the Closed Shop . . . 97
   (a) The Membership Function . . . 97
   (b) The Discipline Function 99
   (c) The Entry Control Function . . . 105

5. FACTORS AFFECTING DEMANDS FOR THE CLOSED SHOP . 107
(1) Problems of Organizing the Labour Force . . 107
   (a) Problems of Turnover and Contact . . 108
   (b) The Problem of Inter-Union Competition . 110
   (c) The Problem of Worker Indifference . . 111
(2) Problems of Controlling the Labour Force . . 111
   (a) The Problem of Enforcing Unilateral Regulations 111
   (b) The Problem of Strike Solidarity. . . 114
   (c) The Example of Coal Mining . . . 115
   (d) The Example of Car Manufacture . . 119
   (e) The Problem of Strike Control . . . 122
   (f) The Example of Iron and Steel . . . 122
(3) Problems of Organizing or Controlling the Alternative
   Labour Force 125
   (a) Unskilled Groups 126
   (b) Skilled Groups 134
   (c) The Examples of Printing and Shipbuilding . 136
   (d) Exclusiveness versus Comprehensiveness . . 141

CHAP.   PAGE

(4) The Influence of Group Morality and the Closed Shop Tradition 143

(5) The Attitude of Unions and their Officials to the Closed Shop 145

(6) The Argument So Far 146

6. AN EXPLANATION OF THE CLOSED SHOP PATTERN . . 148

(1) Limitations on Union Power . . . 148

(2) Groups where the Closed Shop is Prevalent . . 149

   (a) Craftsmen 150

   (b) Lesser Skilled Pre-entry Groups . . . 150

   (c) The Post-Entry Trades 152

   (d) Process Workers in Iron and Steel . . 157

   (e) Entertainment Workers 158

   (f) Employer-Initiated Closed Shops . . . 159

(3) The Relative Importance of the Closed Shop in Different Trades 160

(4) Well-Organized Groups in which the Closed Shop is not Prevalent 161

(5) Summary 175

PART TWO

JUSTIFICATION

7. THE ISSUES INVOLVED 179

(1) Introductory 179

(2) The Common Obligation Argument . . 179

8. THE RIGHT TO EXCLUDE NON-MEMBERS FROM THE JOB . 185

(1) The Removal of Criminal Liability . . . 185

   (a) Legal Justifiability 185

   (b) The Royal Commission of 1867 . . . 186

   (c) The Reforms Proposed by the Majority Report . 187

   (d) The Argument of the Minority Report . . 189

   (e) Voluntary versus Non-Voluntary Trade Union Regulation: the terms of the closed shop debate . 192

   (f) The Results of the Royal Commission . . 198

CHAP.   PAGE
    (2) The Removal of Civil Liability   .   .   . 199
        (a) The Period before 1906 200
        (b) The 1906 Act and After 207
    (3) The Present Position and its Rationale   .   . 214
        (a) The Limits of Existing Immunity   .   . 214
        (b) The Rationale of the Present Position .   . 216

 9. THE RIGHT TO EXCLUDE EX-MEMBERS FROM THE JOB   . 223
    (1) The Authorization Principle 223
    (2) Natural Justice   226

10. CONTEMPORARY CRITICISM   231
    (1) Suggestions for a Restrictive Practices Court for
        Labour   231
        (a) The Existing Court   231
        (b) Objections to the Proposal   .   .   . 236
    (2) Suggestions for Circumscribing the Right to Reject
        Applicants 241
    (3) Suggestions for Extending the Basis of Legal Control
        over Expulsion Rules   245
        (a) Common Law Jurisdiction   .   .   . 245
        (b) Statutory Control   252

11. CONCLUSIONS AND SUGGESTIONS 256
    (1) The Continued Justifiability of the Closed Shop . 256
    (2) Proposals for Reform   262
        (a) Restrictions on the Right to Exclude Non-Members 262
        (b) Restrictions on the Right to Exclude Ex-Members 267
        (c) Possible Restrictions on the Right to Exclude
            Existing Members   275
    (3) Conclusions 279

APPENDIX   282

TABLE OF STATUTES AND CASES CITED .   . 287

INDEX   289

PART ONE
DESCRIPTION AND FUNCTION

. . . they brought in a chap, a clockmaker, and he had no union card, and also he was not a young man. You do find some young fellows who have been in a non-union shop but who have got a good background and you could get round them; but a man getting on for forty or fifty, if he has not come into the union and yet claims he is a tradesman it is a bit tricky.

The shop steward in charge at the time went over and I think they saw the local supervision; they also saw Mr. Langston, of Personnel for the whole plant. I think they put the facts; but nothing was done, and we knew that nothing would be done until the shop stopped work.

The shop did stop; and I think we stood there for about four hours. I remember this man was particularly brave. He stood there for all those hours and watched us all losing pay. It was a shocking 240 minutes, but all the time he just stood there.

MR. J. J. McLOUGHLIN *giving evidence to the Court of Inquiry into the dispute at Briggs Motor Bodies, April 1957.*

Chapter i

THE NATURE OF THE CLOSED SHOP

THIS book is concerned with the nature, extent, functions, effects and justification of the 'closed shop'—defined as a situation in which employees come to realize that a particular job is only to be obtained and retained if they become and remain members of one of a specified number of trade unions.[1]

(1) The Factual Vacuum

It is difficult to account for the lack of any serious and sustained consideration of the closed shop among students of industrial relations. The topic usually attracts the attention of leader-writers whenever a strike to exclude non-unionists is in the news, and almost everybody appears to have opinions about it. This was borne out by the results of a recent Gallup Poll. A representative cross-section of the population were asked:

if the majority of workers in a trade or works are union members, and find that the existence of a minority of non-members weakens the Union in wage and other negotiations, do you think the Union members are or are not justified in putting pressure on the non-members to join the Union by refusing to work with them?[2]

Thirty-three per cent of the sample thought they were justified; 53 per cent thought they were not; only 12 per cent said they didn't know. When members of the working population were subdivided into trade unionists and non-unionists the proportions in favour and against were less equally divided. Seventy per cent of the trade unionists approved, whereas 68 per cent of the non-unionists disapproved. The only substantial number of 'don't knows' were the 'wives of members'. Thirty-six per cent of them thought the action described was justified; 42 per cent said it was not, and 22 per cent answered 'don't know'.[3]

[1] The study is mainly concerned with trade union closed shops, but analogous practices in so-called 'professional associations' are discussed.
[2] *Gallup Poll on the Trade Unions*, 1959, p. 7.
[3] The complete results of the inquiry may be tabulated thus:

WORKING POPULATION

	Total	Trade Union Member	Non-Member	Wives of Members	Others
Are Justified	33	70	23	36	20
Are not Justified	55	23	68	42	61
Don't know	12	7	9	22	19

The difficulty is that the great majority of those who answered this question decided their attitude towards the closed shop in an almost complete factual vacuum. There is, for example, no history of the closed shop. More important still, perhaps, there has been no attempt to study why unions come to demand it, or the effects which it has on individuals in particular and industry in general.

One possible reason for this neglect may have been the conviction that the practice was rapidly dying out—or was of importance in only a few trades. This was the opinion of those who signed the minority report of the Royal Commission on Trade Unions of 1867, and ten years later, one of the trade union witnesses to the Commission, George Howell, appeared to subscribe to it when he wrote:

The common sense of the majority of unionists will soon consign a policy of this kind to the limbo of the past, as it has done in the case of opposition to machinery and many other matters.[1]

However, Howell made no attempt to support this statement and merely remarked, in passing, that 'the practice cannot be defended either on social or political grounds'.[2]

In 1905 another writer on the subject, Geoffrey Drage, expressed slightly less categorical views. Admitting that the closed shop had not disappeared, although most responsible trade union leaders claimed that they 'condemned' all acts of 'violence and intimidation' directed at non-unionists, Drage suggested that 'in recent years there has been some revival of this conduct in connection with the organization of unskilled labour'.[3]

A much more recent and uncompromising opponent of the practice was Dr. Barou. In his book *British Trade Unions*, published in 1947, he wrote:

The 'closed-shop' policy is a child of the most violent period of industrial conflict at times and in countries where capitalists used blacklegs and armed forces for strike-breaking and the workers refused to play their part in the unions' struggle for justice, by joining unions. But that policy contradicts the main principles of modern trade unionism, which claims that the union is a voluntary organization, and objects to its members being forced into membership, either by legal prescription or by brute force. . . .

It is evident that in a democratic State, where the freedom of the individual and his association are protected by law, where the use of brute force in industrial

---

[1] *The Conflicts of Capital and Labour Historically Considered*, Chatto and Windus, 1878. p. 366.
[2] *Ibid.*
[3] *Trade Unions*, Methuen, 1905, p. 10.

conflicts is a punishable offence, and where a highly developed practice of conciliation and arbitration exists, there is not much need, and little justification, for the
unions employing a 'closed-shop' policy.[1]

Similar arguments were used by V. L. Allen in his *Power in Trade
Unions*, published in 1954. Allen suggested that the closed shop
affected only a comparatively small number of trade union members
and considered it essential that this situation should remain. Trade
unions, he wrote, must act 'in an atmosphere of freedom'. A trade
union 'can regulate but it must not coerce, and if it is unable to
retain its members by inducements, by satisfying their wants, then
it is not entitled to have members'. He concluded, 'For the sake of
their own freedom of action and in the interests of democracy trade
unions must, therefore, be voluntary societies'.[2]

Yet although Allen suggested a number of possible reasons for its
growth, neither he nor Barou provided any systematic analysis of
its functions and effects.[3]

But if it is plausible to assume that those who regarded the closed
shop as a vanishing minor menace did not need to study it in any
detail, what reason can be given for its almost total neglect by those
writers who believed that it was both inevitable and desirable?
G. D. H. Cole, for example, set out his own uncompromising but
unsubstantiated views in his first major work on industrial relations,
The World of Labour, published in 1913. He wrote:

. . . the definite assertion of the refusal to work with non-unionists throughout
even one industry would be a tremendous step in advance and could not fail to
have an immense effect on the Trade Union movement as a whole. For every
step the Unions take towards becoming compulsory corporations, preserving free
entry, but allowing no non-unionists in their industries, takes them a long way
towards attaining the competence necessary for a far higher control over industry
as a whole. . . . The delegation of control by the State is the only possible solution;
and instead of lamenting the loss of the 'free labourer' more accurately known to
the populace as the 'blackleg' or 'scab' those who desire real progress should be
concerned in destroying him root and branch.[4]

It seems clear from this passage that Cole was mainly interested in
the closed shop because he saw it as a step toward Guild Socialism.
This is made even more apparent in the book's final chapter, significantly entitled 'The Future of Trade Unions'.

[1] *British Trade Unions*, Gollancz, 1947, p. 95.
[2] Longmans Green, 1954, p. 61.
[3] Moreover, much of what Allen wrote about the closed shop is open to question—see
below.
[4] Bell and Sons, 1913, p. 55.

B

There are the first beginnings, in Trade Unionism to-day, of an attempt not merely to raise the standard of life or to 'better' conditions, but to change the industrial system, and substitute democracy for autocracy in the workshop.

As we have seen already, the first and most obvious sign of this awakening is the rising demand that membership of the Unions shall be compulsory on all workers . . . more and more strikes every year are turning on this point . . . in the Coal Mines and on the Railways, in the Textile industry of Lancashire and even among Transport Workers in some ports the non-unionist is doomed to extinction. The demand may not be granted generally at once; but it is clear from the recent tendency that in the end it will be granted.[1]

Once again, no attempt was made to substantiate such a claim, or to study the working of the practice itself. Eight years later another student of industrial relations, Henry Slessor, echoed Cole's prophesy in an equally sweeping form. He wrote:

The increase of trade unionism, particularly since the war, has been so enormous that it is very probable that, in a short time, practically the whole of the working class will be absorbed into their respective unions and the position of the person who does not wish to join a trade union will be an impossible one.[2]

By 1934 it was no longer feasible to maintain such an extreme view and Milne-Bailey, in *Trade Unions and the State*, admitted that the closed shop was still the exception rather than the rule. Nevertheless he went on to assert that 'over a considerable area there is in fact discrimination against non-unionists', and added, 'Where the habit of organization has become settled and accepted this is bound to be the case'.[3]

Twenty years later even Cole had become less optimistic. In his *Introduction to Trade Unionism*, published in 1953, he admitted that the practice was 'a long way off being general'. More significantly, he no longer appeared to condemn this situation unreservedly. For he continued:

Unions could not keep going on compulsory members; they require a large nucleus of willing volunteers to keep their organization alive and in good condition. A trade union that loses this driving force is in danger of withering away; and employers know they need pay no attention to it.[4]

These might be the words of Allen or Barou. Yet although Cole changed his mind about both the inevitability and advisability of the

---

[1] *Op. cit.*, p. 371. Cole's attitude towards the non-unionist blackleg can be measured by the following, which appears a few pages further on: 'It is not as a rule wise to offer physical violence to "blacklegs"; but there is nothing wrong about it, except in the eyes of the law and the middle class.' (*Op. cit.*, p. 377.)

[2] *Trade Unionism*, Methuen, 1921, p. 119.

[3] Allen and Unwin, 1934, p. 117.

[4] Allen and Unwin, p. 75.

closed shop, he still failed to provide a detailed defence of his position. Like Milne-Bailey and Slessor he contented himself with announcing his beliefs. Moreover, although most recent books on British trade unions have contained references to some of the issues involved,[1] the factual vacuum remains unfilled.

One of the objects of this book is to provide these facts. To do this it is necessary to answer four separate but related questions: (a) What is the nature of the closed shop, what forms does it take and how does the situation facing union members in a closed shop differ from that facing those in other areas? (b) How widespread is the practice; what industries and operations does it cover, and what proportions of union membership does it affect? (c) What functions does it perform and what are its effects? (d) Can it be justified and what are the arguments used for and against it? This chapter is concerned to elaborate and defend the definition of the closed shop set out above, and to define a number of terms which are needed to measure and analyse the practice in subsequent chapters.

(2) OBJECTIONS TO THE TERM 'THE CLOSED SHOP'

The tendency in recent writing has been to drop the allegedly controversial and misleading phrase 'the closed shop' in favour of the apparently more objective and precise term, 'compulsory trade unionism'. But this academic term is, in fact, as controversial as the one it replaces, and is liable to encourage far more serious misconceptions.

For example, V. L. Allen argues that:

The term 'closed shop' has been used so loosely and indiscriminately by writers, politicians and trade unionists alike in Britain in particular, that it is difficult to make precise definitions without being controversial. Under a general heading of Compulsory Trade Unionism my points would not be disputed.[2]

Interviews conducted in connection with this study suggest otherwise. No description of the imposition of trade union membership as a condition of work annoys trade unionists so much as the label 'compulsory trade unionism'. They invariably reply, with some force, that the description is far too analogous to compulsory military service. Unions, they assert, do not compel men to join them in the strict sense of providing no legal alternative. As one shop steward said, 'A man who does not want to join can always go and work

[1] Notably B. C. Roberts in *Trade Union Government and Administration in Great Britain*, Bell, 1956, pp. 37–55.
[2] *Op. cit.*, p. 56.

somewhere else.' There is, of course, an element of disingenuous-
ness in this argument, and the more widespread the closed shop area
the more illusory is the freedom claimed. Yet even in the case of a
trade or occupation entirely covered by closed shops there remains
a sense in which it is perhaps misleading to refer to this in terms
which suggest an analogy with compulsory duties to the state. It is
not merely that one form of pressure is backed by law and the other
is not; but that pressure to join the union, however strong, is always
to *some* extent contingent upon the individual's prior decision to
follow a particular occupation. Thus the union's pressure only
becomes compulsive *after* an act of choice on the part of the individual.[1] But the indignation of trade unionists could be set aside if
the phrase 'compulsory trade unionism' were not open to more
serious objections.

As the Webbs pointed out in their *Industrial Democracy*, unions
seek to impose 'minimum conditions of employment by Common
Rules'—and this necessarily involves a measure of compulsion. It
is a fundamental objective of unions that their regulations should be
binding on all workers, whether they are in the union or not. No
employer is allowed to pay less than the union rate to any worker—
if the union can help it. If the union opposes the introduction of
piecework it intends to prevent *any* worker being in a position to
accept it. But, as the Webbs also stressed,

it is impossible to make common arrangements for numbers of men without
running counter to the desires of some of them. The wider the range of the
Common Rule, and the more perfect the machinery for its application and enforcement, the larger may be the minority which finds itself driven to accept conditions
which it has not desired.[2]

Yet this is not all. When unions strike, their objective is to
prevent anybody from working, and the strike itself is essentially a
weapon of compulsion directed, if necessary, at employer, non-
unionist and the public. In other words, it is more plausible to
argue that all unionism is in some sense compulsory rather than to
appear to suggest that there is a narrow sphere of compulsion or
coercion confined to the area of enforced union membership.

But even this objection is not the most important. It is not merely
that the phrase 'compulsory trade unionism' blurs the distinction

---

[1] This objection loses some of its validity in countries like New Zealand, where the great
majority of manual and clerical workers are forced, *by law*, to belong to trade unions. In
industrial relations generally it is common to refer to the sanctions of the state as 'compulsory'.
In this country there are no areas in which union membership is upheld by legal sanction.

[2] Beatrice and Sydney Webb, Longmans Green, 1897, p. 207.

between compulsion exercised after some act of choice and compulsion without this feature; it is not simply that it seems to imply an absence of any compulsion outside the area of enforced union membership; it is that even within the sphere of union membership it encourages misconceptions about the nature of the closed shop. As subsequent chapters will demonstrate, and as the overwhelming number of trade unionists interviewed freely admit, strong pressures of various sorts are habitually employed to recruit and retain union members without (in the words of the definition set out above) *employees being made to realize that a particular job is only to be obtained or retained if he or she becomes and remains a member of one of a specified number of trade unions*. The extent and nature of these pressures are made apparent as this study proceeds, but the open acceptance, among trade unionists, of the existence and need for them constitutes an overwhelming argument against attempts to describe British trade unions as 'voluntary' bodies, who from time to time depart from their true nature and engage in 'compulsory trade unionism'.

Indeed, more confusion than enlightenment results from attempts to subsume the activities of unions under one or another of these unsatisfactory labels. Unions are neither compulsory associations— like the state—nor voluntary bodies—in the sense in which a tennis club is a voluntary body. Like tennis clubs they provide certain benefits or 'rewards' which are only available to members; but they also aim to accumulate industrial power, to be able to match the power of employers. This means that they require a whole range of sanctions, used, if need be, against both employers and workers. The closed shop merely furnishes them with one of the most penal of these sanctions.

In later chapters, the way in which this is done will be analysed in detail; at the moment all that need be said is that there is often no sharp line between the sanctions employed which justified the use of the labels 'voluntary' and 'compulsory'. Certainly it is misleading to isolate the enforcement of union membership as a condition of employment and single it out for the label 'compulsory'. The 'less controversial' phrase turns out to be even more resented and challenged, and still more ambiguous than the term in everyday use; for these reasons it will not be used again.

But rejection of the phrase does not involve acceptance of the term 'closed shop' in the broad sense in which it has been defined for the purposes of this study. Indeed, many trade unionists would object to the phrase being used in such a way that it covered *any* situation in which union membership is imposed as a condition of employment. The closed shop, they often assert, is what *others* do, and they define it narrowly enough to exclude their own practices.

Those who impose union membership *after* workers have been engaged insist that the term ought to be confined to situations where union membership is a *pre-condition* of engagement. Those who operate this latter kind of closed shop, but do not insist that all labour is supplied through the union office, assert that the phrase should be restricted to situations where this condition is met. Those who behave in this way maintain that they do not operate a closed shop because there is no formal agreement with management which stipulates that workers can only be engaged through the union. In these and other ways trade unionists often deny that they operate a closed shop; what they have, they suggest, is an 'all ticket job', or an 'all union house', or, most common of all, '100 per cent trade unionism'.

It is difficult to believe that this reluctance to admit to a closed shop is rooted in any deeply felt and generally held distinction between the ways in which union membership becomes and remains a condition of work. In practice one finds that a trade unionist's readiness to use the phrase depends not on what is done, but on the view that he takes of the company he is in. In the writer's experience they invariably use the phrase to describe *any* situation where union membership is a condition of employment, so long as they are talking among themselves, or in front of an observer whom they have more or less accepted.[1]

This does not mean that the distinctions within this area, some of which have been mentioned, are not significant or important.

It makes a difference, for example, whether the closed shop is upheld by means of a collective agreement or imposed by means of a strike. The point at which it begins to operate is important too, and when the practice is used to ensure that labour is supplied through the union it takes on additional functions and works in a different way. These distinctions and differences will be explored and explained, and reasons given as to why, in a particular instance,

---

[1] Even those who think the observer is a hostile outsider usually slip into the vocabulary of the closed shop as an interview proceeds. After stressing that what they have is an 'all ticket job', for example, they go on to explain 'how we closed that job'. What unionists seek to do when they act in this way is to introduce a little rudimentary public relations, realizing the phrase is unpopular with non-unionists, they try to avoid tying an unpopular label on their own activities.

the closed shop takes a certain form. Nevertheless, it will also be suggested that the features common to all situations in which trade union membership is an effective condition of employment are important too. Indeed, it will be argued that the closed shop, in whatever form, provides unions with a number of additional sanctions, which assist them in a number of ways. These will be termed the *functions of the closed shop*. The importance of these functions makes it plausible to argue that the really significant distinction is that between the closed and non-closed shop areas of industry, as defined in this study.

There is one final objection to the term which must be discussed before the various forms it takes can be considered in more detail. In 1946 the General Council of the T.U.C. raised an objection to the term being used to describe British trade union practice, which focused neither on the varied *methods* used to enforce union membership, nor on the *point* at which it was imposed. Their objection was that the term implied, quite wrongly, that unions in Britain were accorded exclusive recruitment rights.

They wrote:

The General Council . . . draw a clear distinction between the 100 per cent shop and the 'Closed Shop', as trade unionists generally understand the term. The 'Closed Shop', in the sense of an establishment in which only members of a particular union can be employed, to the exclusion of members of other unions, is alien to British trade union practice and theory.[1]

In the General Council's view the phrase '100 per cent shop' did not 'imply a claim on the part of any particular union to exclusive rights of organization where *bona fide* unions are concerned'. It is difficult to see why it should be assumed that the closed shop *necessarily* implies such a claim, any more than the phrase '100 per cent trade unionism', but the more important point raised by this objection is how far it is true that in fact British unions do not claim such rights.

In their statement the T.U.C. gave some indication of the types of organization whose *bona fides* were suspect. These included 'breakaway unions and other dissident bodies of small influence which could not secure affiliation to Congress', and unions which tried to invade 'the field already occupied by a single National Union'. For despite their remarks about 'exclusive jurisdiction' being an alien concept the Council were forced to admit, on the next page, that:

In the historical development of the British Trade Union Movement where a single National Union has evolved by such processes of amalgamation, exclusive

[1] *T.U.C. Annual Report*, 1946, p. 255.

jurisdiction pertains in these circumstances to that union and is not contested by other affiliated unions, or by Congress.[1]

More important still (if their distinction was supposed to be based upon the presence or absence of effective competition between unions), they went on to deny the existence of any general right to choose one's union. Quoting their own Interim Report on Structure and Closer Unity, they wrote:

... we are striving to secure stability of trade union membership, co-ordination of effort and the abolition of unnecessary competition. A handful of disgruntled members, having fully exploited the services of their union, may feel that member-ship of another union would suit them better. That feeling may be justified or otherwise, but the complete recognition of the right of members to move from union to union may destroy stability of organization, undermine loyalty and lead to an undesirable extension of the number of unions concerned in negotiations with a single employer. Any union facilitating this chopping and changing would probably find that in their turn they would experience the same difficulties as the original union ... if there were complete freedom to remain outside the union, or even to move at will from one union to another, we should have a Trade Union Movement whose authority was completely undermined.[2]

Reading this it seems difficult to see what was so crucial about the distinction upon which the General Council placed such emphasis. On their own admission exclusive jurisdiction is not unknown, and even where it has not developed no general right of choice can be assumed.

How far, in fact, the right to transfer has been removed can be gauged by Shirley Lerner's account of the General Council's own jurisdiction procedure.[3] Mrs. Lerner shows how the Disputes Com-mittee of the T.U.C. progressively narrowed the circumstances in which they would grant the right to transfer from one union to another. In the years before 1927 individual, spontaneous or 'volun-tary transfers' were allowed, so long as they did not offend against what were termed 'good union practices'. Between 1927 and 1929, however, extensive discussions aimed at eliminating so-called waste-ful competition were reinforced by a number of mergers and a more uncompromising attitude towards breakaway organizations. The effect of this was that,

In such a climate, the principle of freedom of choice tended to diminish in impor-tance as compared with the development of friendly and orderly relations between unions.

[1] Op. cit., p. 256.   [2] Op. cit., p. 257.
[3] The T.U.C. Jurisdictional Dispute Settlement, 1924–1957, the Manchester School of Eco-nomic and Social Studies, September 1958, p. 222.

The effect of all these influences was to blur the distinction between induced and spontaneous transfers . . . the Disputes Committee's attention became directed towards whether a union had behaved 'properly' and away from the right of workers to choose their union. Consequently, the concept of 'poaching' was extended to include a wide range of 'improper' union behaviour.[1]

This development found expression in Clause (v) of the 1939 Bridlington resolution which denied unions the right to take in members in 'any establishment or undertaking in respect of any grades or grades of workers in which another union has the majority of workers employed and negotiates wages and conditions unless by arrangement with that union'. In 1946 this was interpreted to forbid taking in ex-members of a majority union which no longer had a majority of workers enrolled as a result of spontaneous resignations; the Disputes Committee commenting that

A literal interpretation of the single word 'majority' is, in the circumstances of the present case, contrary to all established Trade Union practices, customs and relationships.[2]

Whether recruitment by another union would be allowed if all the workers concerned resigned from the union with negotiating rights, and how long ex-unionists have to remain non-unionists before another union can recruit them, is not clear. It seems impossible, however, not to agree with Mrs. Lerner's general verdict that it is at least the intention of the Bridlington Agreement, as it has been interpreted, that

If Union 'A' holds negotiating rights in a given territory while Union 'B' does not, Union 'B' may not recruit workers in that territory if Union 'A' objects.[3]

She argues that this has severely restricted the individual's right to transfer. In effect the right has come to depend on the continual absence of five factors. There must be: (1) no dispute between the employee and his union; (2) no dispute between his union and his employer; (3) no inducement or persuasion to transfer; (4) a *bona fide* union catering for the grade and industry where he is employed prepared to take him into membership; (5) a clearance by the employee's original union in all cases in which at some time in the past it has secured negotiating rights and has at one time recruited a majority of members.

[1] *Op. cit.*, p. 229.   [2] *Op. cit.*, p. 231.   [3] *Op. cit.*, p. 231.

As Mrs. Lerner shows, the last provision has hardly ever been met, and if the union wanting to recruit the member took the original union to the Disputes Committee, then

The net result of the various changes in the T.U.C.'s principles for settling juris-dictional disputes, described above, has been that '*not a single post war award has permitted transfers*'.[1]

Yet even the jurisdictional awards of the T.U.C. do not reveal the full extent to which competition has been eliminated among *new entrants*, as against workers seeking a transfer. It has long been the case that no alternative union is normally available for so-called skilled workers,[2] but what is often not realized is how far competi-tion, on entry, has been eliminated among other groups; in mining, the merchant service, boots and shoes, and pottery, for example, the union is generally recognized by others to have exclusive recruit-ment rights throughout virtually the whole of the manual labour force. In textiles, live entertainment and the non-industrial civil service an entire industry or trade is divided up between a number of unions, each of which has an exclusive right to recruit in specific grades. In yet other cases, i.e. shipbuilding and engineering, although craft unions have monopoly rights in their section of the industry, there are a number of unions with recognized rights to recruit; but it cannot be assumed that even here there remains a right to choose between unions on entry to the job. Unions like the Transport and General Workers and the National Union of General and Municipal Workers have set up a standing joint committee for dealing with inter-union problems, and one of its main tasks is to supervise the dividing out of areas between the two unions. Similarly, the National Union of Vehicle Builders and the Transport and General Workers' Union have recently reached a similar understanding at national level, while at local and regional level gentlemen's agree-ments are quite common between the officials of those unions and those of the Amalgamated Engineering Union. The precise form taken by these agreements or understandings are, of course, exceed-ingly difficult to determine. But the impression gained from talking to union officials is that effective understandings are often reached to refrain from recruiting in certain factories or shops in which another union has a substantial membership, in exchange for similar con-

[1] *Op. cit.*, p. 234.
[2] Craft unions dispute about whether a particular job should be done by their members, but what they are trying to do is to extend their monopoly rights over new processes and grades of work. They would normally scout the idea of taking in workers accepted as being within the province of another union, and would denounce poaching.

cessions elsewhere.[1] In this way whole areas are 'horse traded' between unions and choice eliminated.

Understandings of this sort are not always watertight, and shop stewards may still be willing to take in another union's potential members, and even connive with recalcitrant members to effect a transfer. But it cannot be stressed too strongly that these are exceptions and not the consequence of any generally accepted right to choose between unions. Where choice still exists it is the result of one or another of three factors, which may disappear at any time. They are:

(1) the virtual non-existence of union organization covering a particular factory or job. In this case any worker who wants to start the job of organizing his workmates may be able to choose which union he joins—so long as he is not engaged on one of the jobs which are covered by only one union, as outlined above.

(2) the presence of a union, or members of a union, who are prepared to connive in getting round whatever pattern of agreements or understandings exist for eliminating competition.

(3) The absence of any such agreements, usually as a result of some personal inability to agree on 'spheres of influence'.

The opportunities remaining as a consequence of such factors cannot be regarded as rights. They are temporary privileges, revocable at any time that it suits the unions concerned. It is only if a fourth and extremely uncommon situation exists that we can speak of a 'right' to choose between unions. This is where two or more unions are recognized as having recruiting rights among a particular group, but are *permanently* unable to reach any agreement over areas of influence and are unwilling to allow the jurisdiction committee of the T.U.C. to decide between them.[2] As will be shown in Chapter 2, these areas are not usually covered by closed shop agreements. The great majority of those most closely affected by the closed shop have had little or no freedom of choice at all. For this reason it is impossible to take at its face value the claim of the General Council.

There is no meaningful distinction to be made between British practice and the practice of unions elsewhere, on the grounds of British unions failing to claim 'exclusive rights of organization'. British unions have been campaigning for exclusive rights for the

---

[1] In the Oxford area, for example, there is an understanding between the local officials of the T. & G.W.U. and the N.U.G.M.W. which limits the areas in which each union seeks to recruit workers employed by the British Motor Corporation.

[2] As in the case of the Railway unions.

last thirty years at least—and the General Council's disputes committee has done its best to assist the process. The more one looks
at the General Council's statement the more disingenuous it appears.
Its apparent plausibility lies in the largely irrelevant fact that British
unions have not developed along industry-wide lines. Because of
this there are usually several unions recruiting in any one industry or
factory. But there is rarely more than one union recruiting any
particular class of worker in any particular factory, and if the distinction made is to be of any significance it must surely be presumed to
refer to some degree of personal freedom or choice which the
individual worker enjoys within the so-called '100 per cent shop'.
It is this element which allegedly makes it unfair and misleading to
call it a *closed* shop. Since this is largely non-existent there seems no
reason why the term 'closed shop' should not be used—particularly
since this is the term in current usage among the public, the employer,
the worker, and even members of the General Council when they
are not engaged in public relations.

(3) VARIATIONS WITHIN THE PRACTICE

Having defined the closed shop in broad terms its many variations
must now be examined in more detail. An understanding of these
variations is essential if one is to analyse the extent of the practice
and explain why it has arisen where it has.

The most significant variations within the closed shop relate to
three issues: the *form* which it takes, the *manner* of its enforcement,
and the *scope* of its application.

(a) Variations in Form

The important distinction to be made here concerns whether or
not the individual worker has to join the union, or be accepted by
it, *before* he can be engaged by the employer. If this is necessary we
may speak of the existence of a *pre-entry* closed shop. If, on the other
hand, the employer is free to engage a non-unionist, so long as he
agrees to join the union immediately or shortly after engagement,
then the practice may be described as a *post-entry* closed shop.[1]
Insistence on union membership or acceptance *before* engagement is
always associated with the aim of using the closed shop to control,
or to restrict in some way, entry to the job in question.

[1] In some cases workers must join immediately they are engaged, in other circumstances
a week or so may elapse. The distinction between the pre-entry and post-entry shop employed here corresponds to the distinction made in the United States between the closed
shop and the union shop—the union shop, in this book, is termed the post-entry shop.

This may be done unilaterally, or in association with the employer, and need not necessarily imply a desire to restrict the total number of workers available for employment. It may merely be that unions wish to establish some sort of job preference for existing members. By insisting that workers must join the union before they can begin work the union forces the employer to employ only existing members of the union. Entry to the job is made contingent on entry to the union. By controlling, or restricting, entry to the union, entry to the job is regulated; this practice may be called *job entry control*.[1]

Unfortunately it is necessary to make a number of fairly complex distinctions between the way job entry control is affected within the pre-entry shop, and to mark these with special terms.

The main distinction relates to the degree of skill of the workers in question. If they are relatively unskilled, in order to be able to operate job entry control, the union usually tries to become the main or sole source of the labour supply. All workers may then be supplied through the union office or branch, although employers will reserve the right to object to particular men whom the union supplies, on certain grounds. Where the union becomes accepted as the sole or main source of the labour supply, we may speak of a *labour supply* closed shop. A well-known example of this occurs among newsprint workers in London, where labour must be engaged through the unions.[2]

Sometimes, however, it is not possible to secure control of the labour supply, and the union must accept a modified form of the labour supply shop. The crucial feature of this second kind of closed shop is that the employers, in co-operation with the union, agree to form a recognized pool of labour, confined to workers accepted by the unions. For this reason it may be termed a *labour pool* shop. The best known example occurs among workers employed by the National Dock Labour Board.[3]

---

[1] Job entry control can be enforced without the use of the closed shop. Any group can strike against the introduction of additional workers to an assembly line, or attempt to negotiate certain educational or training qualifications as a condition of employment. Any union can sign a redundancy agreement stipulating that those discharged will be given a preference in respect of re-engagements. These are all attempts at entry control, and can exist without the need for the closed shop. Thus the phrase *job entry control*, as used in this study, refers simply to the aim of workers to exert an influence over the supply of competitive labour for the jobs available to them. The use of the pre-entry shop is merely one effective way of securing this aim.

[2] See p. 38 below.

[3] See p. 42 below.

The main difference between the labour supply shop and the labour pool shop is that it is only in the case of the former that the union functions as a labour exchange. In the labour pool shop the worker is free to transfer from one job to another, without going through the union, once he has gained entry to the pool. So long as he confines his choice to members of the pool, the employer does not need to apply to the union for labour.

Yet the union may restrict the size of the pool, by restricting membership of the union and confining it to certain categories of labour—for example, those who are the relatives or friends of existing members, as is usually the case in the docks. Even where this is not possible they will still be able to object to particular individuals, refuse them admission to the union, and thus exclude them from the pool. Moreover, the principle will be established that first preference in allotting jobs shall be given to existing members. This is, in fact, the main object of forming the pool. Employers undertake to draw labour from the pool, and to recruit additional labour only when the pool is empty. They also agree that membership of specified unions shall be a condition of entry to the pool, and to the job.

Where workers are relatively skilled, entry control may be achieved without the need for the union to become either the source of the labour supply or the joint administrators of a pool. Where accredited apprenticeship is a necessary qualification for the job the union need only limit entry to the union to properly qualified apprentices and then seek to limit the number of apprentices trained. The union insists on a fixed proportion of apprentices to fully trained craftsmen and manages to get this ratio accepted by employers. Entry control is then effected in two ways. First, in respect of juvenile entry, an upper limit is fixed which restricts the number of craftsmen available. Since apprentice selection is often undertaken in association with the unions some kind of preference is often established for the sons or relations of existing union members.

In any case apprentices, at their selection, are asked if they will be willing to join the union during apprenticeship, and those who refuse are not chosen. Second, in respect of fully trained craftsmen, entry control is effected by means of the closed shop, imposed in its pre-entry form. Membership of the union, or the necessary section of the union, is denied those not serving a qualifying apprenticeship in a shop which observes the apprenticeship ratio, and only workers with the necessary union card are allowed to start work. We may say that there exists a pre-entry shop for craftsmen, and a post-entry shop for apprentices, but the former does not take the form of the labour supply or labour pool shop. While he restricts himself to properly qualified union men the individual employer will be under no obligation either to get his labour through the union or from a registered pool. Similarly, workers will be free to move from one employer to another, subject only to their individual contracts of employment. Because the workers involved are accepted as skilled, entry control in this form of closed shop can be enforced by confining entry to workers who fulfil certain craft qualifications—for this reason it will be referred to as the *craft qualification* shop. Perhaps the best known example of the craft qualification shop occurs among skilled groups in general printing works.[1]

But this form of closed shop may also be modified, and the type described above is best regarded as its most extreme form, to which particular closed shops approximate to varying extents. In some cases there is no fixed apprenticeship ratio, or one which is relaxed from time to time. In other instances there is no accredited system of apprenticeship. Craftsmen are recruited from semi-skilled workers in the same establishment. Yet by restricting membership of the union, and entry to the job, to particular semi-skilled workers, often those employed to assist the existing skilled members, the unions organizing craftsmen may still be able to exert a form of entry control. Once engaged on craftsmen's work, and permitted to join the union, these workers may be free to transfer to similar jobs elsewhere. For this reason, and because entry control is still enforced *via* a restriction on union entry based on certain training qualifications, a craft qualification shop may still be said to exist.

However, there are one or two cases where this element of transferability is absent. The workers concerned advance from unskilled to skilled status by means of a rigidly enforced system of promotion mainly based on seniority rules. Loss of position on the ladder of promotion usually involves starting somewhere else at the bottom of another ladder as a relatively unskilled worker. In short there is no *recognized* transferable skill or craft, and so no equivalent of the class of potentially mobile craftsmen who form the basis of a craft qualification shop. Yet, at varying points in the promotion ladder, there will be a pre-entry shop. In effect the union organizing workers at that level insists that entry to a particular job shall be contingent on the next senior man, at the time of promotion, being a member of the union. If he is not, then he will be passed over for

[1] See p. 45 below.

the next senior man who is. This form of closed shop will be termed the *promotion veto shop*. An example at its most developed occurs among iron and steel workers.[1]

The four types of pre-entry shop listed above represent the ways in which the closed shop is used to assist unions to restrict or control entry to the job. In the case of craftsmen this can be done by restricting union entry to those with certain training qualifications; in the case of non-craftsmen entry control cannot be effected in this way. It must be enforced either by getting the union accepted as the source of the labour supply, or by obtaining the right to nominate members of a preferential labour pool.

(b) Variations in the Manner of Enforcement

The crucial variation here relates to the role of the employer in imposing the closed shop. At one end of the scale is the closed shop which is the subject of a written collective agreement. In the case of a labour supply shop the employer may have agreed that all labour shall be recruited through the union, and any worker found to be in arrears, or expelled from the union, will be discharged. This is not to say that the union will have no role to play in ensuring the enforcement of the closed shop; it must ensure labour is available, and may have the job of notifying the employer of the existence of recalcitrants. It is also no guarantee that at some time in the past the employer did not resist this arrangement. Nevertheless, so long as there is a written agreement, and so long as the employer abides by his responsibilities under that agreement, we may speak of the existence of a *formally recognized* closed shop.

A less clearly defined situation exists where the employer has signed no formal agreement, but has, in practice, accepted the fact that his employees will have to be in a specified union, either before or after engagement. The extent of the employers' active participation in a closed shop of this sort varies very much. If the closed shop is of the post-entry sort management may nevertheless 'screen' workers when they apply for jobs, in order to see whether they would object to joining a union; those who raise objections will not be engaged. On other occasions no information will be given to new entrants, and there may even be some reluctance to discharge those who refuse to join, or have lapsed from the union. It may be necessary, sometimes, for the union concerned to threaten a stoppage of work before management will agree to warn recalcitrants that

---

[1] See p. 49 below.

they are faced with dismissal unless they become and remain members of the union. However, so long as the employer is willing to wield this final weapon for the union without the need for an actual strike we may say that there is an *informally recognized* closed shop in existence. Yet even if the employer is not prepared to play any role in enforcing the closed shop, and is actively trying to prevent it, it may still exist. It is possible for workers to impose the practice by means of unilateral action—i.e. by a refusal to work with those who are not members of the union. If this is habitually the case then we may speak of the *union enforced closed shop*.

Perhaps the most effective form of the *union enforced* closed shop is that in which workers refuse to sign on with those who are not already paid up members of the union; i.e. a pre-entry shop enforced at the point of hire. But it is possible to enforce a post-entry shop without assistance from the employer. This is because when notice is given that a strike will take place unless non-unionists or lapsed members make their peace with the union or leave the job, the strike is aimed at the coercion of the recalcitrant employees as much as the employer. In effect all closed shops are aimed, at least in part, at recalcitrant workers; they threaten to prevent men from working unless they become and remain members of specified trade unions. In the case of the unilaterally enforced post-entry shop this threat can only be made finally effective by means of a strike. When such a strike takes place the recalcitrants have three alternatives. They may make their peace with the union; they may leave the job to avoid trouble; they may decide to defy the union's threats. But if they choose this last alternative, and an effective strike takes place, they will be prevented from working in any case. Thus the union is using the strike weapon to force them to choose between making their peace and leaving the job. When this happens, and as a result of the strike the men concerned decide to do one thing or the other, we may say that the union has *unilaterally enforced* a closed shop. In practice it may be difficult to decide whether to regard particular closed shops as unilaterally or bilaterally enforced. Once management realizes workers can enforce the closed shop unilaterally they usually come to terms with it, but the degree to which they are prepared to co-operate will vary. Sometimes the most they will do is to react to an actual strike by agreeing to move a recalcitrant worker, sometimes they will only agree to do this if this does not involve discharging the man from their employ. Sometimes they will agree that all additional labour recruited must

c

join the union, but will not agree to take any action against existing employees. On other occasions they will be prepared to take any action required as soon as a strike threat is made. Sometimes, as soon as there is any chance that the non-unionist issue is likely to result in strikes, they will agree to negotiate a formal closed shop agreement.

Nevertheless, it is necessary to arrive at a working definition of the line between the recognized and unrecognized closed shop. It is surely not meaningful to speak of recognition unless management will take some action aimed at enforcement without the need for strike action to occur. The strike is the weapon of unilateral enforcement; if it is not necessary to use it, then management, in a very real sense, may be said to have recognized the right to the closed shop. In practice the result of such a move is to establish, at the very minimum, an informal understanding that the area in question should, in future, be regarded as closed to those who will not agree to become and remain union members. Some form of 'screening' almost invariably follows. It may still be necessary to threaten strike action to procure the necessary response from management— but this tends to become more and more a matter of procedure, and less and less an indication of an open struggle.

This is not to say that management co-operation is not dependent on an awareness that otherwise a strike would take place. Recognition of the closed shop, and its bilateral enforcement, is usually dependent, to some extent at least, on such an awareness. The threat of unilateral enforcement lies behind bilateral enforcement and co-operation. Most closed shop campaigns begin with attempts to impose the practice unilaterally, though most successful campaigns end with formal or informal recognition.

In a few cases, however, this process is reversed. It is management rather than workers who take the initiative, and it can even be argued that some managements have forced the closed shop on the bulk of their workers. These exceptional cases, and the reasons for them, are discussed further below.

(c) Variations in Scope

So far this chapter has considered differences in the point at which union membership is required, and variations in the way in which it is enforced. Both these variations relate to a given area in which the closed shop operates. What must now be discussed is how this area varies from one type of closed shop to another.

Sometimes the most that is involved in refusing to belong to a union is the loss of a particular job, in a particular place of employment; by agreeing to be moved to a similar job, within the same works or plant, the individual can evade the effects of the closed shop. Where an entire plant is affected there may be variations in the prevalence of the closed shop from one plant, or place of employment, to another, within the same town or region. Even where this is not the case, and the entire area is equally affected, it may be possible to avoid the closed shop—by moving to some other region. There are relatively few occupations comprehensively closed to the non-unionist throughout Great Britain. Certain regions are notably weak in union organization, and there the non-unionist may be able to follow a trade not open to him elsewhere. Conversely, there are some regions where the closed shop is more likely to arise than in others. In these regions occupations unaffected by the practice elsewhere are liable to be closed to the non-unionist. Finally, in cases where a particular occupation is not confined to one industry, it may be possible to avoid the effects of the closed shop by moving from one industry to another.

(d) Minor Variations

The variations in form, manner of enforcement and scope of application discussed above are the most important ones that need to be considered. Two minor variations remain, which concern rather different issues.

The first relates to whether or not the employer agrees to deduct union dues from the wage packet. In the United States this is known as the 'check off' and this term will be employed below. In practice the check off is largely confined to closed shop areas, although there are many closed groups where there is no check off. Sometimes the check off is a substitute for the closed shop, but in practice they often complement each other.

As a result of the Truck Acts, contracts of employment which *force* workmen to take any part of their wages other than in cash are prohibited.[1] This means that before an employer can deduct union dues from a worker's pay he should ensure that the worker freely consents to this, and 'authorizes' the employer's actions. In practice it is easy to discover, at a relatively early stage when interviewing an applicant for a job, whether he would object to joining a union.

[1] See Sir Frank Tillyard's *The Worker and the State*, Routledge and Kegan Paul, 1948, Chap. 3.

If he does not, a check off 'authorization' form can be produced with other papers and most workers will sign it without objection. If objections are raised, either to joining the union or to signing a check off sheet, it is not necessary to quote these as a reason for non-engagement.

For this reason it is, in practice, possible for the employer to impose the check off as a condition of employment—if he wishes to do so.

Finally, it is necessary to mention the question of whether or not workers in a closed shop have any choice as to the union they join. As already noted, membership choice has two aspects; there may be a right to choose between two or more unions when entering the job, and there may be a right to transfer afterwards if one is dissatisfied with the union of one's choice. Both these aspects of membership choice are important, and more will be said about them below.

Each closed shop described in this book is an amalgam of one or other of the varied features outlined in this section. Each one of the forms noted may be combined with one or another of the others; pre-entry shops may be used to effect entry control, in one of a number of ways. The form of the closed shop that results may be formally or informally recognized, or it may be unilaterally enforced. It may cover part of a factory, most of a region, or the whole of an industry. It may or may not be accompanied by a check off, and there may or may not be a choice of union on entry, or a right to transfer. Even the types outlined are themselves over-simplifications introduced as rough conceptual guides to assist in disentangling the complexity of the closed shop as it arises in British industry. Yet no matter how complex the positions analysed in each and every case apply to the definition set out at the beginning of this chapter: i.e. individuals are made to realize that a particular job is only to be obtained and retained if they become and remain members of one of a specified number of trade unions.

(4) THE SEMI-CLOSED SHOP

It was argued in section (2) above that the term 'compulsory trade unionism' is misleading because it implies a simple dichotomy between 'voluntary' and 'compulsory' membership that does not exist. Workers belong to unions for a complex of reasons which are difficult to classify under such labels. What this study is concerned with is the use of a particular type of penalty—the threat of exclusion from the job—which aims at ensuring that all the workers in a particular group belong to unions. But the objective of 100 per cent union membership is pursued without recourse to such a sanction. It may be enough to use friendly persuasion. On other occasions those who resist persuasion may be subjected to stronger pressure, but this may still stop short of the threat of exclusion.

In practice unions do not usually threaten to strike for the closed shop until a majority of workers have been recruited without it; but this does not mean that nothing more than persuasion has been used. The number of workers willing to belong to unions of their own volition is frequently small; many may have to be subjected to various forms of cajolery, persistent badgering, or collective ostracism. Sometimes the methods used approach intimidation, or go beyond it. Union members may ensure that non-unionists are given more than their share of difficult and unremunerative work, complaints will be made about them, and so on. They may be 'sent to Coventry', and their tools and other belongings 'mislaid'.

Moreover, all this is unilateral action, amounting to strong social and economic pressure exercised by workers on their fellows. Sometimes these devices are supplemented by strong pressures exerted by employers. Managers let it be known they would 'prefer' workers to belong to a union, and inform recalcitrants that they 'want no trouble with the unions on this point'. Others agree to restrict overtime, and even, very occasionally, wage increases, to union members.

Where pressures of this sort are particularly strong, what is intended is to create a situation in which the non-unionist feels that there is no alternative to either joining the union or leaving the job. Without actually using the exclusion threat life is to be made as difficult as possible for the man who will not conform. When this situation exists we may speak of the existence of a *semi-closed shop*.[1] The logical distinction between the semi-closed shop and the closed shop proper is easily drawn. If the employer is willing to remove recalcitrants, or the group itself habitually sustain an effective refusal to work with them, we may speak of a closed shop. If neither is the case then, no matter how unpleasant and unremunerative it may be to remain a non-unionist, nothing more than the semi-closed shop exists. The problem in making use of a notion like the semi-closed shop is that it is difficult to define, even in principle, how weak the pressures operating on the non-unionist have to be

---

[1] The notion of the semi-closed shop applies only to workers actually employed on a job —i.e. there is no semi-closed area which corresponds to the pre-entry shop.

before we are no longer justified in speaking of its existence. Obviously, if no social or economic pressures are used to force recalcitrants into unions, then whatever the level of organization they are working in what may be termed an *open shop* area. In other words, the crucial distinction between the semi-closed shop and the open shop concerns the degree of toleration shown non-unionists. Nevertheless, it is to some extent a personal judgement which decides when intolerance is strong enough to qualify as evidence of the semi-closed shop and the precise way in which the term is being used can only emerge as the next chapter proceeds. However, no attempt will be made to measure the scope and size of the semi-closed shop areas of British industry. This is not essential for the purposes of the study. The reasons why it is necessary to make use of the somewhat vague notion of the semi-closed shop are descriptive and analytic, rather than quantitative. It is of importance mainly because the pressures it represents are sometimes an effective alternative, sometimes an ineffective substitute, and sometimes a stage on the way towards the closed shop. The reasons for this, and their importance in explaining the spread of the practice, are outlined in detail in later chapters.

CHAPTER 2

THE CLOSED SHOP PATTERN

(1) SOURCES OF INFORMATION

THE main object of this chapter is to describe and analyse the extent to which different industries and occupations are affected by various kinds of closed shop. A subsidiary object is to provide an introduction to the account which follows of the functions of the practice and the factors influencing its development.

The estimates used are based on over 300 personal interviews conducted on both sides of industry. Over a hundred different trade unions were contacted, about fifty employers' associations, seventy-four individual managements, representatives of the nationalized industries and many government departments—including the Ministry of Labour. In almost all cases those interviewed were extremely co-operative and ready to assist in any way they could. Both their records and their time were freely put at the writer's disposal.

Three different methods were used to calculate the number of workers affected by the closed shop in particular groups. First, it was usually possible to obtain reliable figures of the number of workers employed in the main occupational groups within most industries—either from the Ministry of Labour or the appropriate employers' association. If it was generally accepted within the industry that a particular occupational group was either completely open or comprehensively closed, these totals could be used to calculate the number of workers in the industry affected by the closed shop.

Difficulties, therefore, were mainly confined to what might be termed the 'mixed groups'—i.e. those where there were both open and closed shop areas. Here it was necessary to adopt different methods. Much more extensive inquiries were made among union officials and employers' representatives at all levels within the industry. Those contacted were asked to estimate the size of the open and closed areas known to them, and from these estimates, and the

27

reasons given for them, it was usually possible to arrive at reasonably accurate totals. However, in two important industries—engineering and building—this was not the case.

Because of the size and complexity of these industries, and the lack of centralized knowledge about them, it was felt necessary to undertake further investigations. Questionnaires were distributed to a cross-section of employers and union representatives with the assistance of additional research workers.[1] Over 600 of these were returned and with the aid of the facts they contained more accurate estimates were calculated.[2]

In making estimates for this chapter it has been decided to err on the cautious side throughout. That is to say, in the few cases where a serious doubt remained as to which one of a series of figures was the more reasonable the one chosen was well on the low side of the estimates.

(2) THE EXTENT OF THE PRACTICE

On the basis of the information gathered it can be said that the closed shop affects about three and three-quarter million workers— roughly 16 per cent of the 22,800,000 employees in Great Britain, or one worker in six.

But it may be more significant to ask what proportion of Great Britain's nine and a half million trade unionists are in closed shops?[3] On these estimates the figure is about 39 per cent. Of the 38 per cent of employees in Britain who belong to trade unions roughly two out of every five are employed in closed shops.

On these figures the closed shop affects about 26 per cent of the labour force in manufacturing and extraction; 22 per cent of workers in transport; 10 per cent in distribution; 6 per cent in building and civil engineering, and only 2 per cent of those employed in the service trades.

---

[1] See Preface, above.

[2] See Appendix at page 282 for more detailed information on methods of collecting the material for these estimates, and an assessment of their relative reliability.

[3] The *Ministry of Labour Gazette* for November 1962 gives the aggregate membership of trade unions in Great Britain as 9,541,000—p. 414. (H.M.S.O.) This figure is compiled from sources supplied by the Registrar of Friendly Societies and from confidential returns of un-registered unions supplied to the Ministry. For this reason it is the most accurate figure available, although it probably exaggerates the actual *industrial* strength of unions since it includes retired members—see below.

The industrial breakdown of the workers covered is:

Manufacturing and Extractive Industry:

Engineering	1,200,000
Mining and Quarrying	630,000
Printing	275,000
Iron and Steel Manufacture . . .	210,000
Shipbuilding and Ship-repair . . .	150,000
Textiles	110,000
Small Scale Metal Manufacture . .	45,000
Timber and Furniture	40,000
Clothing	40,000
Food, Drink and Tobacco . . .	35,000
Chemicals and Oil Refinery . . .	35,000
Paper, Box and Carton Manufacture .	20,000
Fishing	10,000
Other Manufacturing	10,000
	2,810,000

Transport:

Sea Transport	80,000
Docks and Inland Waterways . .	90,000
Railways	80,000
Passenger Transport and Car Hire . .	100,000
Road Haulage	30,000
Air Transport	10,000
	390,000

Building and Civil Engineering . . .	100,000

Distribution:

The Co-operative Movement . . .	300,000[1]
Other Distribution	20,000
	320,000

The Services:

Local Government	45,000
Entertainment	45,000
Public Utilities	30,000
Other Services	20,000
	140,000

TOTAL	3,760,000

[1] Including productive workers employed by Co-operative Wholesale Societies.

However, it is necessary to examine the actual groups involved in more detail in order to measure how common the practice is among particular kinds of work. To do this it is useful to classify workers according to how far particular occupations, or clearly defined working groups, are dominated by the closed shop.[1] This involves making a distinction between four different situations in which the closed shop is prevalent to a greater or lesser degree. These will be termed:

(a) The Comprehensively Closed Trades

By classifying an occupation or working group under this heading, it is not meant to imply that it is impossible for a single non-unionist to remain within it. Unless a comprehensive check off is imposed as a condition of employment, temporary lapsing may arise occasionally, and sometimes workers may be able to avoid joining the union for a short period. A comprehensively closed trade is one where within the group as defined the great majority would find it impossible to remain outside a union for any length of time and the amount of non-unionism is very small, affecting no more than a few per cent of the group. Moreover the exceptions are usually, though not necessarily, subject to the semi-closed shop.

(b) Mainly Closed Trades

The majority of workers here are in closed shops, although some open shops exist which are also quite often subject to the semi-closed shop.

(c) Mainly Open Trades

Closed shops exist within these groups, but affect less than 50 per cent of the workers involved. The pressures of the semi-closed shop, if they exist, are usually less widespread.

(d) Comprehensively Open Trades

As far as is known these groups are entirely unaffected by the closed shop, although they may or may not be subject to various forms of semi-closed shop.

The most obvious conclusion which follows from grouping the workers affected by the closed shop under one or another of these

[1] In a few cases occupations such as baking, or shipbuilding, are comprehensively closed over certain extensive and clearly defined working areas, whereas they contain a number of open shops elsewhere. The most important instances where this is so are distinguished below.

headings is the extent to which the practice is at its most prevalent among manual workers. The list of comprehensive trades reads:

Manual Workers:

Coal Miners	600,000[1]
Craftsmen and other manual workers in Printing	250,000
Process Workers and skilled maintenance workers in Iron and Steel . . .	160,000
Craftsmen and other manual workers in Commercial Shipyards . . .	150,000
Sailors and other deck hands . . .	70,000
Dockers in Commercial dockyards . .	68,000
Bus Workers and Maintenance Staff employed by London Transport . .	50,000
Craftsmen in Cotton and other Textiles .	45,000
Hatters	4,000
Scottish Bakers	14,000
Manual Workers in London's Wholesale Markets	10,000
Film Production Workers . . .	7,000

Non-Manual Workers:

Draughtsmen in Commercial Shipyards .	4,000
Teleprinters and Proof Readers . .	5,000
Musicians	25,000
Trade Union and Labour Party Officers and Staff	8,000
TOTAL	1,470,000

These figures cover about 39 per cent of all workers in closed shops and less than 3 per cent of the total are non-manual workers. Moreover, all the workers in the mainly closed category are also employed on manual work, i.e.

Unskilled Manual Workers in Iron and Steel	50,000
Manual Workers in Engineering . . .	1,200,000
Manual Workers in Textile Finishing . .	35,000
Manual Workers in Oil Refinery . .	25,000
Engineers and other craftsmen in the Merchant Service	10,000
Manual Workers in Railway Workshops .	65,000
	1,385,000

[1] Including surface workers.

Together these two groups account for over two and three quarter million workers—roughly 76 per cent of those affected by the closed shop. Over 98 per cent of them are engaged on manual work.

The remaining 24 per cent of workers in closed shops, who are employed in mainly open groups where the closed shop is very exceptional, come from a wide variety of trades. There is one sizeable group—the 210,000 workers covered by the closed shop in co-operative distribution—many of whom would not be regarded as manual workers in the accepted sense; but the great majority of the remaining half million or so are employed on manual work. In mining, printing, engineering, transport, distribution and the services there are small groups of non-manual workers in closed shops, but in trades such as paper, box and cartons, small-scale metal manufacture, textiles, fishing, building and civil engineering, public utilities and local government there are far more workers affected and in these industries the practice is almost entirely confined to manual grades.

If we add all the non-manual groups together (including for this purpose all the workers covered by the co-ops) the number of non-manual workers in closed shops is not more than about 300,000—i.e. roughly 8 per cent of the total number of workers affected. If Co-operative workers are excluded the proportion drops to 3 per cent.

But a more precise method of measuring the relative concentration of the closed shop can be arrived at in another way. There are no known examples of the practice among certain mainly administrative groups in the service industries—i.e. those engaged in banking, real estate, insurance, accountancy, medicine, and so on.[1] These groups together account for about two million workers. There are also, as has been seen, very few examples of the closed shop among clerical, administrative and technical workers, and none among various officer groups in transport. This group of comprehensively open and mainly open trades accounts for a further four million workers.

If we add all the groups listed above together, and subtract them from the twenty-two and three-quarter million workers making up

---

[1] The argument that certain professional associations, like the Royal College of Veterinary Surgeons, operate practices analogous to the trade union closed shop is considered below. At this point we are concerned with the number and distribution of workers affected by the closed shop in British trade unions.

the civilian labour force, we arrive at a figure of about sixteen and three-quarter million workers. For the purposes of convenience this figure may be regarded as the total number of employees engaged on manual work.[1] What proportion of this group is covered by the closed shop?

It is necessary to deduct from the total closed shop figure set out above the non-manual workers affected.[2] When this is done it is found that about 22 per cent of manual employees are in closed shops—i.e. more than one in five. Again, it may be even more significant to ask what proportion of trade unionists in this group are affected, though this is more difficult to estimate. Taking the figures for total trade union membership published by the Ministry of Labour as a guide, and deducting from this figure the total membership of unions recruiting in non-manual groups, and, so far as is known, the non-manual membership of unions recruiting in both sections, the percentage of trade unionists in manual groups covered by the closed shop rises to 49 per cent.

But there is reason to believe that this figure is a slight under-estimate, for the Ministry's estimates include retired members of most trade unions, and in some cases even the widows of deceased members. For this reason it is worth making an alternative estimate derived from the more realistically based figures of unions affiliated to the T.U.C. Virtually all unions of any size recruiting in the manual areas are members of the T.U.C.[3] and they tend to affiliate on their actual industrial strength.

Taking as a basis the membership of the T.U.C. as a whole, and dividing the total number of workers in closed shops into this figure, it may be said that about 45 per cent of the T.U.C.'s members are in closed shops.[4] If we deduct from the total T.U.C. membership the membership of unions recruiting outside manual groups as defined above, together with the numbers, where they are known, of the non-manual membership of other unions, then it is possible to arrive at a figure which can be compared with the total number of manual workers in closed shops. As a result it can be said that

[1] Because of the unsatisfactory nature of employment figures outside manufacturing this figure undoubtedly contains a small number of clerical and administrative workers, but this cannot be helped.

[2] Apart from co-operative workers in closed shops.

[3] Or the Scottish T.U.C. In the estimates that follow, the membership of unions affiliated to the Scottish T.U.C. only are included in the 'T.U.C.' figures.

[4] Taking the T.U.C.'s total membership as 8,312,000 (1962 Report of the T.U.C.). The only union with a closed shop membership not represented is the National Association of Local Government Officers, and in their case the numbers involved are extremely small.

some 51 per cent of the T.U.C.'s membership in manual grades of work are in closed shops.

But it can be argued that even this figure does not adequately represent the total impact of the closed shop on British Industry. So far we have been concerned with attempts to assess the proportions of various groups who are actually in closed shops at the present time. But this gives us no more than a static view of what is essentially a changing situation. At some time all comprehensively closed trades contained some open shop areas and many trades, at the present time, are in the process of moving from one category to another. To assist in describing the tendency of groups to change, or attempt to change, their proportion of closed shops, it is useful to make use of the notion of the *closed shop prone trade*.

If any trade which is not comprehensively closed makes frequent and widespread demands for the closed shop it may be regarded as closed shop prone. Such a group is characterized by a state of dis-equilibrium. The unions organizing in it are anxious to enforce the closed shop wherever and whenever they can. As the level of union-ization rises, and union strength grows, pressure for the closed shop increases and the open sections of the group grow smaller. Because the elimination of non-unionism is a basic union objective in a closed shop prone group, the open sections of it usually contain elements of the semi-closed shop.

In situations of this sort the closed shop is a factor of importance not merely to those employers and workers who have come to accept it, and work within it, but also to those whose plants or jobs are likely to be affected. This is particularly true if they are working in sections of industry where the practice more or less predominates —i.e. sections in which there is a likelihood of demands for the closed shop arising throughout the trade, and where it is clear that the majority of workers have already been affected. This is precisely the position among the mainly closed trades, who are all closed shop prone.

In estimating the total impact of the closed shop, then, there is a case for considering not merely the proportion of workers in closed shops, but also the proportion of workers in open shops in the mainly closed trades. There are about 1,350,000 workers in this latter position, and, as was mentioned above, they are all manual workers. If we add this figure to the 3,760,000 workers actually in closed shops we may say that there are 5,110,000 workers who are either in closed shops or in jobs in which not to be in closed shops is exceptional. That is to say 22 per cent of all the employees in the civilian labour force. Expressed as a proportion of the manual labour force this is about 31 per cent.

Since most mixed trades contain at least some groups who would like to extend the closed shop if they could it is, in the last analysis, a matter of personal judgement that decides how strong demands have to be before a group can be classified as closed shop prone. But in the light of interviews conducted it is possible to say something about the degree to which various mainly open trades are closed shop prone.

In the manufacturing and extractive trades there is a widespread correlation between the level of unionization and the degree to which workers are closed shop prone. The bulk of clerical and administrative workers in these trades are not organized at all, and the few that are make virtually no demands for the closed shop. Among the great majority of the lesser skilled engaged on manual work in the food and drink trades, as well as in chemicals, glass manufacture and woollen and nylon textiles the position is roughly the same. The level of unionization is generally low, and demands for the closed shop are few and far between. In iron foundries and the small-scale metal using trades, demands for the practice are virtually confined to the more skilled groups, who are by far the best organized. In cotton textiles, however, the position is more complicated. As has been stated, the craftsmen in the industry are dominated by the closed shop, but there are also frequent demands for the closed shop among the better organized sections of the lesser skilled operatives and, viewed as a whole, cotton textiles may be regarded as a closed shop prone trade.

The same may be said of the clothing industry, apart from the boot and shoe trade. Here the overall level of organization in the larger factories is probably as high, if not higher, than that in cotton textiles and the Tailor and Garment Workers' union presses for the closed shop wherever it has the chance. Similar features may be observed in the better organized parts of the fishing industry, as well as in tobacco manufacture and the furniture trade. All these relatively well-organized groups are closed shop prone.

Similar correlations between unionization and the emergence of widespread demands for the closed shop can be found outside manufacture and extraction. In the gas industry demands are most common among the highly organized groups, such as retort house workers. In passenger transport it is only in the larger garages, where most workers are already organized, that campaigns to obtain the closed shop usually arise.

But the correlation, though widespread, is not universal. There are some trades where demands for the closed shop tend to arise even when the level of unionization is low. This was the case among merchant seamen long before they became a comprehensively closed trade. It applies to-day among building labourers. Similarly there are some groups, like porters, or signalmen, or railway goods-yard workers, where quite high levels of organization can be reached without widespread demands for the closed shop emerging. More significant still, there are some trades in which very high levels of unionization are reached and maintained without those groups becoming in any sense closed shop prone.

The most important examples of these trades are the following:

(1) Non-industrial civil servants.
(2) Teachers and other non-manual groups employed by local authorities.
(3) Sections of the Industrial Civil Service.
(4) Firemen.
(5) Footplate workers on the Railways.
(6) Clerical and Administrative workers in nationalized industries.
(7) Electricity workers employed by nationalized undertakings.
(8) Boot and Shoe Operatives.

All these trades are over 90 per cent organized, and many workers within them are employed in situations where the unions have recruited every worker on the job.

It is worth noting what they have in common. First, four of them are employed by the government, three by nationalized undertakings, and only one is in the private sector. Second, three consist of government workers, mainly employed on manual work. Third, all the manual groups contain some workers who are subject to pressures of the semi-closed shop sort. It is necessary to explore this point a little further.

Interviews reveal that the semi-closed shop arises in two different situations. In the closed shop prone trades it is usually a stage on the way to the closed shop itself; an unstable feature representing all that can be obtained at the moment. In the case of the manual groups above, however, this is not so. Here the semi-closed shop is a permanent phenomenon, representing the most the unions care to demand, rather than a temporary halting place along the road to a universal closed shop.

The reasons why groups like the footplate men, the electricians and the boot and shoe operatives exhibit such untypical tolerance towards the few non-unionists at work within their trade will be explored in full in later chapters.

Summarizing what has been said so far about the extent of the closed shop it may be said that demands for it tend to arise as the level of organization rises in most, though not in all, trades. At the moment it directly affects less than about one worker in six, although roughly one worker in four is either in a closed shop employed in a group where the practice predominates. It is much more likely to arise among manual rather than non-manual workers. Roughly one in four manual workers are in closed shops and one in three is either covered by the practice or employed in one of the mainly closed trades. Among union members the proportion of workers in closed shops rises still further. Two out of five trade unionists are in closed shops, and among working trade unionists in the manual occupations every other member is in a closed shop. It can surely be concluded from these estimates that the closed shop is a common feature of British industrial relations, which among well organized trade unionists is the rule rather than the exception.

(3) Variations in Form

Most closed shops are of the post-entry kind, although there are probably just under three-quarters of a million workers in one pre-entry shop or another. The precise limits of the pre-entry shop are difficult to estimate, though the following are the main groups which can be measured and classified:

The Labour Supply Shop

Newsprint and Periodical Workers[1] . .	85,000
Textile Finishing Workers . . .	35,000
London Market Workers	10,000
Film and Television Production Workers .	7,000
Hatters	4,000
	141,000

The Labour Pool Shop

Dockers	68,000
Seamen	70,000
Fishermen	7,000
	145,000

[1] Skilled workers in this group are also subject to the craft qualification shop—see below.

D

The Craft Qualification Shop

Shipyard Craftsmen	80,000
Craftsmen in General Printing . . .	75,000
Craftsmen in Iron and Steel . . .	12,000
	167,000

The Promotion Veto Shop

Process Workers in Iron and Steel . .	148,000
Craftsmen in Textiles	45,000
	193,000
TOTAL	646,000

Something must be said about the form the closed shop takes in each of the groups on this list.

(a) The Labour Supply Shop

This reaches its most developed form among newsprint and periodical workers, where it affects both skilled and unskilled operatives, as well as clerical groups such as proof-readers and press telegraphists. It does not affect journalists, although a small proportion of these are in post-entry shops.

The recognition of the union as the source of the labour supply, which is the distinguishing characteristic of the labour supply shop, reaches its most rigorous expression in what are termed 'casual' engagements. Many large newspapers and national magazines are produced by a small permanent labour force supplemented by influxes of temporary workers. It is one of the strictest of printing union rules that *all* this labour must be supplied through the union office, where it is shared out among union members who desire to supplement their income in this way.[1] Naturally it is the semi-skilled labour force, recruited by the National Society of Operative Printers and Assistants and the National Union of Printing, Bookbinding, and Paper Workers, which are mainly affected.

Since the eight separate unions organizing craftsmen in printing all confine their membership to accredited apprentices, and have agreements with the newspaper and magazine owners recognizing their right to demand apprenticeship ratios, they may also be said to operate a craft qualification shop. In fact, however, the employers

---

[1] Much of the work is done at night or at week-ends.

in newsprint and periodicals do not train their full quota of apprentices and usually ask the unions to supply them with fully trained
craftsmen who have served their time in general printing. Since the
rates paid in newsprint are generally higher than in other sections
of the trade, there is often a waiting-list, which again is operated by
the union concerned.

Similar waiting-lists exist for the lesser skilled. In major towns,
like London, Manchester or Glasgow, there is a queue for vacancies
in the newspaper and magazine section of the industry. When jobs
arise existing members of the unions employed in other sections of
the trade are given first priority. Moreover, just as newspaper and
magazine proprietors do not take up their apprenticeship ratios they
also employ few juniors among their semi-skilled or unskilled labour
force. The result is that most workers on the larger papers have
received their training in general print and have transferred, to
Fleet Street and elsewhere, via the union's vacancy list.

In the case of several of the larger branches in the big towns there
also exists a list of would-be new members known colloquially as
the 'Sons and Brothers' list. When the branch is ready to admit any
additional members it takes those on the top of the list and allots
them a Probationary Card. After twelve months they are eligible
for permanent membership. But power is also given in the rules of
the Printing Trade Operatives for the creation of a class of 'Temporary Members'. It is not normal to allow 'temporary members' the
right to transfer to another job—say in the more lucrative newsprint
section of the trade.

The Labour supply shops in textile finishing, which cover the
majority of workers involved, are the result of agreements between
the unions and employers stipulating that employers must first
apply to the unions for labour. In the eventuality of the unions
being unable to meet their requirements within twenty-four hours
the employers are free to engage who they like, but those employed
must agree to join a union. The more skilled groups are organized
by the National Union of Dyers, Bleachers and Textile Workers,
while the General and Municipal Workers Union is prominent
among the lesser skilled.

In the London wholesale markets branches of the Transport and
General Workers' Union operate informally recognized labour
supply shops. The form these take can best be exemplified by a
description of the situation in Smithfield. Meat arrives in the market
on lorries driven by members of the Transport and General Workers'

Union who operate a post-entry shop. It is drawn onto the tailboard by 'drawers back', carried to wholesalers' stalls by 'pitchers', moved within the stall by 'humpers', and carried from stall to stall by 'bummarees'. When bought by customers with their own van it is carried out of the market by other 'bummarees', though if it is to be transported by carriers 'carriers porters' will do this job.

Bummarees operate in gangs, informally attached to a particular butcher. No gang will take the work of another gang, and until recently they would object to a butcher carrying his own meat, or using his own employees for this purpose. Before the war butchers were allowed to use their own staff for this purpose if their usual bummarees were not available.[1] When rationing ended in 1954, and Smithfield returned to normal, they wished to resume the pre-war arrangements.[2]

Under the by-laws of the market they were entitled to do so yet:

the Transport and General Workers' Union, to which the bummarees belong, refused to permit them to do so. Employees of the wholesalers, who were members of the same union, were instructed by the union to deliver meat only to licensed porters. If the butchers persisted and entered the stalls to take possession of their meat, the union threatened to withdraw the services of all other employees in the market.[3]

Since only labour supplied by the Transport and General Workers' Union was employed for drawing back, pitching, humping, and other work, this threat was effective.

Workers in the market are all members of the Smithfield Market branch of the union and its Central Committee is composed of representatives of each section of the labour force. It is the committee that decides whether a man can be admitted to one or another of the sections, and in the case of bummarees this has resulted in a long waiting-list. This form of entry control has been criticized on the grounds that it results in a shortage of labour, especially bummarees. The union replies that it also makes possible the decasualization

---

[1] See the Report of the Court of Inquiry into the *Causes of Industrial Unrest in Smithfield Market*, H.M.S.O., 1958.

[2] During the war wholesale markets were disbanded and the Ministry of Food allocated supplies from smaller depots on the outskirts of the towns concerned. In 1946 trade returned to pre-war market-places, but under the control of the Ministry, which employed the necessary labour. The Conservatives decided to wind up these activities of the Ministry, and so, in 1954, the pre-war set-up in Smithfield and elsewhere was introduced.

[3] Simon Rottenburg, 'Monopoly in the Labour Market: The "Bummarees" of London's Wholesale Meat Market', *Industrial and Labour Relations Review*, New York, October 1959, p. 57.

of the labour force and a stable level of employment for existing members of the union.[1]

The position in Smithfield is analogous to that in the three other important London Markets—Billingsgate, Spitalfields and Covent Garden. Portering is covered by the labour supply shop, and elsewhere the post-entry shop is the rule.

In films and television the labour supply shop covers the membership of the Cinematograph, Television and Allied Technicians Union, apart from their members employed by the B.B.C., who are in open shops. Most B.B.C. employees belong to the Association of Broadcasting Staffs. In their agreement with the commercial television programme contractors the Cinematograph Technicians have obtained a formal recognition of their right to supply labour similar to that obtained by the unions in textile finishing.

In practice the companies obtain their labour through the union office up to the level of assistant director. Naturally they operate a veto on those the union sends, and can insist on obtaining the services of individual union members if these are free. In the past it has been alleged that the union has wanted the labour shop to restrict total supply, and this is said to be the reason for the employers' insistence on their own right to provide labour if the union cannot meet their requirements. The union denies this, however, and maintains that they only desire entry control to give a preference to existing members and to mitigate the effects of an extremely casual form of employment. Certainly the union has been known to close its registers when the film industry has faced a slump.

Finally, we come to the position of the 4,000 members of the two felt hatters unions—one for women and one for men—sharing the same general secretary. They are both based on Denton, where the trade is concentrated. The form taken by their version of the labour supply shop is set out in the rules of both unions. Rule 28 of the men's union states:

Any member going to any shop to seek employment without his 'asking card' shall be fined 2s. 6d. Such 'asking cards' must not be granted to members owing more than four weeks' contributions.[2]

The obtaining of such a card from the branch secretary is a prerequisite of engagement, since labour is supplied solely through the union office. In addition an apprenticeship ratio operates for all

[1] See Rottenburg, op. cit., for a detailed discussion of the case for and against the practices of the Union. Also the Court of Inquiry cited above.
[2] Rules of the A.S.J.F.H. & A.W., 1948, p. 39.

male workers, except a small group called 'outdoor plankers and other outdoor workers'.

(b) The Labour Pool Shop

The Labour pool shop reaches its most developed and complex form among dock workers employed by the National Dock Labour Board. The main unions involved are the Transport and General Workers, the Stevedores and Dockers, the Watermen's Union, the Scottish Transport and General Workers, and the General and Municipal Workers.

The form taken by the practice is largely the result of the long campaign for the decasualization of dock labour and the stabilization of dockers' earnings pioneered by the Transport and General Workers and its first general secretary, the late Ernest Bevin. Bevin's objective was to create a register of dockers confined to union members, jointly administered by union and employers. Establishment on the register would entitle the worker to a basic minimum wage and a priority claim to vacancies.

In February 1946 these aims were given legal expression by the passage of the Dock Workers (Regulation of Employment) Act. The consequence of this act was that recruitment, payment and allocation of all manual workers in the great majority of ports came under the control of the National Dock Labour Board.[1] Before workers can obtain employment they must be accepted for registration by local Dock Labour Boards, made up of an equal number of representatives of employers and unions. In practice this means that would-be applicants must secure membership of the local union branch.

Entry control is effected in a number of ways. First, the register is divided into different categories. There is the Main Register, the Probationary Register, the Temporary Register, and the Seasonal Register. The register has a 'Sanctioned Strength' which is altered from time to time according to the labour requirements of the industry. If labour demands expand, those on other registers may secure promotion to the main register and a small number of un-registered workers may also be temporarily engaged. If labour demand contracts recruitment stops, and, if necessary, the sanctioned

[1] The ports covered by the N.D.L.B. scheme are Tyne and Wear, Middlesbrough and Hartlepools, Hull and Goole, Grimsby and Immingham, Wash Ports, East Anglia, London, Medway and Swale, South Coast, Plymouth, Cornwall, Bristol and Severn, South Wales, Liverpool, Garston, Manchester, Preston, Fleetwood, Barrow, Cumberland, Ayrshire, Greenock, Glasgow, Aberdeen, East Scotland.

strength is reduced. Normal wastage is expected to take care of the secular fall in the demand for labour and the Board tries to avoid discharging permanent employees on grounds of redundancy. Theoretically this could be done by taking advantage of the need to re-register every six months, but recently the Board has dealt with reductions in labour demand by a temporary release scheme, placing those released to find work elsewhere on a 'dormant register' which carries with it the right to be recalled at short notice. There is a financial incentive to leave the scheme during periods of slackening demand, when jobs are in short supply and workers find it impossible to maintain their normal level of earnings. Nevertheless, there is still no shortage of workers wanting to join the scheme, and as a result the Board recognizes the priority claim of dockers' sons to be taken on to the Main Register.[1]

These arrangements amount to a joint control over the *size* and *distribution* of the labour force shared by union officials and employers at national and local level. Yet, quite apart from this bilaterally regulated control, there also exists within the branches an additional control over the composition of the labour supply which is unilaterally regulated. This is made possible by taking advantage of the union's nomination rights, which are used to confine dock work to those the branch approves of, and for the most part these are existing members of the union who have some personal connection with other dock workers.

As a result of these arrangements it can be said that within the area covered it is virtually impossible for a non-unionist to gain entrance to the docks. What cannot be said is that men find it impossible to drop out of their union, or get into arrears, once they are engaged upon dock work. The unions have not managed to secure quite such an effective control over the maintenance of the closed shop as they have over its original imposition on new entrants, but this is a subject which will be discussed in more detail when considering variations in the way in which the closed shop is enforced.[2]

The form taken by the labour pool shop in the merchant service is the outcome of the long struggle on the part of the National Union of Seamen to obtain a pre-entry shop imposed at the point of hire. One of the main aims was to use this to secure the elimination

[1] The 1961 Report of the N.D.L.B. shows that some 18 per cent of the Main Register's Annual Intake was made up of dockers' sons—p. 25.
[2] See p. 55 below.

of casual labour, as was described in the case of the dockers above. During the First World War the employers' association, known as the Shipping Federation,[1] was forced to bargain with the union and to seek their aid in obtaining labour. With the creation of the National Maritime Board, in 1918, the war-time arrangements were put on a permanent basis. The Board was composed of representatives of employers and unions, and set itself two objectives. First, the negotiation of wages and conditions. Second,

The establishment of a single source of supply of Sailors and Firemen jointly controlled by employers and employed in accordance with the following general principles:

(1) The Shipowner shall have the right to select his own crew at any time through a jointly controlled supply office. . . .
(2) Equal rights of registration and employment must be secured for all seamen. Raw recruits to be registered as such.[2]

To implement the second objective district panels were set up who appointed Port Consultants. These were chosen from both sides of the industry and among their duties was the administration of the joint labour supply scheme. Until 1921 the employers were nominally entitled to employ non-unionists, since there was no formal stipulation that the men supplied had to be members of a union. In that year the arrangements were varied so that each man signing on had to produce a form—known as a P.C. 5.[3] stamped by both local port consultants, one of whom was an official of the seamen's union.[4] Since no official of the N.U.S. would stamp the P.C. 5 of a man out of compliance or not already a member of the N.U.S., this resulted in the union achieving a comprehensive pre-entry closed shop.

In 1947 this system was modified to allow for a measure of decasualization. British-born members of the N.U.S., with a certificate of navigating competency, or over twelve months' service at sea, were allowed to become members of the Establishment Service Scheme. This gives them a priority over non-members when applying for ships, and when they are out of employment the right to 'establishment benefit'. The total number of established personnel is settled by negotiation, and men may choose to belong to either

---

[1] This organization of employers works in association with the Association of the Port of Liverpool; together they cover over 90 per cent of British ocean-going vessels, outside fishing fleets.
[2] Constitution of the N.M.B.
[3] P.C. stood for Port Consultants.
[4] At the same time the Seamen's Union was given a monopoly of bargaining rights for sailors and other deck hands—see p. 126 below for an account of this period.

the establishment of a particular company or to what is known as the General Service Establishment. Unlike the docks there is no attempt to use the closed shop to secure a limitation on *total entry*.

The system is effective, although it has three drawbacks. First, only employers who are members of the Shipping Federation or the Port of Liverpool are covered. This means that a minority of owners, for the most part engaged on coastal shipping on small vessels, are unaffected. On their ships non-unionism is rife. Secondly, workers who enlist for one voyage, and do not agree to a check off, may escape paying arrears if they then leave the sea. Thirdly, it is sometimes necessary to sign on seamen in foreign ports, where the system of control is not watertight.

In fishing similar labour pool shops are operated by the Transport and General Workers in many ports. There are decasualization schemes and the union assists in the administration of these. Once again there is no attempt to control total entry, although in some ports unions have the right to act as a labour agency.

(c) *The Craft Qualification Shop*

It will be remembered that the distinguishing characteristics of the craft qualification shop are the restriction of union entry to ex-apprentices, and the acceptance of some limitation on the number of apprentices to be trained. This form of closed shop reaches its most developed form among skilled printing workers.

Nine unions are involved. Three recruit typographers, while others organize among lithographic workers, electrotypers and stereotypers, monotype casters and typefounders, and silk screen and process printing. One union, the Printing, Bookbinding and Paper Workers, organizes craft workers in the binding room, and lesser skilled workers in binding and elsewhere.

All these unions insist on apprenticeship ratios, and entry to the job is confined to accredited apprentices who have been chosen as a result of a process of joint-selection in which the union plays a major role. This usually enables them to give a preference to the sons and relations of existing members. The apprenticeship ratios are formally recognized by employers and set out in national collective agreements with each union which link the number of apprentices the employer is allowed to the number of journeymen he employs.

As has been noted, in newsprint the unions also function as a source of labour supply. This is not usually the case in general printing, although employers often approach the union where labour is particularly short and local branches sometimes have an understanding with individual employers which accords their members first preference for any vacancies. However, most employers in general print are free to advertise for labour, so long as they confine themselves to union men.

Unlike the press owners, employers in general printing tend to employ their full ratio of apprentices, and complain that they cannot take on more. They also criticize the rigid job demarcations between one craft and another, and the fact that the unions will not allow them to promote semi-skilled workers to certain types of work now regarded as the exclusive province of craftsmen. The unions reply that these restrictions are necessary in order to protect their craft status and job security.[1]

In shipbuilding and ship-repair the craft qualification shop takes a slightly less rigorous form. There are about a dozen craft unions engaged in this industry, the most important of which are the Boilermakers and Shipwrights, the Engineers and the Woodworkers. Between them these unions have about three-quarters of the craftsmen in the industry.

To-day entry to most of the skilled sections of the craft unions is confined to accredited apprentices. Members would not allow the unapprenticed man to be promoted on to craftsmen's work by the employer, although during two world wars they were prevailed upon to accept non-apprenticed 'dilutees' and many of these men have managed to retain their jobs and have come to be accepted as the equal of the qualified craftsmen.

Unions largely confined to the industry, such as the boilermakers, or the shipwrights, impose rigid apprenticeship ratios, although these are not embodied in any formal collective agreements, as in printing. Other unions, like the Engineers, or Woodworkers, with the bulk of their membership in industries other than shipbuilding, are not able to be quite so inflexible. They also maintain a 'backdoor' into the industry for the non-apprenticed man in that outside shipbuilding non-apprenticed members find it easier to get promoted on to craftsmen's work without having served an apprenticeship. Once they have managed to do this, and gained acceptance to the

---

[1] See p. 238 below for a further discussion of this point.

skilled section of the union, they may be able to transfer to work in a shipyard without being asked to show their indentures.

Another difference between the closed shop position among craftsmen in printing and shipbuilding relates to the failure of the shipbuilding unions to impose effective craft qualification shops in Admiralty shipyards. In printing there are a few very small firms, particularly in the south-west, who have evaded the effects of the craft qualification shop, but there is no significant difference in this industry between public and private enterprise. The Stationery Office employs over 3,000 printers, and they have to submit to the same apprenticeship ratios and restrictions as any other printer. They would be in a position of some difficulty if one of their established personnel refused to pay his union dues, but in this unlikely eventuality the workers concerned would be able to force such a recalcitrant to either pay up or leave the job by the use of unilateral strike action.

In contrast it is disputable whether the craft qualification shop exists in an effective form among the 40,000 or so workers employed by the Admiralty to construct and repair ships in naval dockyards. The most important union here has always been the Shipwrights, who were over 90 per cent organized and had some union enforced closed shops. Pressures of the semi-closed shop sort would undoubtedly be employed against those who tried to lapse, but it seems clear that the sanctions upholding union membership are nowhere near as strong among this group as in commercial shipyards. The Boilermakers' union never enjoyed the dominant position in Admiralty yards which it secured elsewhere. For the most part the workers it recruited as skilled craftsmen in commercial shipbuilding are regarded as semi-skilled by the Admiralty. At the moment most of them are recruited into one of the general unions. Unlike printing employers, and their counterparts in commercial shipbuilding, the Admiralty is not affected by the same rigid demarcation rules as apply in these trades. They are more free to promote their lesser skilled workers, and make a more flexible use of the labour force.

A third group of workers who are subject to a more or less rigorous form of craft qualification shop work on maintenance and construction work in the iron and steel industry. The unions involved include the Amalgamated Engineering Union and the building unions, such as the Amalgamated Union of Building Trade

Workers. In this industry the craft qualification shop takes a form which is similar to that in commercial shipbuilding.

Apart from the trades described above, where the numbers covered by the craft qualification shop can be measured with reasonable accuracy, there are a large number of craft unions organizing in other industries who attempt to impose a modified form of the craft qualification shop whenever they have the strength to do so. For example, in the manufacture of small-scale metal products, such as chisels, hammers and cutlery, there are local craft unions, as well as national unions like the Sheet Metal Workers and Coppersmiths, who have the craft qualification shop as one of their traditional objectives. Similar practices are aimed at among metal mechanics and brassworkers.

In engineering there are over 600,000 workers nominally classified as craftsmen, but it is impossible to reach any reliable estimate of how many of them are in craft qualification shops. What can be said is that this is most likely to be the case among the relatively small unions whose membership is mainly or solely confined to the more skilled sections of the labour force—e.g. the Boilermakers, the Iron Fitters and so on. Numerically much more important are the mixed unions—who organize among skilled and unskilled—such as the Foundry Workers, the Vehicle Builders, and the Engineers—and the position in these unions is much more difficult to determine.

The Amalgamated Engineering Union, which is far the largest of this group, with three-quarters of a million workers in the industry, has a third of its membership in what is termed 'Section One' of the union—which is confined to so-called skilled workers. But it is impossible to say how many of these are ex-apprenticed. In any case, in the Engineers the traditional object of entry control via a rigidly enforced apprenticeship ratio is all but extinct. Dilution and upgrading on a more advanced scale than in shipbuilding had resulted in the union abandoning the notion of the ratio as an object of national policy before the Second World War. In some localities ratios were still unilaterally imposed on individual firms by craft groups, but these were weakened by the developments of 1939–45. In 1940 agreements were made with the unions which allowed for the unrestricted introduction of non-apprenticed dilutees. The result of this has been that although apprenticeship is still a common practice in the trade as a recent survey claims:

The continued post-war expansion of these industries has retained these clauses in the agreements covering employment, and there are now a very large number of men now engaged on jobs rated as skilled who have been upgraded from other work. In addition to these there are probably many—though how many it is impossible to estimate—who have upgraded themselves.[1]

The same writer comes to similar conclusions about the building industry, another trade in which the craft unions have been power-less to prevent the continued promotion of the non-apprenticed. Her investigations underline what union officials in the industry readily admit. Many building firms are unwilling to take the responsibility for training apprentices and a situation has arisen in which an increasing number of new entrants are 'picking up their skill rather than being trained'.[2] Most union branches have long accepted the fact that this development makes the recruitment of the non-apprenticed a regrettable necessity. As in engineering, well-organized branches may still operate a limited form of entry control —objecting to further promotions while some of their members are still unemployed, or objecting to individual workers on grounds of incompetence, or because of their trade union record, but this does not take a form which is systematic or rigorous enough to merit classification as an example of the craft qualification shop.[3]

(d) The Promotion Veto Shop

The most important example of this form of closed shop occurs among process workers in iron and steel manufacture. These workers are recruited from among the unskilled labourers who assist many of whom are organized by one of the general unions in post-entry shops. Once on process work they must become a member of either the British Iron and Steel and Kindred Trades Association (commonly known as Bisakta) or the smaller Blast-furnacemen's union, which recruits among process workers in blast-furnaces outside Scotland. From this point on further promotion depends, in the main, on seniority, with one important proviso: promotion opportunities will be vetoed by the union if the candidate for promotion is not, at the time the vacancy arises, a fully paid up member. In this case promotion will normally go to the next senior man who is in compliance.

---

[1] *Recruitment to the Skilled Trades*, by Gertrude Williams, Routledge and Kegan Paul, 1957, p. 69.
[2] Williams, *op. cit.*, p. 98.
[3] The problem sometimes is that the worker has *no* trade union record—i.e. he has never belonged to any union before. This was the case of the watchmaker whom management tried to start in the tool-room at Briggs—see p. 1 above.

Since there is no right to a similarly skilled job in another production team if a worker decides to leave, or if he is discharged or made redundant, loss of position on the promotion ladder usually involves starting somewhere else as an unskilled labourer. Since this system restricts skilled jobs to certain specified workers who are also existing members of the union it is a form of entry control operated in conjunction with the closed shop. But since there is no recognized transferable skill the mere possession of a union card carries with it no recognized craft status and does not even entitle its owner to a degree of job preference.

Preference is governed by the promotion system, which, nowadays at least, is fully accepted by the employers. All the closed shop does in this instance is to provide a negative sanction, or veto, denying the job to those who would qualify, on other grounds, if they were not in compliance. Thus, when one management wanted to promote a man who was in arrears, representations were made to the union branch asking that an exception should be made, if the man concerned paid up. When the next worker in line for promotion objected, the man originally selected was passed over.

What the practice also results in is the use of the branch to settle internal disputes about promotion opportunities in general. If a promotion opportunity arises which is not considered to be very desirable the 'senior' man, who would normally take it, may attempt to waive his right in favour of the next most senior man. If this is done because there is reason to believe that this will result in the senior man ultimately obtaining a more preferable job, there may be an objection. The next most senior man will insist that the senior man *must* take the job in question, or waive his right to promotion permanently. Similarly, if a particularly desirable job falls vacant, or is about to fall vacant, two or three men may claim it on the grounds of seniority. For the most part, management is nowadays only too pleased to let the union sort out such difficulties within the branch.[1] In disputed cases of this sort it is the union that selects the man for the job, and it has to develop its own custom and practice for this purpose.

The other industry where the promotion veto shop is widespread is textiles. In mule spinning, for example, there is no system of apprenticeship, and promotion to the rank of spinner is usually reserved, as a result of union pressure, for the senior assistant in the

---

[1] In the past, of course, promotion was the prerogative of management, and this led to complaints of favouritism and unfairness.

mill, who must be a member of the spinners' union. This does not usually give rise to difficulties since the great majority of spinners' assistants are already members. However, the rule on engagement of spinners varies between mills. In some areas there is an agreement that a spinner who loses his position can apply for *alternative* vacancies in other mills, the remainder being reserved for promoted assistants. If this is the case, of course, the spinners may be said to be operating a modified form of the craft qualification shop. However, it seems generally agreed that even where such an agreement exists it is rarely applied. As one writer has put it, 'the one thing which invariably brings the piecers to mutiny is a threat to their promotion prospects'.[1]

As was argued in the previous chapter, the crucial difference between the post-entry shop and all forms of pre-entry shop is that it is only in the case of the latter that the closed shop can be used to effect *any* kind of entry control. It can be seen from this account of actual examples of the pre-entry shop, however, that the objectives of entry control, and the extent to which they are realizable, vary from one form of pre-entry shop to another, and even between different examples of the same form. Sometimes the practice is used to restrict total entry, share out casual work, and retain job monopolies for members of the family. Sometimes it is used to enforce rigid job demarcations, in defiance of the wishes of employers in the industry. On other occasions all that is desired, or at least obtained, is a form of job-preference for existing union members, or a veto over promotion and the right to sort out disputed promotion issues within the union branch.

Unfortunately, it is often difficult to say with any certainty whether, in practice, the groups in question effectively pursue one or other of these objectives. It is particularly difficult to estimate how far the pre-entry shop is being used to restrict total entry. As can be seen in the case of the bummarees, entry restriction is a complex affair; what one side regards as an unjustifiable attempt to limit the total number of workers available, the other side describes as a mere sharing out of available work, so as to avoid short time and redundancy. Similarly, the mere existence of apprenticeship ratios is not conclusive evidence of a restriction of total numbers. In printing, the employers have in any case agreed to these ratios, and some of them support the contention of the unions that the ratios allow ample margin for growth. In shipbuilding this is not

---

[1] H. A. Turner, 'Trade Union Differentives and the levelling of Wages', *Manchester School*, Vol. XX, p. 264, 1952.

so, and management generally resents the unilaterally enforced
ratios of the boilermakers on precisely these grounds. Yet the
boilermakers, like the bummarees, and the dockers, reply that all
'reasonable' requests for the introduction of more apprentices are
not opposed, and that they, like other trade unionists, are really only
interested in maintaining and protecting the existing jobs of their
members. In other words, they represent their actions as examples
of the operation of job preference, rather than the restriction of total
numbers to 'unjustifiable' levels. These complex matters are discussed further in subsequent chapters.

(e) Post-Entry Shops

On the most generous of estimates the number of workers affected
by the pre-entry shop in all its forms is unlikely to be more than
three-quarters of a million. This means that for every worker in
a pre-entry shop there are four in post-entry shops. Almost two-
thirds of these—or just under two million—are employed in one of
two trades—engineering or mining. Just under a third of the
remainder—or about 300,000—consist of various semi-skilled and
unskilled groups who either service or work alongside workers
covered by comprehensive pre-entry shops—i.e. non-craft workers
in general printing, shipbuilding and textiles, as well as labourers in
iron and steel.

Of the remaining 700,000 or so workers covered by the closed
shop almost half are employed by co-operative societies. The rest
come from a wide variety of trades, the most important of which
are building and various types of transport work. Small numbers
of workers are affected by the post-entry shop in numerous sections
of manufacturing industry.

For the most part, in all the groups where the closed shop exists in
its post-entry form it is necessary to join the union immediately or
very shortly after starting work. But the variations in how this
comes about within different post-entry shops is best explained in
the next section.

(4) VARIATIONS IN ENFORCEMENT

As in the case of variations in the form taken by the closed shop
it is impossible to prescribe the precise limits of formal and informal
recognition in every industry, or to measure the extent and force of
unilateral enforcement by the union in each trade.

What can be done, however, is to list the more important groups where the formal closed shop operates, and classify the trades that remain under three broad headings. The list of formally closed areas reads:

Coal Miners	240,000
Dockers	46,000
Scottish Bakers	14,000
London Transport Workers . . .	43,000
Entertainment Workers	15,000
Co-operative Society Workers. . .	300,000
TOTAL	658,000

Something must be said about the way the closed shop is enforced in each of these groups.

(a) Coal Miners

When the National Coal Board took over the industry the closed shop was already formally recognized throughout a number of regions—for example, in Durham, Wales and Warwickshire—and in particular coal pits. Elsewhere the great majority of miners were already in informally accepted closed shops, and those who were not were often covered by the union enforced closed shop, imposed, if necessary, by means of a stoppage of work. There were, in addition, a number of pits in which the semi-closed shop operated. In some parts of Lancashire, for example, non-unionists could not get piecework, and in Cumberland they were subjected to other restrictions.

This was the position facing the N.C.B. when the National Union of Miners, in January 1948, asked for an agreement formally recognizing the closed shop. The Board replied that although there was a widespread acceptance of such a practice,

To make Union membership compulsory throughout the industry was a different matter. There was now only one employer. To grant the N.U.M.'s request would mean discharging all workmen who did not wish to join the Union regardless of their efficiency and length of service; these workmen would not merely be discharged from their particular jobs but from the industry, and they would be unlikely to find jobs elsewhere in which they could use the experience and skill they had gained. Further, if a man were expelled from the Union for a breach of Union regulations, the Union would be able to get him dismissed from the Board's service even though the Board had no complaint against him. The introduction of a 'closed shop' would also change the voluntary nature of the union.[1]

[1] N.C.B. Annual Report, 1948, p. 48.

E

Nevertheless, although they refused to accede to the union's request, they added that they too wished to see the 'complete and orderly representation of workmen' and were prepared to 'continue existing District arrangements for maintaining Union membership, and, in Districts where there were no arrangements, to tell their officials to do what they could to persuade all workmen to join the union'. Moreover, they also decided to accede to the union's demand for a check off—where written consent could be obtained from the individual concerned.

The effect of this compromise has given rise to a situation in which the N.C.B. can only be said to recognize the right of the Miners' Union to a formal closed shop in places such as Durham, where it was accepted by the previous owners of the industry. In practice, however, over a wide area, the check off is used to assist in the implementation of an *informally* recognized closed shop.

Management has been prepared to print and distribute forms authorizing deductions from wages for trade union contributions, and for a small commission their officials undertake to carry out all the administration involved. One indication of the comprehensiveness of this system is that, with the exception of Durham, it is not now the general practice of the National Union of Mineworkers to issue subscription cards. The Durham District remains the exception only because it decided, in 1948, not to take advantage of the check off offer; as a result it still needs to collect contributions at the pit head.

A sure index of the extent to which the closed shop has come to be accepted within coal mining is the fact that strikes over non-unionism have largely disappeared from this most strike-prone of British industries.[1]

Nowadays, the need for unilateral enforcement is only likely to arise in a situation in which a miner is expelled from his union for a disciplinary offence. Most colliery managers would be reluctant to accept the need to discharge such a man, and officially the N.C.B. would disapprove. Individual managers might be prepared to move him to another job, or even another pit, if they thought this would help. Fortunately for the N.C.B. this does not appear to have been a problem very often. The overwhelming majority of miners sign a check off when they enter the industry without any difficulty, and they continue paying dues until the day of their retirement.

[1] See p. 65 below.

(b) Dockers

The position in respect of the enforcement of the closed shop among dockers employed by the National Dock Labour Board is in many ways analogous to that of miners who work for the N.C.B. Before the creation of the N.D.L.B. there were local agreements which required nominees for work to produce clearance certificates from their union. These agreements covered workers employed in the London, Liverpool, Manchester and Bristol Docks. The existence of these agreements, which nowadays affect about 46,000 workers, may be construed as evidence of formal closed shop arrangements. The remaining 22,000 dockers employed by the N.D.L.B. must be presumed to be covered by a form of closed shop which is at most informally recognized.

However, it is important to note that even in the case of the dockers of London, Liverpool, Manchester and Bristol, there is a sense in which their formal closed shop arrangements have to be supplemented by unilateral enforcement. This difficulty arises partly out of the statutory nature of employment under the N.D.L.B. scheme. In the dockers' contract with the N.D.L.B. there is no mention of union membership, and it may be doubted whether, once it had admitted a man to the register, the Board would be entitled to discharge him for non-payment of union dues or expulsion from the union. Certainly, the man concerned would have the right to appeal to a special tribunal, and might sustain a suit of breach of contract in a civil court. Theoretically it would be possible to deny such a man the right to re-registration, which is required every six months, but even this could be challenged and the Board would be most reluctant to court such publicity.

Fortunately for the Board, the unions have always preferred to *maintain* the closed shop, where this was necessary, by unilateral pressure, unconnected with the individual's right to remain on the N.D.L.B. register. This involves a collective refusal, operated at the point of hire or 'call', to work with anyone who is in arrears, or has been expelled from the union. Those threatened in this way may still draw their guaranteed weekly wage, but they will be unable to earn above this because no docker will sign on with them.

The unilaterally operated refusal to work with non-unionists or lapsed members has a long history in the docks. It was the traditional way of enforcing the closed shop before bilaterally regulated decasualization. In those days its main objective was to enforce a measure of entry control.

The system works thus. When gangers wish to engage men they stand at recognized points while those wanting work present themselves for hire or 'call'. If the ganger is a member of the union he will only call paid up union members; if he is not, then paid up members will not work with non-members, and if necessary will subsequently refuse to work with the non-union ganger. To let fellow members know they are in compliance they hold up union cards stamped on the front with a figure which changes every quarter. In this way it is easy to detect a man more than thirteen weeks in arrears and deny him work.

In the past, the card check at the point of hire could be used to impose a measure of decasualization, by limiting the total supply of cards at branch level. But the system had its disadvantages, and union officials, at least, long desired to supplement it with the creation of a recognized register or 'pool' of labour, to whom employers agreed to pay a basic wage, whether work was available or not.[1]

(c) Scottish Bakers

Members of the Scottish Association of Master Bakers, together with a number of other Scottish Master Bakers, have a formal agreement with the Scottish Bakers' Union on the closed shop. This agreement results in the enforcement of a comprehensive post-entry shop over all the large baking and confectionery establishments in Scotland.[2] In conjunction with this agreement, it must be added, the Scottish bakers are also party to another which provides for arbitration and forbids strikes and lock-outs for 'any other form of direct or coercive action whatsoever'.[3]

(d) London Transport Workers

The formally recognized post-entry shop which covers members of the Transport and General Workers' Union employed in operating and servicing London Transport vehicles is the outcome of an

---

[1] See Jean T. McKelvey, 'Dock Labour Disputes in Great Britain', *Bulletin No.* 23, New York State School of Industrial and Labor Relations, March 1953. In recent years the continued reliance on the card check to *maintain* the closed shop resulted in its breakdown in parts of the Northern Ports. This is discussed below in the section on Variations in Scope.

[2] National Working Agreement between the S.U.B.A.W., the Scottish Association of Master Bakers and others, p. 19.

[3] National Agreement of the National Joint Committee for the Scottish Baking Industry, p. 16. The relationship between closed shop agreement and non-strike clauses is discussed further below.

agreement reached with the London Passenger Transport Board, as it then was, in August 1946.

Before that time the farthest the company would go in openly accepting the closed shop was a declaration posted in all garages, 'encouraging' union membership. From the moment that London Transport was nationalized, in 1934, to the passage of the Trade Dispute and Trade Union Act of 1946, recognition of the closed shop was statutorily illegal in any publicly owned establishment,[1] and so the L.P.T.B. would not have been able formally to recognize the practice, even had they wanted to.

However, in 1946 the Board was able to agree to a union request formally to recognize the practice. It is generally admitted that the main reason for the demand for the closed shop was the elimination of a breakaway organization—the National Passenger Workers' Union. This organization was founded after the settlement of a strike in 1937 and, although it never managed to secure recognition from the L.T.P.B., it continued to hold the allegiance of several thousand busmen. Friction continued between the two organizations, producing sporadic strikes, until the Transport and General Workers' Union notified the L.P.T.B., in 1946, that their members would no longer work with workers who were not members of the union.

To 'avoid strikes and maintain public order' the Board decided 'not to continue in their service any employee in the grade concerned who is unwilling to join the Transport and General Workers Union'.[2]

(e) Entertainment Workers

Among entertainment workers the closed shop arises among three groups: (1) musicians, (2) actors and other performers, (3) certain production and back stage staff in theatres, films and television. In each group there are some formally recognized closed shops.

The Musicians' Union has an agreement in commercial television stipulating that all players must be members of the union before the date of the performance.[3] A similar agreement covers London Theatres. Equity, the actors' union, has an agreement with the Society of West End Theatre Managers establishing a register of

[1] This was the effect of Clause 6 of the 1927 Act, which was repealed by the 1946 Act.
[2] J. T. McKelvey, 'The Closed Shop Controversy in Post-War Britain,' Industrial and Labour Relations Review, Vol. 7, No. 4, p. 559.
[3] Exceptions are made for service bands, church organists, and a number of other small groups—see below.

approved managers and artistes. In practice, all members of Equity and the Society of West End Managers 'become registered and remain registered so long as they are members of those associations'.[1] The Association of Cinematograph and Allied Technicians have a formal agreement covering union membership in both films and commercial television.

When the closed shop arises outside these areas in entertainment, it is usually informally recognized—or at least tolerated by employers—for example among actors and other performers in the larger provincial centres. The only important group in which its enforcement still relies on unilateral regulation is musicians.

For the most part, those who employ musicians on a permanent basis have come to terms with the closed shop, but the great majority of members of the union are engaged on a series of temporary and shifting jobs, varying from one-night stands in make-up bands to more or less permanent employment in a single orchestra or band under the control of a particular conductor or musical director. In such a situation the enforcement of the closed shop necessarily depends on the attitude adopted by individual musicians, who may be together for no more than a few hours or days.

In these circumstances it is the practice to call for a card inspection if one member of the band is suspected of being a non-unionist. Those found to be out of compliance are told to join or pay up before the performance and any who are unable to comply with the request because of shortage of funds will normally be allowed to wait until after they have been paid. Existing members will often be able to purchase union subscription stamps from an activist on the job, or from the local branch secretary.

(f) Co-operative Workers

The co-operative movement consists of about a thousand retail societies, three national federations, eighty-seven local federal societies and roughly fifty productive societies and specialist organizations. The total labour force is just under 400,000 workers. The majority of these are organized by the Union of Shop, Distributive and Allied Workers, although the Transport and General Workers is active among transport workers and delivery roundsmen.

About 560 societies employing approximately 300,000 workers have recognized the closed shop. About 90,000 of these workers

---

[1] This does not result in a labour pool shop. Managers remain free to engage anyone they wish.

are engaged in various forms of manufacture, and in the service trades. The rest are in distribution and the majority serve in co-op retail shops.

The formal closed shop in the co-op is the outstanding example of what may be termed the *employer initiated* closed shop. But it would be misleading to imply that the practice is in any sense enforced against the wishes of the unions; if it can be said to be imposed on anyone it is on the workers themselves. As V. L. Allen puts it: 'Closed shop conditions in the Co-operative Movement are not the result of collective bargaining but are, in effect, employer imposed conditions, arising primarily from the theoretical identity between the aims of the Co-operative Movement and the trade unions'. Allen goes on:

The procedure is for Co-operative members' meetings or meetings of the boards of management of individual societies to pass resolutions to employ trade-union labour only. Trade unions come indirectly into the picture by getting their members who are also active Co-operative Society members to sponsor such resolutions.[1]

This is an accurate summary of what happens in most retail societies. In Oxford, for example, the closed shop drive came almost entirely from trade unionists not in the employ of the society. Early minutes of the Trades' Council abound with references to attempts to establish union organization within the local society and demands that the management committee should discriminate in favour of union labour. To this end the Council ran 'trade union' candidates for election to the Management Committee until, by 1937, they had a majority. They then forced the General Manager to issue a circular 'encouraging' workers to join. The result was disappointing, and the chairman remarked that apparently 'the employees don't want trade unionism'.[2] By 1938 the trade unionists on the committee had committed the society to the closed shop. A provision was introduced into the society's rule book stipulating that membership of union affiliated to the T.U.C. 'shall be a condition of employment'. Commenting on the effect of the resolution, the then Chairman has said, 'There was a terrific opposition among the majority of non-unionized employees', though he continued,

[1] Allen, *op. cit.*, p. 41.
[2] The Chairman was the late George Wallis, J.P., later President of the Society. He was a printer by trade, and a great trade union stalwart, who led the fight for the unionization of the Oxford Co-op.

'this was speedily overcome and it was not necessary to give any-body the sack.'[1] Since that date, an effective post-entry shop has been imposed on the great majority of permanent full-time workers without the need to threaten enforcement of the provisions of the society's rule book.

This is mainly because of the early introduction of a check off, along the lines outlined already in respect of coal-miners. In fact, the check off was suggested by a local union official unable to find enough active workers to collect subscriptions. But management has been reluctant to force the closed shop on temporary and part-time workers, and maintain that if it did many of them would not be prepared to work for the society. This means that there remains within the Oxford Co-op a small pocket of non-union labour, which probably amounts to about 10 per cent of the total.

Apart from the fact that Oxford, as a high-wage town where labour is short, is more than normally dependent on temporary and part-time staff, this account of the growth and scope of the closed shop is accepted as typical. Pockets of non-unionism, even among the part-time staff, are less likely to be tolerated in the more militant union areas, but there are no known examples of the demand for the closed shop coming, in the first instance, from determined pressure from below. The check off is widespread, though there are no figures available.

Among the 600 societies or so that have not passed formal resolutions imposing the closed shop, the situation is difficult to determine. Most of them are very small and on average employ about 150 workers each; taken together they account for less than a quarter of the total labour force, and they probably have more than their share of part-time workers. It is said that some impose an informally recognized closed shop, but it is doubtful if anything like the majority do so effectively. Where the closed shop works in the co-op it is, in almost all instances, formally recognized and employer initiated.

Apart from the six groups listed above, there are some formally recognized closed shops in other trades, but the numbers involved in each case are usually small. In the course of interviews the writer has uncovered individual firms who have formally recognized the closed shop in trades as different as engineering and clothing, or

---

[1] Interview with the late George Wallis.

chemicals and road transport. In one important instance, local government, the practice, where it occurs, is also often managerially initiated.

This is the case among about forty local authorities where the Labour Party has, at some time or another, controlled the council and has introduced a closed shop resolution along the lines of the Oxford Co-op. Their motives in acting in this way are the same as those of local co-operative management committees; indeed, they are often the same people. In several cases, moves to obtain the closed shop can be traced back to an identical source—a resolution passed in the local Trades' Council demanding action from fellow trade unionists in their capacities as employers.

As in the co-op it would be misleading to imply that in most cases this means that the closed shop is being enforced against the wishes of the unions who benefit, although there was one case where this was so. This occurred in Durham when the County Council, in November 1950, decided that *all* its employees, both professional and manual, must belong to a union. The National Union of Teachers instructed its members to refuse to produce the required evidence, and announced its total opposition to the principle of the closed shop.[1]

After Parliament had debated the issue, and a Conservative vote censuring the Council had been defeated by fifteen votes, the Council, in response to ministerial pressure, modified its demands. Abandoning attempts to dismiss existing non-unionists, it insisted only that in *future* all new teachers would have to join the union. The Teachers Union then called on all its members to resign *en masse*, and in face of what was, in effect, a strike threat the Minister directed the Council to refrain from questioning applicants for teaching posts about their union status. But, in August 1951, the Council ruled that applicants for special leave, or extended sick leave, must file an application through the union. Once again the union protested and the Council was prevailed upon to refer the Dispute to the Minister of Labour under Order 1376. When a Board of Arbitration, set up by the Minister, decided that the sick leave rule of the Council conflicted with its prior agreement with the union, the Council capitulated and announced that in future it would not seek to impose the closed shop on non-manual workers.

[1] The British Medical Association reacted in a similar way.

The Durham dispute is interesting mainly because so far as is known it is the one case where a union has positively refused the closed shop, and has threatened to organize a strike to avoid its enforcement. As will be seen in future chapters, not all unions are equally closed shop prone—i.e. they do not all tend to demand the practice with equal determination as and when the opportunity to obtain it arises. Nevertheless, it is most unusual for a union to go out of its way to launch a campaign *against* the closed shop, and even in the case of the teachers this has only happened in Durham, so far as is known.

A closer study of the Durham Dispute reveals that even in that case there are special political and personal factors involved. In Durham the initiative for the closed shop came from the local Labour Party, who made no secret of the fact that they wished to symbolize their post-war ascendancy by adopting what one student of the dispute has termed 'a policy of discrimination in reverse'.[1] Moreover, the most active member of the Labour Party Group engaged in this fight was the father of a Labour M.P., who was himself a member of the union. He was subsequently expelled from the union for his part in the affair.

(g) The Limits of Informal Recognition

On the basis of the estimates quoted above, just under a fifth of all workers covered by the closed shop work in situations where the practice has been accorded some kind of formal recognition, although, as in the case of dockers, it may still be necessary to employ certain types of unilateral pressure as well.

What are more difficult to determine are the limits of informal recognition, and the extent and scope of unilateral enforcement. The most that can be done is to list workers not covered by the formal closed shop, under three broad headings. These are:

(1) Those in which informal recognition is widespread or virtually universal, resulting in the great majority of employers being prepared to 'screen' prospective employees and inform them that they will be expected to join a union. Those that refuse will eventually be discharged, or removed to other work, without the necessity of an actual strike threat.

(2) Those in which few or no employers are prepared to act in this way. In which the closed shop, when it arises must be mainly enforced by means of the strike threat—directed as much at the recalcitrant worker as at the employer.

[1] McKelvey, *op. cit.*, p. 569.

(3) In between groups, i.e. those where many employers have accepted the closed shop, for the most part informally, but others have not. Where it is sometimes necessary to threaten a strike to produce the grudging co-operation of the employer.

The first category contains about a million workers, most of whom are employed in comprehensively closed groups, where the way in which the closed shop is enforced has already been described —i.e. miners and dockers and musicians not covered by the formal closed shop, shipyard workers, sailors, iron and steel workers, hatters, workers in London markets, and a number of small craft unions.

The second category includes less than 50,000 workers, all employed in mainly open groups where the closed shop is very exceptional—i.e. sections of the industrial civil service, such as those employed in certain government engineering factories, and workers in paper, box and carton manufacture.

Among the 100,000 or so industrial civil servants employed in government engineering factories, unionization is extremely high, and strong social pressures amounting to a semi-closed shop operate over a wide area. As is usual with government departments, there is no question of official recognition of the closed shop, but it is realized that in places like the machine shop, or the tool room, unilateral pressures, amounting if necessary to a refusal to work, would make the position of a non-unionist virtually impossible. In the paper box and carton trade, similarly strong unilateral pressures ensure that many craft workers remain within their respective unions. Pressures are less strong on the semi-skilled and unskilled workers, and employers generally adopt a quite different attitude to that now ruling among their associates in printing. Indeed, it would be true to say that the employers in this industry are still determined to resist the spread of the closed shop, as and when they can. Generally speaking, it is only when paper firms are also printers of long standing that they have agreed to come to terms with the closed shop.[1]

Over three-quarters of the two million or so workers in the third group are employed in one of three industries: engineering, construction and road transport, but they actually span a wide variety of trades, including textiles, timber and furniture, clothing, chemicals, and many other trades. They are best typified by engineering—where over half the workers involved are employed.

[1] For example, the Oxford University Press.

In engineering there is a very wide variation in the degree of acceptance of the practice, and in the role of unilateral enforcement. The survey of individual firms conducted in the industry revealed that, in many cases, the existence of the closed shop was openly admitted, and even defended by management. In other cases there was an element of conscious deception; men rejected as unsuitable because they objected to joining a union during the 'screening' process were not informed that this was the reason, and when recalcitrants were discharged it was ostensibly for some other cause. In other firms it was openly admitted that non-unionists who were the cause of a threatened stoppage would be discharged, but the union was more or less expected to make such a threat before management would act. In different establishments management actually required a strike before it would act, and in a few cases even after this they refused to move.

The mixture of unilateral and bilateral regulation differs from one industry to another in this group, but there is little point in trying to list the groups in this category in any declining order of managerial co-operation. Such a list would be extremely rough and would signify little. What can be said as a result of the foregoing analysis, is that almost half the workers in closed shops are either in formally recognized closed shops or in industries where the great majority of employers are prepared to co-operate in its informal implementations. Of the remainder less than one in forty are employed in industries where management co-operation in any form is very unusual, and the remainder in industries where the situation varies, along the lines outlined in engineering.

(h) Closed Shop Strikes

Despite about half the workers in closed shops being employed in industries where the practice sometimes has to be enforced unilaterally, the closed shop issue has never been responsible for a substantial proportion of British strikes. In the published records of the Ministry of Labour, strikes to enforce the closed shop are grouped with those for union recognition, and those against the alleged victimization of union members, under the general heading 'Trade Union Status Disputes'. Knowles has shown that between 1911 and 1945 strikes over 'Trade Union Status' were invariably a small proportion of all strikes—on average they accounted for a mere 6 per cent of strikers, 1·5 per cent of strikers directly involved.[1]

[1] Knowles, *op. cit.*, p. 314.

In connection with this study a more detailed analysis was made by the writer of actual closed shop strikes known to the Ministry of Labour for the years 1945–57 inclusive. This showed that altogether there were 462 recorded strikes over the closed shop in this period. 162,000 workers were directly involved and 562,000 working days were lost. On these figures less than 2 per cent of recorded strikes were over the closed shop, fewer than 2·5 per cent of all workers directly involved were striking about the closed shop, and less than 1·5 per cent of all working days lost as a consequence of recorded strikes were due to this issue.

Turning to the industrial distribution of the strikes it was found that since then there have been no recorded strikes among many of the comprehensively closed trades, such as printers, merchant seamen, and so on, to enforce the closed shop. This has also been the case, since the early post-war years, in one other group, miners. There were, however, a number of comprehensively closed groups, such as craftsmen in the shipyards, or process workers in iron and steel manufacture, where the state of the statistics does not allow one to reach a separate conclusion. (It may well be that all the twenty-two recorded strikes in shipbuilding occurred among the unskilled and semi-skilled, but on the available information this cannot be known for certain.)

Dominating the remaining industries affected by closed shop strikes were the two large closed shop prone industries, engineering, and construction. These two industries accounted for 45 per cent of recorded strikes, 78 per cent of workers involved and 45 per cent of working days lost. The other trades most affected were road transport, the small-scale metal trades, iron foundries, paper box, wood and cork manufacture, clothing and other manufacturing. Between them, these account for eighty-eight strikes or just under 20 per cent of the total. The remaining strikes were spread over a wide area of industries and included workers in textiles, distribution, public utilities, chemicals, fishing, railway workshops, and many others.

Unfortunately, it is not possible to accept the statistical records of the Ministry as a complete and accurate measure of *all* closed disputes.

In the first place, there are many minor strikes over non-unionism that are too small to get into the statistics. The Ministry does not record strikes involving fewer than ten workers and those which last less than a day, unless the aggregate number of working days exceeds 100. The writer has been informed of many actual closed shops strikes which were too small to be recorded on these grounds.

Secondly, the Ministry has no completely effective techniques for collecting information about strikes. It relies on information received by its local officers, who are dependent on their own contacts, and the local press. Every effort is made to be as comprehensive as possible, but it is clear that quite a few small strikes slip through the Ministry's net. For example, local employers' associations in the engineering industry collect their own strike statistics. In the experience of the writer they invariably show evidence of a level of strike activity considerably above that recorded in the official statistics.

But if this is so with closed shop strikes it is also the case with the rest of the official statistics; there is no reason to suppose that the information gathered about strikes other than closed shop strikes is any more complete than that gathered about strikes over non-unionism. There is also no reason to believe that the official figures are more inaccurate in one industry than another.

If this is so, then the attitude to adopt towards the official statistics is one of qualified acceptance. While they are not comprehensive, they are also roughly representative. They must be regarded as incomplete parts of indeterminate sized icebergs. Since it is plausible to suppose that roughly the same proportion of each iceberg is hidden, one can use them as an index of the relative importance of closed shop strikes, and as signs of their industrial distribution.

One can also use them to establish how far strikes called to enforce the closed shop are likely to succeed. The records reveal that between 1945 to 1957 some 11·3 per cent of all strikes called to enforce the closed shop were decided in favour of the employers—that is to say the men concerned remained at work and the exclusion threat failed to work. 42·9 per cent were decided in favour of the workers—that is to say the non-unionists or lapsed members involved either left the job or were forced to pay up or join the union. The ultimate result of the rest of the strikes is not so easy to determine. In the majority of them 'work was resumed pending negotiations'. Whether the outcome of the negotiations was the de facto acceptance of a closed shop situation or a decision to move or to put pressure on particular recalcitrants it is impossible to say. In about half the cases examined, a successful strike to maintain or impose the closed shop was won when the non-unionists concerned left to find other employment.

(5) VARIATIONS IN SCOPE

(a) Craftsmen

There are few types of work unreservedly closed to non-unionists throughout Britain; what does exist is a whole range of occupations in which the closed shop is only avoidable at considerable cost and inconvenience.

The group in which the impact of the practice is probably at its most all-pervasive is process workers in iron and steel. There are few regional or other variations, and the result of expulsion from the union is the denial of an opportunity to practise a highly specialized and well paid craft. Since the skills used are of little use outside the occupation in question, this means that the worker concerned must become and remain an unskilled worker, until or unless he can learn another craft. Almost as pervasive is the effect of the closed shop among skilled cotton groups—such as the spinners, or the tape-sizers.

A slightly different situation arises in the case of skilled printing workers, or among certain classes of shipyard craftsmen. There are pockets of non-unionism in these trades, in the first case mainly among small printers in areas like the south-west, and in the second case largely in Admiralty shipyards. If an expelled printer or boiler-maker is lucky he may be able to gain admittance to one of these areas. Similarly, a boilermaker may be able to escape into a less well organized industry, such as engineering. Nevertheless, the strength of the union in such industries is not inconsiderable, and it may well be that before long the worker will be forced to come to terms with the union again. Moreover, as in the case of iron and steel, the skill of a printer or boilermaker is relatively useless outside the trade, and those permanently excluded from a required union may be forced to become, if only temporarily, unskilled workers.

Among skilled groups in other industries, the closed shop is generally less all-embracing. For example, a tool-room worker in engineering may learn his job and find work without becoming and remaining a member of the Engineers—although he may have to confine himself to the smaller establishments. The questionnaires circulated to both sides of the engineering industry showed that the closed shop is much more prevalent among the larger establishments, where it is the rule rather than the exception in places like the tool room and machine shop.

Less comprehensive still is the impact of the practice among construction workers. A questionnaire circulated to a representative cross-section of branch secretaries of the Amalgamated Society of Woodworkers, for example, indicated that about 30 per cent of the building and civil engineering workers covered by the sample were in closed shops. The Woodworkers which recruits among about 30 per cent of the craftsmen in the industry, is far the best organized of the building unions. Once again, the practice is less easy to evade on the larger sites, and is virtually universal in areas like the Tyne Wear and Tees, Liverpool and Birkenhead.

Among craft workers employed on maintenance work in the manufacturing industries, such as electricians, plumbers, painters, and so on, the strength of the closed shop varies according to how far the industry they serve is itself dominated by the practice; thus, if an electrician wants to work in Fleet Street, he will have to become and remain a member of the Electrical Trades' Union. If he is content to service workers in a pickle factory he may well be able to lapse.

If he transfers to commercial electrical contracting he will enter a well-organized industry, where the larger firms have long since come to terms with the closed shop and the practice is difficult to evade. If he enters the service of an electricity board, and avoids the more militant parts of the country, the most he will have to resist are the pressures of the semi-closed shop.

In general terms it may be said that the impact on and importance of the closed shop to any craft group will depend mainly on two factors: (1) the extent to which the union organizing the craft has managed to impose a comprehensive closed shop throughout the industries in which it recruits; (2) the extent to which the skill which makes it possible to follow the craft is non-transferable. It may be argued that there is a third factor which is sometimes important—i.e. the extent to which equally attractive jobs open to craftsmen in similar trades where the skill would be of use, are themselves effectively covered by craft unions operating comprehensive closed shops. If this is the case, then the recalcitrant who is expelled, or who leaves his original union, may still find that he is compelled to become and remain a trade unionist—if he is allowed to do so by those working at the trade.

(b) Non-Craftsmen

The closed shop cannot hope to make quite such an all-pervasive impact on lesser skilled workers, but there are many occupations where it can only be evaded at a price. This price is probably highest among dock workers. Here the chance of remaining on the most remunerative work while dropping out of the union is small, and the chance of obtaining entry to the docks without gaining acceptance by a union is largely non-existent outside the small areas covered by Admiralty docks. Generally speaking, the earnings of dockers are above those of similarly skilled labourers in other trades, and in a few instances dockers can obtain earnings far above the average.

Similar factors operate in shipyards. The more remunerative jobs are usually well organized and require the retention of a union card. Of course, the labourer in shipbuilding who wants to drop out of his union can leave the shipyards and go into engineering, or building, without suffering any significant drop in earnings. Still, the areas round most shipyards are well organized, and drives for the elimination of non-unionism often arise in both these trades. If he is determined to avoid the effects of the closed shop, or if he is in dispute with his union because of lapsed dues, the would-be non-unionist may have to leave the district altogether, or find a job in some relatively underpaid industry where the closed shop is unknown.

Another type of work in which the closed shop can only be evaded with difficulty, and at a price, is mining. Only outside the coalmining section of the industry can this be done. The situation here is analogous to that among seamen. If a man wants to be a member of a mercantile marine he is more or less forced to become and remain a member of the National Union of Seamen; similarly, if he desires to make felt hats he will have to be prepared to renounce non-unionism. In cases of this sort it cannot be said that the trade preferred requires some peculiar expertise, which will be wasted if another sort of job is taken; still, every type of work has its own attractions, and if the enforcement of a comprehensive closed shop means that it can only be followed by remaining a member of a specified trade union, this is a price which must be weighed.

In most other instances of the closed shop among the unskilled, or sections of the semi-skilled, the most that is involved is the disadvantage of moving from a particular area or firm. A baker who refuses to join a union must keep away from Scotland, a bus driver cannot move to London. The clapper-boy who drops out of the Association of Cine-Technicians may find employment with the B.B.C., and the shop assistant who dislikes his union will find that outside the area of the co-op he will seldom encounter it. In many

F

more instances, in the chemical industry for example, or above all in engineering, the most that will often be involved is a readiness to move to another part of a particular plant.

But in the case of engineering the chances of evading the closed shop will also be higher if the would-be non-unionist is prepared to confine himself to certain sections of the industry. What is conventionally termed the 'engineering industry' is in fact a vast and complex group of over thirty metal-using trades, and the prevalence of the closed shop varies very much from one trade to another. The motor manufacturing trade, for example, is one of the most affected areas, and it can be said that well over two-thirds of the manual workers employed therein are either employed in firms where the closed shop is generally accepted, or by firms that are ready to come to terms with it whenever it looks like causing trouble. Among other sections of vehicle manufacture the prac- tice is not quite so widespread, although it is common in aircraft production and cycle manufacture. It is much less prevalent among the 60,000 workers engaged in the custom built coach trade, and virtually unknown among the 200,000 workers employed in motor vehicle repair. In machine tools the closed shop predominates, and it is almost as strong in marine engineering. In electrical engineering and machinery it is rather less widespread, although even here it probably affects a majority of the semi-skilled manual groups outside the very small firms.

But, of course, inter-industry variations of this sort are themselves largely the product of variations in the level of unionization. As has been said, manual workers in engineering tend to demand the closed shop with growing force as the level of unionization rises. They are naturally less successful among such largely unorganized groups as motor vehicle repair, and more able to exploit their position within highly organized motor-car firms.

Variations in the level of unionization are also largely responsible for the fact that, viewing engineering as a whole, the closed shop is much more likely to be found within the larger establishments. This particular variation in the scope of the closed shop was well brought out in a questionnaire returned by about ninety firms with a combined labour force of over 200,000 drawn from most of the main sections of the industry. The 30 per cent of firms with fewer than 500 workers were the least affected by the practice. Half of them had no closed shops, most of the rest claimed it was confined to skilled groups, and only 10 per cent maintained that it affected a majority of all manual workers employed. Of the total manual labour force employed in these smaller firms, 70 per cent were employed in firms where there was no closed shop, about 10 per cent in firms where it was confined to skilled men, and only 20 per cent in firms where the great majority of manual workers were affected.

By contrast, a mere 10 per cent of firms with more than 300 workers were quite unaffected by the closed shop. Twenty-three per cent said it was mainly confined to skilled workers, and over 25 per cent accepted that it covered the great majority of lesser skilled grades. Only 8 per cent of the workers employed in these larger firms were in factories where there were no closed shops; 34 per cent were in firms where the closed shop was confined to skilled groups; 20 per cent in firms where it was widespread but covered only a minority of manual workers, and 38 per cent were employed in firms in which the great majority of workers were covered by closed shops.

Similar inter-industry and size variations affect the impact of the closed shop in several other large industries. For example, the closed shop is more prevalent among multiple clothing firms in Leeds and London than it is in such sections of the clothing industry as shirt-making and pyjamas, where unionization is almost universally low, and the mass of small firms are without any effective workshop organization at all. It is also less common among builders labourers' groups in small-scale speculative buildings.

Once again it is possible to list, in general terms, the factors involved in any estimation of the impact and importance of the closed shop among semi-skilled and unskilled manual workers. These are: (1) the extent to which a comprehensive closed shop has been imposed throughout the occupation in question; (2) the uniqueness of the features of the job in question which the individual workman finds attractive; (3) the degree to which similarly attractive jobs are available in open areas elsewhere.

Naturally, the same sort of considerations operate for non-manual workers in closed shops. In the case of musicians, for example, continued membership of the union is essential to earn one's living in the profession on a full-time basis. With draughtsmen it is easy to evade the closed shop outside the ship-building industry, and with most other examples of the practices among non-manual workers it is not usually necessary to do more than leave a particular place of work.

It has already been stated that the closed shop is less likely to be encountered if one avoids manual work, what has not so far been considered is how far one's chances of having to come to terms with it are increased by progressing from unskilled to more skilled types of manual work. The main difficulty encountered in trying to decide this question is the unsatisfactory nature of the customary classifications of 'skilled', 'semi-skilled' and 'unskilled' and the difficulty of classifying workers affected by the closed shop under one or another of these headings. A number of craft groups where the closed shop exists—e.g. in shipping, printing, textiles, building, railway workshops, and so on—may be easily classified and identified as skilled. Others—e.g. labourers in shipyards and building and civil engineering—are clearly all unskilled. Similarly, groups such as drivers and workers in distribution seem best regarded as semi-skilled. But, in addition to these groups, there are many more who are mixtures of all three categories—e.g. engineering workers, miners, dockers, sailors, and so on. Probably the best description for most of the workers in these groups is semi-skilled—but it is not possible, in many cases, to measure the precise size of the semi-skilled sections, or to agree about where such sections merge into the skilled and semi-skilled sections on either side. For these reasons one cannot go very far in classifying workers covered by the closed shop in terms of skill, and it is impossible to arrive at reliable over-all figures.

Very roughly it can be said that something like three-quarters of a million 'craftsmen' are affected, and it seems plausible to suppose that a considerably higher proportion of 'skilled' workers are in closed shops than in other groups. But it must be appreciated that no statistically respectable figures can be given to support this contention.

(c) Regional Variations

It has been stressed throughout this chapter that even within the comprehensively closed groups there are usually traces of regional variations. Very broadly, and in the overwhelming majority of cases, these regional variations fit into a definite pattern which is of considerable importance when considering the scope of the closed shop and its impact upon the individual worker.

Whatever the over-all prevalence of the closed shop within a particular industry or occupation, it tends to be more effectively imposed in some regions of the country than others. The so-called 'good' areas here are the industrial North, particularly the North-East Coast, and Clydeside. Somewhere round the south of the Wash, the position changes, apart from the industrial centres of South Wales. The Home Counties are regarded as 'bad' areas, and the South-West, apart from Bristol, is considered to be the grave of trade unionism in general and the closed shop in particular.

Some degree of ambiguity arises over the position in the great conurbations around Birmingham and London. Some union officials regard the Midlands as a bad area, and London as worse. Others take a different view, and a few maintain that they have a relatively large proportion of closed shops in those areas. On further examination, however, this apparent paradox is largely removed. Usually the plants in question are large, sometimes unusually so. It may be that some cases the larger conurbations have more than their share of big firms. As was seen in the case of the engineering industry, the closed shop tends to be more prevalent among the larger firms, and this may compensate for the fact that these areas are not otherwise particularly good ones for trade unionism and the closed shop.

The only important exception to this pattern occurs in the Northern Ports of Hull, Merseyside and Manchester, and there are very special reasons for this. After bitter disputes between militants and officials of the Transport and General Workers' Union over the conduct of several unofficial strikes many dockers in the north became increasingly reluctant to pay their union dues. The situation was made worse when, in 1956, some of them took the lead in introducing a London union, the National Association of Stevedores and Dockers, to the Northern ports. The Transport and General Workers' Union took this union to the Disputes Committee of the T.U.C. on a charge of 'poaching', and it was ordered to expel its northern membership. At this point an ex-Transport and General Workers' Union member brought a successful action against the Stevedores and Dockers to restrain them from expelling him.[1] The Stevedores and Dockers announced that they must regard this judgment as affecting the whole of their northern membership and refused to negotiate an agreement with the Transport Workers providing for their withdrawal from the North. The result was that in 1959 they were expelled from the T.U.C.

But this expulsion did not finish the Stevedores and Dockers and even now they have a few thousand members in the northern ports.

[1] Spring v. N.A.S.D., 2 All E.R. 221.

Unfortunately for the Transport Workers, several thousand dockers, observing the squabbles between the two unions, decided to hold no cards at all, and for this reason the closed shop in the docks may be said to be less comprehensive in the north than elsewhere.

There is no simple way of summarizing the effect of all the many variations in the scope of the closed shop which have been discussed in this section, except to say that they indicate that the consequences of non-unionism and the penalty of exclusion from a union can vary very much from job to job and from individual to individual, quite apart from the differences which arise from variations in the actual *area* over which a particular closed shop extends. There is also the question of the alternative type of employment open to each worker, and this depends on his skill, inclination, ability to move, and even the area of the country in which he happens to be born. The significance of these variations in the impact of the closed shop upon different individuals will be discussed in more detail in the second part of this book.

6. MINOR VARIATIONS

Two minor variations were mentioned in Chapter 2: the question of the check off, and the issue of membership choice.

Inquiries revealed that the check off is very rare, outside mining, seamen, local authority employees, and the co-operative movement. A number of small groups are affected in industries such as road transport, engineering, chemicals and the small-scale metal-using trades. Very broadly, the maximum number of members affected by the check off in closed shops cannot be more than a million—and almost three-quarters of these are miners. The conclusions on the issue of membership choice are not so easily quantifiable. All one can do is to list the groups where a degree of choice still exists. For the most part these are confined to non-craft workers, and even here there are few examples of post-entry choice. A choice on entry, however, often exists among many workers in such groups as the semi-skilled and unskilled in shipyards, road transport, railway workshops, iron foundries, furniture manufacture, civil air transport, building and civil engineering, distribution and a number of other manufacturing groups where small numbers of workers are covered by the closed shop. In one area of the docks, it was noted, union rivalry recently has resulted in a measure of membership choice, while in some industries, such as engineering or local government, the absence of rigid local agreements, or the determination of officials to evade the Bridlington principles, has caused a growth of post-entry membership-choice of a kind.

However, it is submitted that the general conclusions to be drawn from the survey underscore what was written on the subject of membership choice in Chapter 1. The growth of exclusive juris-diction practices, the implementation of the principles laid down by the T.U.C. Disputes Committee, and the development of 'gentle-men's agreements' at local level have all contributed to the narrowing of membership choice within the major areas covered by the closed shop. Temporary revocable privileges may remain, in some places, but there is not much acceptance of the right of members in a closed shop to choose between one of a number of unions, and to transfer from one to another when dissatisfied.

7. ANALOGOUS PRACTICES IN THE PROFESSIONS

In their standard work on the professions, Carr-Saunders and Wilson define these as 'those vocations which by common consent are called professions, together with others which claim that title or whose organization or other characteristics resemble in some degree those of acknowledged professions'.[1] The distinguishing mark of such groups is the possession of a particular technique or expertise which may be of a scientific, institutional or even aesthetic sort, such as enables members of the group to render a 'specialized service to the community'.[2]

Some members of the professions, such as teachers, are also members of trade unions, and their position in relation to the closed shop has already been described.[3] However, far more professional workers are members of what are termed 'professional associations' and some of these associations operate practices analogous to the closed shop. It is not the object of this study to measure, analyse or evaluate the activities of professional associations as such,[4] but it is necessary to refer, if only briefly, to the extent to which they follow analogous practices to those of the trade union closed shop.[5]

When the state is concerned with the competence and prestige of 'professions' it seeks to regulate entrance and secure the observance

[1] *The Professions*, by A. M. Carr-Saunders and P. A. Wilson, Oxford University Press, 1933, p. 284.
[2] *Ibid.*
[3] See p. 61 above.
[4] In fact this is exactly what Carr-Saunders and Wilson set out to do in the work quoted above.
[5] This matter is relevant to arguments used in justification of the closed shop which follow later in this book.

of particular 'professional standards'. This usually results in a publicly regulated 'register'. Thus, solicitors, doctors, dentists, nurses, mid-wives, patent agents, pharmaceutical chemists and architects have an official register of duly qualified persons. It is an offence for an unregistered person to present himself as a registered person, and an effective monopoly of the technique is secured for those on the register. In all the so-called 'registered' professions there are pro-fessional associations. These associations share with the State a con-cern for the competence and prestige of the profession, and confine their membership to registered persons. They, or their predecessors, have usually taken the lead in demanding state registration, and they are usually involved, in some way, in the process of regulating entry to the register, and supervising those already on it. Thus the Benchers of the Inns of Court admit to the profession, participate in the prescription of qualifications, and are empowered to decide who shall be debarred from practising. Similarly, the Law Society keeps the register of solicitors, participates in the prescription of qualifica-tions, and members of the Council of the Society are selected by the Master of the Rolls to sit on the committee which disciplines the profession. In the case of bodies like the British Medical Association, or the British Dental Association, control is more indirect. The doctors' register is, in effect, controlled by the General Medical Council, but a number of registered 'practioners' are elected to the Council, and those who are supported by the B.M.A. are 'invariably elected'.[1]

It should be stressed, however, that membership of most pro-professional associations in the registered professions is not an effective condition of employment, even when, as in the case of the Law Society, the association is in virtual control of entry, qualifica-tions, examinations and the disciplinary code. It is not necessary to be a member of the Law Society in order to practice as a solicitor, and it is admitted that the Society is not 100 per cent organized. Similarly, contrary to the general opinion of trade unionists, the B.M.A. is in no sense a closed shop. A substantial minority of doctors are not members of the B.M.A.—and sometimes, one is told, established practitioners drop out of the B.M.A. due to some dispute or disagreement with the society. No doubt non-membership may be something of a social bar to a struggling G.P., but it seems clear that it is not in any meaningful sense an effective condition of

[1] Carr-Saunders and Wilson, *op. cit.*, p. 92.

employment.[1] In a similar position are the rest of the medical profession, and registered commercial groups like the architects.

In the case of barristers and veterinary surgeons, however, membership of their respective associations is a condition of employment. No one who is not a member of one of the four Inns of Court is allowed to plead a case before any of the higher courts, while the Royal College of Veterinary Surgeons is required, under the Veterinary Surgeons Act, to admit to membership all those who pass their examination and thus qualify for the register. In fact, the register of qualified veterinary surgeons consists of the membership of the R.C.V.S.

With the unregistered professions the position is different again. To quote Carr-Saunders and Wilson, 'It is the purpose of the professional associations to achieve, and of the State, where it intervenes, to grant, some degree of monopoly of function to the practitioners.'[2] In the case of the registered professions, the monopoly clearly resides in those on the state-upheld register. It follows that unless the state confines the right of registration to those who are members of the association it is possible to practice the profession without membership of the association—though it may be necessary to subject oneself to its rules and orders. In the case of the unregistered professions what is often protected by the state is not the right to the privileges of the registered but the right to use the title of a member of the association. Thus:

a professional title, not necessarily descriptive of membership of any association, or indeed descriptive of anything at all, will be protected by injunction if it can be shown to have become associated in the public mind with membership of a particular body, and if, which is important, membership of that body implies a certain standard of training and qualification.[3]

In this way, such groups have secured a measure of legal protection for the monopoly they have sought to establish. Moreover, sometimes specific acts of parliament and governmental decisions have aided the establishment of a group monopoly. Thus, only a barrister, a solicitor, or a member of one of the two associations of accountants may represent taxpayer in an appeal before the tax authorities.[4]

---

[1] On this point, Carr-Saunders and Wilson quote the opinion of the miners' leader, Herbert Smith, before the 1926 Coal Commission. They go on to comment: 'He is not the only person who has confused the B.M.A. with the G.M.C.' In this isolated instance even these authors are confused. No doctor has to be a member of the G.M.C., and very few doctors are. What a doctor *must* do is get on to the register which is kept by the G.M.C.

[2] *Op. cit.*, p. 319.

[3] Carr-Saunders and Wilson, *op. cit.*, p. 360.

[4] *Op. cit.*, p. 214.

But even where there are not legally upheld monopolies, what Carr-Saunders and Wilson term 'institutional advantages' or monopolies often accrue to associations which can make membership a hall-mark of qualification. Moreover, they continue, 'It is the aim of every association in the unregulated professions to do this'.[1] The degree of institutional monopoly varies from profession to profession, and these authors argue that there are certain circumstances which are more favourable to its arising than others. For the purposes of this study it is not necessary to consider in any detail either the precise degree of institutional monopoly now enjoyed by members of various unregistered professions or the reasons for it. All that needs to be said at this point is that there *are* a number of professional associations who have secured effective monopolies of particular techniques, and membership of one or another of them has become an effective condition of employment. This is the case in respect of 'registered' groups, like barristers and veterinary surgeons, and among the more established 'unregistered' groups. Moreover, among 'unregistered' groups generally, even where this is not the case, there is an intention that eventually it should be. Thus it may be said that in a sense *all* the unregistered professions are closed shop prone.

8. GENERAL SUMMARY

Summarizing briefly what this chapter has revealed, it may be said that the closed shop is an extremely varied phenomenon, which affects different groups in differing degrees and in different ways. About one worker in six is in a closed shop, and only about a quarter are employed in closed shops or areas in which they predominate. However, two out of five trade unionists are covered, and among working trade unionists in the manual occupations every other worker is in a closed shop.

In several skilled trades the entire craft is more or less comprehensively closed to the non-unionist, and among some semi-skilled and unskilled groups a number of rather specialized occupations are widely affected. In most industries, however, a pattern of common regional variations can be observed, with the industrial North and parts of South Wales disproportionately affected by the practice.

---

[1] *Op. cit.*, p. 338. The same authors also point out, such institutional monopolies may arise within the registered professions. Thus the Royal Colleges of Physicians and Surgeons, by imposing higher qualification for admission to the Fellowship grade, have given it a higher prestige than that which accrues to the ordinarily registered G.P. *Op. cit.*, p. 358.

There is also a tendency for the closed shop to arise, to a greater extent, among employees of the larger firms and among skilled craftsmen generally. Employers associated in some way with the Labour Movement itself are also likely to impose the closed shop on their employees in areas in which it would otherwise not arise.

About a fifth of workers in closed shops are in some sort of pre-entry shop and are subject to various forms of entry control. About half are in formally recognized closed shops, or are employed in industries where the great majority of employers will co-operate in its implementation. Outside mining, few are affected by the check off, and there is little membership choice.

There is a widespread correlation between the open shop, an absence of demands for the closed shop, and low levels of unionization; but there are notable exceptions. Several open shop groups which are not closed shop prone have a high level of unionization. Some of these are affected by the semi-closed shop, but some are not. Elsewhere the semi-closed shop has arisen in situations where the industry is closed shop prone.

Strikes to impose or maintain the practice have remained a fraction of all strikes, but they serve as a rough index of demands for the practice and the extent to which employers have come to accept it. In both respects the high proportion of strikes in engineering and construction are of significance.

The survey shows that many sweeping judgments about the closed shop, which were quoted in Chapter 1, cannot be validated. The practice is not an historical relic, affecting a small minority of trade unionists; it is an increasingly common contemporary phenomenon. Yet the non-unionists' position is not equally intolerable throughout industry. The practice has not been pursued with similar vigour wherever the 'habit of organization has become settled and accepted'.[1] Both those who foresaw the gradual disappearance of the closed shop, and those who suggested that it would become universal whenever unions grew to any strength, were wrong. If one wishes to explain why the practice has arisen where it has, and has taken so many complex forms, one must look for a more complicated explanation. The chapters which follow are an attempt to provide this.

[1] Milne-Bailey, *op. cit.*, p. 117.

CHAPTER 3

SOME EXPLANATIONS FOR THE CLOSED SHOP

ASKED to consider why workers demand the closed shop, most trade unionists reply solidarity. Union members, they suggest, resent the continued presence of the non-member, regarding him as a 'free rider' who benefits from their efforts. Believing collective action is essential if standards are to be defended and advanced, they conclude that there is a common obligation, binding on all workers, to become and remain members of their appropriate union. Those who refuse to accept such obligations 'voluntarily' may be justifiably forced to do so. By refusing to work with such men, trade unionists are expressing their 'solidarity'.

But it is possible to argue more or less in reverse. W. M. Leiserson, an American writer, sought to show that it was the degree of 'solidarity' among British trade unionists which accounted for their comparative indifference to the closed shop. Contrasting Britain with the U.S.A. he argued that:

the presence of great numbers of immigrants, the relatively ample opportunities for workers to rise out of the ranks of labor . . . made the development of . . . a feeling of class solidarity impossible.[1]

Threatened by those who were willing to accept existing low standards 'American trade unions saw in the closed shop their only protection'.

V. L. Allen rejects this argument, pointing out that:

both in the U.S.A. and in Britain, it is precisely from those unions that are strongest that demands for 'closed shop' agreements emanate. It is where solidarity is greatest that one finds 'closed shop' principle firmly established. In Britain the mines and the docks are renowned for their community spirit and the workers' solidarity, yet it is there that the feeling about compulsory trade unionism is most intense.[2]

He concludes,

Solidarity . . . is in all cases, in fact, a prerequisite for negotiations for 'closed shop' agreements. A trade union must organize a high proportion of workers in an establishment before it is in a position to claim the right to force non-unionists into the union, for, stated simply, the 'closed shop' is the imposition of the will of the majority on the minority.[3]

[1] *Encyclopaedia of the Social Sciences*, 1930, quoted by V. L. Allen, *op. cit.*, p. 52.
[2] *Ibid.*   [3] *Ibid.*

How does the pattern uncovered in the previous chapter bear out such assertions? And how far can the demand for solidarity be accepted as an adequate explanation for the shape the pattern takes?

(1) THE DEMAND FOR TRADE UNION SOLIDARITY

At first glance there seems to be a close correlation between the closed shop and solidarity. There is a tendency for the comprehensively closed groups to be particularly trade union conscious, or 'solid'—i.e. dockers, miners, shipyard workers, printers, and so on. Similarly, the regional area variations outlined in Chapter 2 showed that there was a general tendency for the more union conscious areas to be more closed shop prone than others. In some cases it is plausible to go further and argue, not merely that the closed shop is more likely to arise among the most solid groups, but also that these groups sometimes infect adjacent groups and touch off demands for the practice in relatively unlikely places.

Yet a closer examination of the pattern leads one to raise objections and queries. Are hatters more 'solid' than electrical supply workers, or boot and shoe operatives? Are London busmen more aware of the need for solidarity than the busmen in the municipalities, or workers on the railways, or even employees on the London underground? Are film workers more solidarity conscious than dockers employed by the Admiralty, or woodworkers in the pay of the Ministry of Works? Are Post Office engineers so less 'solid' than their counterparts outside? What sort of solidarity is it that actors have but firemen do not, that is possessed by musicians but not by teachers, by sailors but not by civil servants? More generally, what is meant in the above quotations by the term 'solidarity', and can it be maintained that such a quality is correlated with the degree of prevalence of the closed shop, in whatever form it takes, among each and every group discussed in Chapter 2. The concept of solidarity, as used by the writers quoted above, would appear to be in need of some definition.

Three notions seem to be involved, which it is essential to separate if one is to understand the effect of solidarity on the growth of the closed shop. First, there is the sense in which all that solidarity implies is a general disposition to act together as a group and interpret the demands of collective action in terms of loyalty to the union, its rules, orders and leaders. In this sense there is a case for saying that many groups relatively unaffected by the closed shop—such as the railwaymen—are as 'solidarity conscious' as many of the groups

classed as closed shop prone in Chapter 3. It is implausible to assert
that solidarity, in this vague or general sense, is correlated with the
closed shop. What it may be correlated with is the over-all level of
unionization. Workers employed on labour only subcontracting in
the building industry are said to have no sense of solidarity, coal
distributors are described as 'individualists' who are largely unorganizable. Thus among these groups an absence of solidarity, in
the sense of group consciousness, makes for low levels of unionization and unless unionization without the closed shop is relatively
high, a move to obtain it by means of a refusal to work is impossible.

But references to the 'solidarity' of workers in closed shops may
mean something more closely connected to the issue of non-
unionism as such; i.e. the strength of the objection to non-unionism.
A group may be 'solid' in the first or general sense without being
'solid' in this particular way. Yet, even here, we must realize what
is the crucial difference between one group and another. It is not
that outside the closed shop areas unionists generally reject the 'free-
rider' argument. The reverse is the case. When talking to union
members in open trades, one is struck by the extent to which they
too regard the non-unionist as a parasite. This contention is well
borne out by the Gallup Poll of union opinion quoted in Chapter 1.[1]
Another question they put to a representative cross-section of trade
unionists was:

Some people say that a worker who does not join a union is evading his responsibilities to other workers. Do you on the whole agree or disagree with this view.[1]

81 per cent of those questioned agreed, 14 per cent disagreed, and
5 per cent said they did not know. On the basis of this survey, there
are twice as many trade unionists who think the non-unionist is
evading his obligations as there are trade unionists in a closed shop;
three out of five trade unionists are employed outside the closed
shop, but only one in five does not criticize the free-rider. Yet the
majority who feel this way do *not* try to force their fellow workers
into the union via the closed shop. It may thus be argued that the
form of solidarity which is most relevant to the closed shop should
be even more narrowly defined; it is not simple solidarity in the face
of non-unionism (expressed as a mere resentment or feeling of
injustice) it is much more an additional readiness to take positive
collective action against the non-unionist or lapsed member, with

---

[1] See p. 3 above.

the object of threatening exclusion from the job unless the individual concerned conforms. What must be asked is how widespread are such feelings among trade unionists, and why is it that they arise where they do?

Here the answers to the question which the Gallup Poll asked concerning the enforcement of the closed shop, which was quoted in full in Chapter 1, are of interest.[1] It will be remembered that 70 per cent of trade unionists questioned said they thought workers were justified in 'refusing to work' with a non-unionists minority whose presence 'weakens the union in wage and other negotiations'.

At first glance this answer would also appear to have uncovered the existence of a form of solidarity directly relevant to the growth of the closed shop over a much wider area than that covered by the practice. Once again, almost twice as many trade unionists as are in closed shops appear to approve. Not only do eight out of ten trade unionists think that the non-unionist is evading his obligations; almost as many (i.e. seven out of ten) think that trade unionists are justified in taking collective action to enforce these obligations upon him. But we must beware of interpreting the answers to this question too sweepingly. It should be noted that, as worded, the question does not make clear that what is at issue is whether the non-unionists should continue to be employed—i.e. it asks for approval for a 'refusal to work', not an attempt to get recalcitrants discharged or moved. Again those questioned are asked if they approve—not how they would act in similar circumstances. Most important of all, it is stated as a fact, and not a mere allegation, that the continued presence of the non-unionist weakens the union in its job of maintaining standards. It is arguable that all three features are calculated to produce a maximum affirmative response from trade unionists. Thus while both these questions help to show the extent to which trade unionists generally resent non-unionists, and even sympathize with those who take militant action against them, they are an imperfect index to the narrow form of solidarity most relevant to the closed shop.

In any case, can one accept the existence or non-existence of solidarity, however defined, as an adequate explanation for the complex pattern outlined in the previous chapter? Solidarity, in the general sense, may be one of the prerequisites of all successful group action. Solidarity, in the sense of a resentment of free-riders,

[1] *Ibid.*

may play a part in touching off particular closed shop campaigns: solidarity, in the narrow sense of a readiness to take collective action to eliminate non-unionism, is present when workers strike to impose or uphold the closed shop; but one still has to discover how it comes about that a particular group exhibit one form of solidarity more than another, and why it is that it is only among certain groups that solidarity takes the form of a strike to impose a particular type of closed shop. To solve these questions it is necessary to go beyond the immediate resentments and fears of trade unionists, to consider both the general factors influencing union strength, and the more precise influences in any industrial situation, which bear directly on the rise of the demand for the closed shop.

But there is one other aspect of the relationship between the closed shop and solidarity, in the more general sense, which should first be discussed. This is the effect of the closed shop on solidarity once it has been imposed. V. L. Allen also comments on this.

(2) THE EFFECT OF THE CLOSED SHOP ON SOLIDARITY

Allen seems to be uncertain about the effect of the closed shop on the disposition of workers to act together as a group and to interpret the demands of collective action in terms of loyalty to the union. He admits that the closed shop may 'be demanded because the union wishes to improve its financial position, or increase its bargaining strength, or increase the hold of the leaders over the members', but stresses that it has disadvantages which are 'more important', and continues:

Compulsory trade unionism may make a union better able to pay strike pay, but this is only one element in the maintenance of solidarity and not the most important. Trade union members must sincerely believe in the aims and methods of their unions and their allegiance to a union must emanate from this belief. . . . A trade union is like a fresh stream: when it is damned up it collects a lot of muddy water and the scum rises to the top. Men who are forced into a union are not only passive they are also often focal points of disaffection and disruption, and form a nucleus to which the dissatisfied voluntary members may cling. Their resentment at being press-ganged into a union affects others, but though the group symptoms may be the same the real causes of the disaffection may be vastly different. Fundamentally, trade unionists want a strong union, and the size of the union is often a good guide to strength. They may, however, be impressed by the boost to membership figures given by 'closed shop' agreements; it is, however, purely fictitious and misleading. Some trade union officials, unfortunately, prefer to be misled and treat the 'closed shop' agreement as an institution-building device.[1]

[1] *Op. cit.*, p. 57.

But having dismissed the closed shop as a threat to solidarity, Allen goes on to write as if the union officials might be right after all. He admits that despite its disadvantages the closed shop

... streamlines union organization; the recruitment function is removed from the shoulders of trade union officials, where it should lie, to those of management, and it (i.e. the closed shop) removes, therefore, the need for union officials to justify the activities of the union to potential members. In all cases the employer becomes an ally in the maintenance of discipline in unions; even the collection of dues is sometimes transferred to the firm's administration. A trouble saving device of this nature certainly has its attractions in a movement subject to so many vacillations and vicissitudes and afflicted with what Peter Drucker has called 'insecurity neurosis'.[1]

This is, of course, an inaccurate picture of what happens in most closed shops. Employers do not take over all the union's recruitment functions. Officials no longer have to persuade new entrants to join; but this need not involve, as Allen implies, the end of rank and file control.[2] But, even if it did, it would be difficult to equate what Allen says about the closed shop as a 'trouble-saving device' with what he says about it as a focal point of disaffection and disruption!

Either the closed shop strengthens union discipline, in which case it cannot result in growing indiscipline, or it does not, in which case it should not be condemned for causing the extinction of rank and file pressure on the leadership. Either the practice is compatible with the growth of solidarity, which is apparently the point Allen made in answer to Leirerson, or it tends, on balance, to reduce solidarity, in which case it is difficult to see why Allen says that 'it is where solidarity is greatest that one finds the "closed shop" principle firmly established'.

Allen's difficulty here is his mixture of the empirical and the *a priori* which so often mars other writing on the closed shop. His known facts seem to show that the closed shop adds to union power, yet he believes on *a priori* grounds, that men forced into the union *cannot* be a source of strength.

Let us look at some facts. Virtually all union officials and employers contacted with a personal knowledge of the closed shop deny that it weakens the unions. Perhaps the most significant comment was by Mr. George Smith, General Secretary of the Amalgamated Society of Woodworkers. As he put it:

If you pay towards an organization you want to justify it, and so you tend to accept the organizations' principles. On the other hand, as a non-member you tend

---

[1] *Ibid.*   [2] *Op. cit.*, p. 59.

G

to justify that position too. You have a different set of principles, act as an individualist, and resent the interference of the union in your affairs.

An active member of the Transport and General Workers' Union working for the Oxford City Motor Company agreed. He said:

Those who join the union as a result of pressure are not usually a source of weakness, often men join rather than have a lot of trouble but they become good enough trade unionists. Trade unionism can become a habit—just like anything else.

There were frequent references to this habit-forming effect and several shop stewards stressed that men who 'had to be forced in' became 'at least as active as the rest'. Two union officials gave examples of active workers who began by refusing to join the union, and the Imperial Father of a printing chapel explained how he had to be 'pushed' into the union by a strike threat in 1936.

On this point it is worth quoting one piece of American research. Miller and Rosen studied membership attitudes towards shop stewards and the union in a large American plant which had operated a post-entry shop for many years.[1] They found that while 'the vast majority of the members were satisfied on every item', yet, 'on most items about one-fourth of the members expressed dissatisfaction'. However, in respect of what they called 'union solidarity', i.e. 'what the attitudes of union members reveal with regard to their potential support of the official goals and practices of the unions', they discovered that,

survey data suggest membership acceptance of the 'union way' and of union policies and programmes. This conclusion is drawn, primarily, from the members' norms—which agreed, by and large, with 'official' union objectives. Similar findings have been reported by Rose, Purcell, and Rosen and Rosen.[2]

In other words, a detailed examination of the attitudes adopted by workers, some of whom had been forced into the union by the operation of the closed shop, exhibited no signs of pronounced disaffection and disruption. On this specific point, Miller and Rosen summed up their findings thus:

Another proposition which has been demonstrated by other research and is supported by the local data, is that being forced to join a union because of a union shop contract clause is not a major deterrent to union solidarity.[3]

[1] 'Members Attitudes Towards the Shop Steward', by Glenn W. Miller and Ned Rosen, *Industrial and Labor Relations Review*, Vol. 10, July 1957. N.Y.
[2] *Op. cit.*, p. 529.   [3] *Ibid.*

Indeed, it has been the American experience that not only do workers forced into a union through the operation of a closed shop come to accept the union's official goals and practices; they also come, in time, to accept the necessity for the closed shop. Under the Taft-Hartley Act, passed in 1947, the existence of a post-entry shop agreement could be challenged, by demanding an authorization poll to be taken in the work-place concerned. If 30 per cent of workers wished to 'de-authorize' the existing agreement a poll had to be held. If a majority of those voting were against, it was revoked for at least a year. In 1951 a new law, Public Law 189, abolished the authorization poll, since of the 46,145 elections held, 97 per cent went in favour of the union.[1]

There is, unfortunately, no equally decisive and comprehensive evidence as to the attitude of the mass of trade unionists in the closed shop areas in this country, but all the available evidence goes to show that Allen's *a priori* fears are groundless; the practice has a habit-forming effect.

Yet even if one accepts that the closed shop both requires solidarity and stimulates its further growth, it is obvious that a satisfactory explanation of the closed shop pattern cannot be found in terms of a group striving after solidarity. The relationship between solidarity and the closed shop is important at this point mainly because it suggests that one should seek an explanation for union motives less in terms of intolerance and resentment, and more in terms of concrete organizational advantages.

The practice is not a useless *chimera*, pursued by ill-informed and misled union officials; it has its uses, and it is the task of the next chapter to explain in detail what they are.

However, there is one final point to be made against the simple solidarity theory, which raises important issues with which it is useful to deal at this stage. The theory sets out to explain why unions demand the closed shop; it does not explain why employers concede it. This is an important omission in any explanation of the rise and spread of the closed shop, and in his own explanation V. L. Allen sets out to remedy it. In fact, he overstresses the importance of the employers' role, and in other ways his theory is not satisfactory. Nevertheless, it raises the main issues which need to be considered, and warrants consideration.

[1] *Right to Work Laws: A Study in Conflict*, by Paul Sultan, Institute of Industrial Relations, University of California, 1958, p. 50.

(3) THE EMPLOYERS' ROLE

Allen regards solidarity, in its general sense, as a limiting condition. He assumes that most groups will try to obtain the closed shop, if they have the power. From then on the crucial issues seem to revolve round the response of employers to such demands.

The basic factor affecting employer attitudes, says Allen, is the relationship between the price of labour and the price of capital. If labour is cheap employers use extensive methods of production and come to depend on the continued availability of cheap labour. Where this occurs

the acceptance of a labour policy which removed from the jurisdiction of employers the right to choose and eliminate workers according to their efficiency would be entirely uneconomic for employers. This explains in part the British employers' attitude to compulsory trade unionism under which, except in the crafts, the union card and not efficiency is the key to employment.[1]

Yet, he continues, the development of industry has not been uniform. Some industries, because of technological advance, make use of highly mechanized methods. Here management may prefer to accede to closed shop demands, rather than risk expensive machinery standing idle during a strike. Even where this is not so it may concede—'where the efficiency of individual workers may be relatively unimportant'.

It is notable that Allen fails to distinguish between the pre-entry shop, with entry control, and the post-entry shop, without entry control; but this is not his only confusion. He is also confused about the relationship between the closed shop and efficiency. There is a sense in which the pre-entry shop circumscribes managerial hiring rights—although even within the labour supply shop employers are allowed to object to inefficient applicants. In the promotion veto shop there are restrictions on the right to promote, but this does not mean that employers must promote inefficient men simply because they are trade unionists. In the craft qualification shop, and even in some forms of labour supply and labour pool shop, there may be restrictions on total entry, but even here the result is not the retention of *inefficient* workmen. The closed shop, in all its forms, does not operate so as to prevent the employer discharging a worker on grounds of inefficiency, it cannot force an employer to retain men he regards as unfit for the job.[2] It is arguable that the craft qualifica-

[1] *Op. cit.*, p. 52.
[2] Of course, any group may resent one of their number being discharged on grounds of inefficiency, and may stage a strike to prevent what they regard as 'victimization', but this can just as well happen in an open shop and it has nothing to do with the closed shop as such.

tion shop in industries like printing and shipbuilding helps to perpetuate an inefficient division of work, but this does not seem to have been in Allen's mind, for he says that it is *outside* the area of the crafts that the union card, and not efficiency, is the key to the job. It is true that within a closed shop the employer cannot engage efficient workers who refuse to join the union, and must discharge those who lapse, but this will only affect efficiency if the employer finds it impossible to obtain equally efficient trade unionists. Allen at no time suggests this.

Yet he is right to stress the significance of employer attitudes, and in assuming that different attitudes can be largely explained in terms of the cost of resisting or conceding closed shop demands. He is wrong in suggesting that this cost can be measured solely, or even mainly, in terms of the difference between labour or capital intensive methods of production.

The main factors determining most employers' attitudes to demands for the closed shop were set down with refreshing candour in a recent report which the personnel department of a leading manufacturing firm made to their Board of Directors. The firm had been plagued with strikes to impose the closed shop, and instructed their personnel department to find out about the attitude of other firms, who had been faced by similar problems in the past. Over seventy firms were contacted, in over fifteen trades.[1]

It was discovered that, in general, the more serious the consequences of a strike, and the greater the likelihood of it taking place, the greater the chance that the employer would concede. On the whole, only firms who had experienced no trouble on the non-unionist issue maintained a position of 'complete impartiality'. Yet it was also found that there were often marked discrepancies between the declared policy of a firm, and what it actually did. At top level, management would maintain that it had never conceded a closed shop; lower down workers were effectively screened, and discharged if they refused to pay union dues.

In discussing attitudes towards the closed shop with employers, in virtually all the important industries listed in the last chapter, it was notable that the answers given reinforced the findings of this report. 'Impartiality', or complete opposition to the principle of the closed shop, is largely confined to employers in open or mainly open trades. Employers in closed shop prone trades are less sure of their position and, generally, their attitude varies according to the amount of

[1] See Appendix.

pressure they have experienced. In mainly closed groups, like engineering, or oil refining, those who have experienced pressure admitted that it was only common sense to recognize the practice if demand for it was strong. Where the closed shop has long been the rule—e.g. among printers, or shipyard workers, management not only recognizes its necessity, but is prepared to admit its own role in upholding it.[1]

But interviews with individual employers also show how Allen has oversimplified the relationship between management's fear of a strike, and its readiness to concede the closed shop. There are other circumstances where employers who do not rely on the extensive use of expensive equipment may still be particularly concerned to avoid a strike. If schedules are tight any strike may involve a loss of essential output needed to fulfil important orders. If employers are handling a perishable product they may be left with it on their hands. If it is particularly costly to resume production once it has been interrupted, they will be unusually vulnerable. Allen has isolated only one factor which tends to make employers ready to concede union demands rather than risk a strike.

More important still, employers are not only concerned with the immediate cost of resistance. They are sometimes even more concerned with the long-term cost of concession—it is here that Allen's theory is at its weakest. As has been shown, the cost of recognizing the closed shop is not necessarily a less efficient labour force, but there may be a cost nevertheless. In the next chapter it will be argued that by helping unions to overcome certain problems the practice generally leads to a growth in union power. Most employers are aware of this. The demand for the closed shop is usually most insistently made by workshop representatives, who make no secret of their conviction that it will add to their influence. As the Secretary of one Employers' Association said of the struggle to advance the closed shop in his industry:

> This is an issue about power—and we know that as well as anybody.

To the extent that management takes into account issues like this, Allen's distinction between capital and labour intensive methods is quite irrelevant. An employer particularly concerned to secure maximum utilization of expensive capital is as likely to want to

---

[1] The only important exceptions to this pattern occur in the case of groups employed by the Labour Movement, where employers initiate the closed shop, and Government employees, where management is more than usually determined not to concede the practice—these two exceptions are discussed further below.

resist a growth in union power as one who relies on cheap labour. The latter may fear this will lead to a rise in the price for labour, but the former may be afraid that it will result in restrictions on the introduction of machinery, opposition to redundancy, and even output limitations.

The employer's attitude to any of these developments, like his attitude to strike threats, is determined not by the capital labour ratio, but by the estimated effect on costs. Costs are important because of their effect on demand and profits. In this sense, demands for the closed shop are judged in a similar way to any other union demand; the cost of resistance is weighed against the cost of concession, so far as this can be calculated. When employers think that the former outweighs the latter, they will usually concede.

Yet there are significant differences between closed shop strikes and others. An analysis of the records of the Ministry of Labour reveals that strikes to obtain the closed shop tend to be smaller than most other strikes, and less prolonged.[1] When resisted they are more likely to be called off than other strikes, partly because no immediate and pressing issue of wages and conditions is in dispute, and partly because it is often the deliberate policy of groups demanding the practice to use the strike as a short, sharp, recurring weapon. In this way the most effective pressure can be put on employers and non-unionists.

Closed shop strikes are also different from most other strikes in that they are aimed *directly* at workers as much as at employers, so that success can be achieved by action on the part of recalcitrant workers alone.[2] This may account for the fact that from the statistics available it looks as if closed shop strikes are more likely to succeed than other strikes.[3]

---

[1] See also K. C. J. C. Knowles, *Strikes: a Study in Industrial Conflict*, Blackwells, 1952, p. 312.

[2] Closed shop strikes are not unique in this respect. Any refusal to work with those who will not observe union rules and group customs comes into this category.

[3] Unfortunately the statistics are incomplete. By consulting the records of the Ministry of Labour it was possible to estimate that between 1945 and 1957 about 43 per cent of all strikes to impose the closed shop were successful, in that the non-unionists concerned either joined the union, left the job, or were given the sack. Unfortunately there are no *published* statistics for strike results in general during this period, and it would have taken considerable research to have extracted these from the records. All one can do, therefore, is to compare the 1945–57 closed shop results with over-all results for earlier periods when the Ministry did publish such figures—i.e. from 1911–43. These show that at no time were more than 28 per cent of all strikes settled in favour of the workers. In attempting to infer from these two figures allowance must be made for the fact that the period 1945–57 was one of full employment in which unions were stronger than they were before the war. Nevertheless, the contrast is striking and it is worth noting that the period 1911–47 includes several full-employment periods, where unions were strong, and relatively militant as well (see Knowles, *op. cit.*, p. 243).

From the employers' viewpoint there are three differences between granting the closed shop and conceding most other union demands. First, there is no *immediate* economic cost involved in concession. This sometimes makes employers more willing to give in, or at least less willing to incur the losses involved in resistance. Second, in so far as there is an immediate cost it usually takes the form of 'bad publicity'. Because the notion of the closed shop is unpopular, or is thought to be unpopular with the public, employers are often reluctant to accept it, unless this can be done in a 'private' and unpublicized way. Largely for this reason, recognition often takes the form of an 'unofficial understanding', rather than a formal agreement. Third, in some cases this reluctance is reinforced by a sincere conviction that the closed shop itself is morally unjustifiable, and employers who feel this way may be prepared to suffer heavier costs, in terms of strike action, than would be justified on strictly economic grounds. What has been written so far is not intended to deny this. On the other hand, it is suggested that the great majority of employers are mainly conditioned by their appraisal of the immediate costs of resistance, modified, in many cases, by their view of the longer term costs of concession. This is not advanced as a criticism, but as a conclusion arising out of the inquiries conducted in connection with this study. Whether it is a justifiable attitude or not is considered at length below.

Like any other union demand, the closed shop can be the subject of bargaining—unions are asked for concessions in exchange for recognition. The most important concession management can demand is a limitation on the right to strike, and in several industries formal recognition has been accompanied by an arbitration agreement containing a no-strike clause.[1] Since the closed shop adds to the ability of the union to discipline dissident members who refuse to abide by such agreements, and foment 'unofficial strikes', the readiness of the union to sign and honour such an agreement has been a crucial factor affecting managerial attitudes towards the closed shop in some industries.

More generally, however, management expect to obtain less precise advantages from recognizing the closed shop. As one employer said:

We found that it helped to have every man in his respective union, in this way local leaders come to feel more secure, and they were more willing to help in putting over management's view to members.

---

[1] For example in Scottish Baking.

Other employers stressed that the closed shop concession showed that the firm was not 'rabidly anti-union', and that 'once stewards are given the right to speak for all in the shop they are more relaxed and willing to take a sensible view'. Another official argued that by using unions as a kind of 'sieve' management can 'save a lot of time in dealing with odd, fiddling issues'. But, he added, 'it is essential to insist that they must all be in the union, otherwise the stewards will not handle the complaints of the non-unionists'. In other cases unions have promised management a priority on types of labour in short supply in exchange for a labour supply shop.

Yet, important though these considerations are, it is not suggested that many managements have been induced to recognize the closed shop mainly because of its advantages to them. Having recognized the practice they usually come to accept it as a norm, and are even prepared to advocate its extension to others, but they do not usually convince those of their number who have not yet experienced similar pressures.

For the most part recognition waits on union pressure, pushed to the point where a strike is likely. It is only then that the cost of resistance is compared with the cost of concession, and management is interested in striking a bargain. So although employer attitudes are sometimes crucial, and may determine the success or failure of many individual closed shop campaigns, one cannot go far in explaining the complexities of the closed shop pattern by means of an analysis of employer attitudes.

(4) The Questions to be Answered

This chapter has considered a number of explanations for the rise and spread of the closed shop. It is useful to summarize what has been discovered, and clarify the issues that remain to be settled.

Since employers mainly respond to union pressures a precondition of success in obtaining the closed shop is an ability, on the part of trade unionists, to develop sufficient power to be able to make enough of a nuisance of themselves on the non-unionist issue. This entails a measure of solidarity, in the sense of a willingness to organize and act together. But it is not possible to explain the variations in the closed shop pattern simply by reference to the strength of this type of solidarity, even if due allowance is made for the attitude of individual employers along the lines outlined in the last section.

Two crucial questions are left unanswered. First, why is it that the extent to which groups come to demand the closed shop is not more closely correlated with the growth of union power; in short, why is it that there are a number of groups where there is a high level of organization and yet few if any demands for the closed shop? Second, why is it that when the closed shop does arise it takes the complex forms that it does?

The key to an answer to both these questions lies in studying the closed shop as a response which unions make to particular problems related to the organization and control of workers, it is largely because it helps to overcome these problems that the closed shop is desired, and results in a growth of union strength and solidarity.

To be able to answer both questions it is first necessary to pose two more. They are: (1) What advantages do unions gain from the closed shop? (2) In what circumstances do they come to feel that they need these advantages?

Chapter 4, which follows, considers the first of these questions; the second is the subject of Chapter 5. When they have been answered an attempt will be made to apply what has been discovered to an explanation of the rise and spread of the closed shop in particular industries. These matters are the subject of Chapter 6.

CHAPTER 4

THE FUNCTIONS OF THE CLOSED SHOP

(1) Job Regulation and Union Sanction

UNIONS seek to regulate the terms of their members' employment in two main ways: (1) by *bilateral regulation*, or collective bargaining, where an attempt is made to reach an agreement with employers; (2) by *unilateral regulation*, or the collective enforcement of the union's own rules and customs, without the need to reach an agreement with the employer.[1] When unions succeed in affecting the terms of their members' employment by either or both of these methods it may be said that they are participating in *job regulation*.

To the extent that job regulation is effective a distinctive system of rules is introduced into the workplace. Of course these are not the only rules that exist. The state lays down rules, which may not be the result of union activity, and the employer can make rules of his own, if neither the state nor the union prevents him. The distinctive feature of the system of rules which result from union job regulation is simply that the workers, via their membership of trade unions, participate in their formulation. In most industries where unions are recognized there is a national agreement, prescribing the rules for raising grievances, settling claims, and avoiding disputes. There are also national agreements prescribing terms and conditions to be observed by all members of the employers' association. But in addition to this system of *external* rules laid down outside the workplace there is usually a variety of internal or *workplace* rules, which are the result of bargaining at local level. Finally, there are the unilaterally enforced rules of the union.

When participating in job regulation unions have three objectives:

(1) To bring as many workers as possible within the grades they organize within the scope of the rules.
(2) To ensure that the rules are actually observed at the workplace level.
(3) To maintain and improve the content of the rules, from the workers' point of view.

---

[1] In practice the distinction between unilateral and bilateral job regulation may be difficult to draw. Employers are prepared tacitly to accept the continuance of certain union customs, yet they may still be reluctant to put their signature to an agreement making them the subject of bilateral regulation.

Unions believe that none of these objectives can be realized unless they possess sanctions which can, if necessary, be used against the employer. The most effective sanction is usually a collective refusal to work, except on terms demanded by the union.[1] It may be necessary to use this sanction to ensure recognition, or the toleration of union rules and customs. It may be necessary to threaten to use it to ensure that individual employers observe negotiated agreements. Even where the use of such a sanction is rare, or virtually unknown, trade unionists tend to assume that an employer who agrees to bargain over terms of employment, or continues to employ union members who are working according to union rules which he objects to, is doing this at least partly because he realizes that such a sanction exists.

But unions also maintain that effective job regulation depends on the existence of another type of sanction: the sanction of the union over workers. Only by agreeing to obey orders, and act in unity, can a group impose effective collective sanctions on employers. This requires a measure of discipline.

Moreover, if employers are to be induced to recognize the union, and honour the agreements they negotiate, it must be relatively certain that workers will accept the terms of settlement; that they will not try to resist their implementation, or take independent action to impose different terms. To ensure the obedience of workers, union leaders must have at their disposal certain disciplinary powers. The closed shop assists in the enforcement of union sanctions over both workers and employers by placing at the disposal of the union the threat of exclusion from the job—a sanction which is at the exclusive disposal of the employer outside the area of the closed shop. In this way it helps to ensure that workers act together, and in unity, and thus assists the union to impose the most effective sanctions on employers. To the extent that improvements in the scope, observance, and content of job regulation depend on the existence of such sanctions, the closed shop can also be said to aid the unions in their task of maintaining and improving conditions.

Union sanctions over members and non-members are used for three purposes, and in each case the attainment of the closed shop adds to the strength of the sanctions available. First, they can be used to increase and maintain the numerical strength of the union; the use of the closed shop for this purpose will be termed its *membership function*. Second, they can be used to enhance the union's

---

[1] Other sanctions include the 'go slow' or 'work to rule'.

internal strength; the use of the closed shop for this purpose will be termed its *discipline function*. Third, they can be used to control entry to the job; this use of the closed shop will be termed its *entry control function*.

(2) THE FUNCTIONS OF THE CLOSED SHOP

(a) The Membership Function

This function of the closed shop has two aspects: recruitment and retention.

The recruitment aspect involves the use of the exclusion threat to force employees to join one of a specified number of unions. In some cases the threat is needed to recruit any substantial number of workers; when this happens the closed shop is unattainable unless imposed by employers. Elsewhere, and in the majority of cases, the exclusion threat is not used until the majority have been recruited without it. This does not mean, as was stressed in Chapter 1, that before this no sort of pressure was used, and sometimes this amounts to a semi-closed shop. But if there continues to exist a comparatively small minority of workers who refuse to join, it is against them that the additional and final sanction of the exclusion threat is directed.

When the closed shop is neither formally nor informally recognized, the exclusion threat involves unilateral action in the form of a collective refusal to work unless those concerned join the union or leave the job. If the threat is ineffective, or is successfully resisted, it may be repeated at intervals until 100 per cent membership is achieved. In this way both non-unionists and employers are subjected to a form of pressure which is more compelling than that mobilized in any other way. Employers are threatened with interruptions of work until, and unless, they discharge non-unionists, remove them from the job, or put pressure on them to make their peace with the union. Workers are threatened with eventually losing their position, and becoming, meanwhile, an object of discord and contention. They are encouraged to feel that their action, or lack of it, is precipitating a dispute in which others suffer besides themselves. Something of the atmosphere of a strike to eliminate a non-unionist has, I think, been admirably captured by the quotation from Mr. J. J. McLoughlin's evidence to the Briggs Inquiry, which precedes this study.[1] Mr. McLoughlin said there that it was

[1] See p. 1 above.

a 'shocking 240 minutes', and from his evidence he was not an unusually squeamish man.

But the use of the exclusion threat does not always generate such resentment. Often it is resorted to reluctantly and with genuine regret, after everything has been done to avoid having to use it. Most trade unionists in any way responsible for enforcing a closed shop volunteered the information that they did not like having to threaten a workmate with the sack, though this does not imply that most of them would hesitate to do so if they thought it necessary. Most tended to regard the exclusion sanction as a last resort and stressed the way in which the news that a demand for the closed shop was about to be made helped to push recalcitrants into the union. Where the closed shop has secured a measure of recognition, it is not necessary to make threats of this sort; consequently, the issue of non-unionism may be dealt with in a less heated way. Where recognition involves screening even fewer problems arise. Management can recruit members for the unions, if necessary without openly acknowledging the existence of the closed shop.

The *retention* aspect of the *recruitment function* involves the use of the exclusion sanction to force employees to remain in the union and to pay contributions they have failed to remit. It is also not normally used unless other forms of pressure have failed, and it may or may not be recognized. If recognition is granted, then it is more difficult for employers to play their part in enforcement by stealth. If they agree to accept the union's right to demand the removal of lapsed members they will sometimes be called on to take overt action against particular employees. For this reason some employers are less willing to co-operate, if this involves discharging the men concerned.

Between them the recruitment and retention aspects of the membership function ensure that all entrants to the job become and remain fully paid-up members of their respective unions. Their importance in contributing to union strength is obvious. 100 per cent membership is a major objective of virtually all union groups. It adds to union finances and to the power to sustain strike action. Moreover, where 100 per cent membership is achieved via the closed shop, union leaders are not merely more powerful—they are more secure. In effect a ratchet is placed under the level of organization achieved. Workers may evade the union temporarily—if there is no check off, or the collecting system collapses—but when the union is able to reassert itself it is easier to regain ground. Entrance fees and arrears can be extracted, if need be, by means of the exclusion threat. Those responsible for subscriptions do not have to be constantly chasing reluctant payers or persistent evaders; faced with recalcitrants they can adopt the role of the judge rather than the appellant.

Naturally their position is easiest if management recognizes their right to the closed shop; though there is a limit to the security provided by recognition, formal or informal. If membership falls too low for too long, management may refuse to co-operate. In this sense the practice is ultimately dependent on the willingness of union members to impose it unilaterally, although the more management is aware of this, the less likely it is that unilateral enforcement will be needed.

(b) The Discipline Function

The closed shop's function here is to use the exclusion threat, and the status which is conferred on those who control it, to force members to obey the union's rules, customs, and leadership. All union rule books contain disciplinary provisions, which can be classified under two headings: (1) *substantive rules*, i.e. rules setting out codes of conduct with penalties for those who break them; (2) *procedural rules*, i.e. those governing the process by which the union decides whether an individual has committed an offence which warrants a particular penalty. This chapter is not primarily concerned with procedural rules, such as appeals provisions, the right to a fair trial, and so on, but with the penalties and offences of the substantive rules.

Penalties and offences can also be classified in a number of ways. In the case of penalties the most important classification relates to the seriousness of the penalty. Sometimes all that is involved is a loss of benefits, as when the rule book says:

No dispute benefit shall be paid to any member who tenders his notice or throws up his situation without having first obtained the sanction of the Executive Council.[1]

On other occasions a fine is imposed. But all rule books contain more drastic penalties, the most important of which is expulsion from the union.

In the case of offences, the most important classification refers to how specific the offence is and how clearly it is defined in the rules. In the rule quoted above, the offence was fairly specific—failing to

[1] U.S.D.A.W. Rule Book, Rule 34, 1957.

obtain permission. Other fairly frequent examples of specific offences are 'threatening or assaulting union officials . . . disobeying official orders . . . refusing to join an official strike . . . violating rules of work agreed by the union', and so on.[1]

The most common specific expulsion rule, and far the most important, is that relating to expulsion for non-payment of subscriptions. The period of allowed lapsing is invariably specified, and varies from as little as five weeks to several months. One common feature of such rules is an automatic lapsing provision, as the rules of the Confederation of Health Service Employees provides:

Any member whose contributions are in arrears for a period of three calendar months shall be deemed automatically to have lapsed his membership of the Union.[2]

Apart from these specific offences there exist, in virtually all rule books, what Cyril Grunfeld terms 'rules which confer on the appropriate union body a general or blanket power of expulsion'.[3] As examples of these he lists a number taken from actual rule books, for example, power to expel a member guilty of:

conduct whether in connection with the (union), the trade or otherwise, which is, in the opinion of the committee, directly or indirectly detrimental to the interests, welfare or reputation of the union.[4]

F. P. Graham examined the rule books of eighty unions, representing 94 per cent of the T.U.C.'s total membership. He discovered that sixty-six rule books included a clause of this type. Many attempted an objective definition of the offences covered, but in some cases the rules provided that members could be expelled when 'in the opinion of the executive Committee' their conduct had fallen below the required standard. In a few cases deliberate attempts were made to avoid the necessity of spelling out the offence in even the most general terms.[5]

---

[1] See Cyril Grunfeld, *Trade Unions and the Individual*, Fabian Society, 1957, p. 9.

[2] C.O.H.S. Rule Book, Rule 6, 1953. In law rules which *automatically* terminate membership are not, strictly speaking, expulsion rules at all. A distinction is drawn between a rule which states that members who allow their arrears to exceed 26 weeks 'shall be expelled' (A.E.U. Rule Book, Rule 27), and a rule which says that 'when a members' arrears amount to 20s. he shall cease to be a member'. (Boilermakers' Rule Book, Rule 22). The latter are regarded as a case of *defeasance*—i.e. the termination of a contract through the operation of a condition subsequent. For the purposes of this chapter, however, the distinction is not crucial; by an automatic lapsing provision is meant *any* rule which may result in a member being struck off the books merely because he is in arrears. The relationship between union rules, the law of contract, and the right to expel is discussed in Chapter 9.

[3] *Ibid.*   [4] *Ibid.*

[5] See F. P. Graham, *A Legal Analysis of Trade Union Discipline in the United Kingdom*, unpublished D.L. thesis, Oxford, 1960.

It is easy to see the connection between almost all the specific offences quoted and the unions' internal strength and authority. Perhaps the need for the general clauses is not so obvious, but the reason for them is the impossibility of covering every eventuality by specific rules. Rule makers cannot foresee all future misdeeds, so most unions must buttress their list of specified crimes with an unspecified list, giving those in authority a measure of prerogative power. Sometimes it is not even thought advisable to make them give reasons at all; though this does not mean that the object of such rules is to enable expulsion to take place without reasons.

The connection between disciplinary rules and the closed shop is complex. As has been stated, the fact that workers are employed in closed shops enormously strengthens the penalty of expulsion. According to how far the trade is comprehensively closed, how far the skill needed is transferable, and how far alternative occupations (equally attractive) are available, the strength of the penalty varies from individual to individual; nevertheless the effect of threatening any worker with exclusion from any job must add to the strength of the expulsion penalty whatever the situation in which it is employed. But this is not all; the closed shop adds much more generally to the union's powers of disciplinary enforcement.

It is not only where the immediate penalty is expulsion that the closed shop is important. Where less draconic punishments are prescribed by the rules, such as fines, a refusal to pay these penalties usually renders the member liable to more extreme measures. Thus the rules of Bisakta empower branches to fine members 2s. for 'interrupting or disturbing the business of a branch meeting'. If the member continues to defy branch rulings he may be ejected from the meeting and his case 'forthwith reported to the Executive Council'. If they consider this constitutes an offence against a general rule, of remarkable comprehensiveness, they may impose a fine of not more than 40s. or may decide to expel the member from the association.[1]

In the Engineers refusal to pay a fine may result in expulsion. Rule 22 states:

all fines shall be paid within 14 weeks from the imposition of such fine, if not then paid (they) shall be treated as arrears of contributions.[2]

But an A.E.U. member is liable to automatic expulsion if he owes the union more than 26 weeks arrears of contributions—i.e. about

---

[1] Bisakta Rule Book, Rule 14, 1957.   [2] A.E.U., *op. cit.*, Rule 22.

H

£2. It follows that the member who fails to pay a fine of more than £2 within 14 weeks is also liable to automatic expulsion. Where a more extreme penalty lies behind a less extreme one, and may be invoked if the latter is ineffective, it may not be necessary to employ the former because its very existence strengthens the effectiveness of the latter. The engineer who refuses to pay a fine, like the member of Bisakta who continues to disrupt the work of the branch, is ultimately risking his livelihood.

By strengthening the sanctions behind all the penalties prescribed in the rule book, the closed shop also helps to buttress the power and authority of those the rule book charges with the task of leading the union and taking decisions in its name. In most rule books specific reference is made to the obligation of members to obey orders given by union officers in the execution of their duties. Members are informed that they must obey the chairman's ruling, that they must accept decisions of the branch committee as final (subject to specified rights of appeal), that they must show their cards to shop stewards, or that the executive council shall have power to 'adjudicate in all matters affecting the union'.[1] In the Engineers it is laid down in the rules that penalties may be imposed 'if any member be satisfactorily proved to have . . . refused to obey these rules, or to comply with any order by them authorized'.[2] Moreover, quite apart from such specific statements, it is obvious that disobeying the decisions of authorized leaders of the union can constitute grounds for punishment under general rules, whether they specifically mention disobedience as an offence or not. It can be plausibly argued that disobedience, or its results, weakens the union, or is inconsistent with the duties of a member, or is in some other way detrimental to union interests. By adding to the strength of the penalties for such disobedience the closed shop makes it more likely that those authorized to take decisions will be obeyed.

Finally, the closed shop also has a less direct but nevertheless potent effect on union discipline in a less tangible way. Most union members are extremely hazy about the contents of the rule book, what it authorizes and penalizes and who it permits to decide issues in the name of the union. Thus the ultimate threat of possible exclusion on grounds of disobedience is rarely tested or critically examined by those against whom it is employed. It is not merely that the rule

[1] N.U.P.B.P.W. Rule Book, Rule 3, 1956.   [2] A.E.U., *op. cit.*, Rule 22.

book is often complex and vague; it is that union members do not often consult their rule book, even where it is clear. Union officials openly admit that this is so, and much of union business proceeds on this assumption.[1] What the members *do* realize is that if they work in an open shop the worst that will happen is that if they disobey the union or its representative they will lose certain friendly benefits and be subjected to a varying degree of social ostracism; the worst that can happen in a closed shop is that they will be forced out of the trade altogether. It is an awareness of this general contrast, rather than any detailed knowledge of the penalties prescribed for disobedience in the union rule book, that helps to uphold union discipline.

Theoretically, of course, the contrast need not necessarily be as extreme as all this. It is possible for any group to refuse to work with one of their number who has broken a union rule or order, or even some unwritten informal custom of the group. If they are prepared to act collectively to this end the worker concerned may be forced to leave the job and may even be discharged by an employer to avoid trouble. Thus, even if he works in an open shop, a worker may find that the penalty of disobedience is exclusion—at least from that particular job. Similarly, even if he works in a closed shop, the same worker may discover that he is excluded without having been charged with committing any offence against union rules.

However, workers who operate group customs, which they are willing to enforce via a refusal to work with those who break them, are usually closed shop prone. In practice this type of exclusion threat is unlikely to arise within an open group.[2] The substance of the contrast between the penalties for disobedience in open and closed shop areas remains, and is in fact strengthened. The individual worker comes to feel that the power which the union, its officers, and its members exert varies substantially according to whether he enters a closed or open group. For this reason all those who belong to and lead a union in a closed shop situation tend to be aware that in the field of membership discipline they enjoy a power, and consequently a status, which is significantly different from that enjoyed by those employed in open shops.

[1] For example, it is quite common for union leaders to authorize strikes, and even pay out dispute benefit, in ways not strictly covered by union rules, yet they are not usually challenged by their members.
[2] See page 111 below for an account of the relationship between such group customs and the demand for the closed shop.

The extent to which these disciplinary powers are actually used is difficult to measure, since only the most extreme cases attract publicity. Union officials say that the number of exclusions for reasons other than lapsing are exceedingly small. Generally speaking, unions appear to use their expulsion powers with restraint, particularly in closed shop areas.

The most impressive example, known to the writer, of the strength of the exclusion threat when used by a closed shop union concerns Bisakta. When their executive council agreed to the continuous working week, in 1947, many branches refused to operate it in practice. The executive replied by sending notices of expulsion to the men involved. Before the notices expired contact was established between Head Office and representatives of the branches. The men capitulated and the notices were withdrawn.

But such wholesale and peremptory action is not typical. Commenting on the attitude of the Transport and General Workers' Union to indiscipline in the docks, V. L. Allen argues that even the 'leaders were treated lightly and the assurances which the majority of them gave to abide by the constitution of the Union in future were accepted in good faith'.[1] Yet it is impossible to gauge the effect of the threat of expulsion in closed shop areas by such examples. A sanction does not merely operate on those against whom it is employed; it conditions the behaviour of those aware of its existence, however vaguely, who, as a result, obey the union's rules, customs and leaders more than they otherwise would. It affects not only the active and militant but also the inactive and moderate—who may, at times, regard the demands made upon them by the most conciliatory leadership as too heavy.

Taken together, the membership and discipline functions represent the advantages of the post-entry shop. Their object is to ensure that each entrant is recruited, retained, and subjected to the discipline of the union. In this way they help to ensure that workers act together, under the control of the union, so that it is possible to impose the most effective sanctions on employers who refuse to concede their demands. In most cases this is all that is required, but in certain circumstances unions feel their bargaining position requires them to obtain a measure of control over entry to the trade. To this end they seek to use the exclusion threat to secure the performance of yet another function. This is described below.

[1] *Trade Union Leadership*, Longmans Green, 1957, p. 209.

(c) The Entry Control Function

This use of the closed shop is confined to the pre-entry shop. The closed shop's function here is to use the exclusion threat to force would-be entrants to obtain prior acceptance by the union. As has been said, any union can bargain over the entry of labour, or strike to secure the exclusion of any individual or group, whether they are members of the union or not. The need for the pre-entry shop only arises when such alternative methods of securing entry control are considered impractical or ineffective.

The pre-entry shop takes different forms, and is used to effect different degrees of entry control which were outlined in Chapter 1.[1] The main feature of the entry control function to be stressed here is its relationship to the membership and discipline functions.

Obviously the attainment of the pre-entry shop for the purposes of entry control carries with it the chance to use the other functions of the practice, and attempts to obtain it are usually motivated by the need for more than one of these functions. Yet sometimes unions are faced with a choice between the pre-entry and post-entry shop, and the choice they make depends partly on the extent to which they feel the need for one group of functions or another. What is in dispute here, is how far it is to the advantage of the group to restrict the area of recruitment and to try to control entry, as against widening the area of recruitment at the cost of more or less abandoning entry control. If the first policy is pursued there is a demand for all these functions of the closed shop to be used in the interests of a comparatively narrowly based group; if the second option is chosen it represents a choice in favour of the membership and discipline functions alone, exercised in the interests of a more widely based group. In the next chapter the influences affecting this decision are described in detail.

One final distinction between the entry control function and other functions must be made. In the case of the membership and discipline functions the workers against whom they are directed can avoid the additional sanction of the exclusion threat by becoming or remaining members of the union and obeying its orders. It is only if they refuse to conform in this way that the sanction is imposed. In the case of the entry control function this element of choice is not usually present. The conditions constituting a qualification for membership cannot always be met, and it is not the intention

[1] See p. 17.

of the union that they should be. In short, the entry control function may be used to exclude workers who would be quite willing to join the union, and abide by its rules. This distinction between the entry control function and other functions is important, and more will be said about it when the question of justification is considered.

CHAPTER 5

FACTORS AFFECTING DEMANDS
FOR THE CLOSED SHOP

AT the end of Chapter 3 two questions were posed. The first of these—what advantages do unions gain from the closed shop? —was answered in the last chapter. This chapter is mainly concerned with the second question—in what circumstances do they come to feel that they need these advantages?

It is not suggested that closed shops arise because trade unionists analyse its advantages, or functions, in the systematic way outlined in Chapter 4, and decide they would be in a stronger bargaining position if they obtained it. What is suggested is that in carrying out their task of job regulation unions come up against certain problems concerned with the organization and control of workers. These problems can be discussed under three headings. They are: (1) *Problems of Organizing the Labour Force*; (2) *Problems of Controlling the Labour Force;* (3) *Problems of Organizing and Controlling the Alternative Labour Force.* The closed shop is demanded because it helps unions to overcome one or another of these problems, and the attitude which individual union leaders adopt towards the practice is mainly determined by their experience of its utility to them in this respect. However, it will also be suggested, in a final section of the chapter, that once the closed shop has operated for any time it tends to give rise to a *closed shop tradition*. This normally results in the continuance, and even the extension of the practice, in situations in which the problems that gave rise to the need for it have declined in importance.

(1) PROBLEMS OF ORGANIZING THE LABOUR FORCE

When unions set out to affect the terms of employment covering a particular job they must organize and control a high proportion of the workers who are doing the job; otherwise their attempt to impose sanctions on the employer are likely to be ineffective. In this section we shall consider four of the difficulties which arise when unions try to obtain and retain a high and stable level of membership, and the effect of these difficulties in giving rise to demands for the membership function of closed shop.

The two most important may be considered together under the heading of problems of turnover and contact.

(a) Problems of Turnover and Contact

Wherever there is a fairly rapid rate of labour turnover the problem of recruiting and retaining members becomes difficult. This is an issue affecting unions recruiting semi-skilled and unskilled workers, and is perhaps at its worst among building labourers. Unless the union's recruiting methods are swift and regular, workers leave before enrolment and sudden drops in unionization are inevitable. Moreover, the more workers move from job to job the more difficult it is to obtain reliable collectors and the more important it is to secure the kind of ratchet effect that the closed shop represents.

Turnover is a great problem in a union like the Transport and General Workers, organizing among unskilled workers in a large number of trades. Goldstein calculated that during the 1935–47 period turnover, as expressed in terms of lapsed membership, was on average 33·3 per cent of the total membership of the union.[1] During this period the union grew by 9·4 per cent a year, and an average of 38·3 per cent of each year's membership consisted of 'new members'[2] Goldstein also calculated the average percentage of 'new' and 'lapsed' members in the thirteen trade groups of the union between 1936–47. His results are worth quoting in full.

National Trade Group	Average Annual New Membership %	Average Annual Lapsed Membership %
Building	85·7	84·0
Chemical	53·8	41·0
Engineering	51·1	46·1
Government Workers	46·8	49·7
General Workers	44·5	39·6
Municipal Workers	44·2	25·0
Supervisory	33·6	25·3
Road Transport Commercial	32·8	27·3
Milling	28·0	22·2
Agricultural	27·8	17·5
Road Passenger Transport:		
— Cab Section	25·4	28·5
— Bus Section	25·8	21·5
— Tram Section	19·5	19·6
Docks	11·8	11·6[3]

[1] *The Government of British Trade Unions*, Allen and Unwin, 1952, p. 73.
[2] *Ibid.* Actually a substantial proportion of those Goldstein regarded as 'new' members were probably ex-members, who had 'lapsed' as a consequence of moving to badly organized jobs. [3] *Op. cit.*, p. 78.

Goldstein maintains that these figures show that the union consists of a large number of workers who are new to the organization and have had little time to identify themselves with it. He believes that this rate of turnover 'prevents the creation of a large body of members capable and desirous of making the new members feel a sense of belonging' and makes it difficult for the union to become 'unified into a well disciplined body'.[1]

This seems an extreme statement to make of a union where two-thirds of the membership is stable over a period of twelve months, but it is substantially true of the membership in building and, to lesser extent, chemicals and engineering. It is difficult to say how far membership in these latter trades consists of a hard core, which remains or changes slowly, surrounded by a shifting membership. The larger and more stable this core is, the easier is the problem of membership maintenance. This is undoubtedly the case, for example, among the union's membership in the industrial civil service, and among municipal workers. Among the more isolated engineering and chemical works, where alternative employment is less likely to be available, or where pay and conditions are relatively good, there is probably a smaller hard core who remain, but this is less likely for many of the trades covered by the general workers' group. In conversation, officials have stressed how difficult it is to maintain membership in this group; only building presents greater difficulties.

In jobs where turnover is high the problem of membership maintenance often lies behind attempts to obtain the closed shop. This is clearly so in building, but is also the case in chemicals, engineering, and other miscellaneous, lesser skilled groups. Often the entry of enthusiastic and militant activists results in a campaign to lift membership above the hard core. When this runs up against resistance, the closed shop is demanded both to break it down and to place a ratchet under the results of such a drive.

This is more likely if job conditions impose the further difficulty of contacting workers on the job or at the branch to attend to their problems and collect dues. This problem affects a number of groups, the most important being merchant seamen, dockers, road haulage and building, civil and engineering workers, and maintenance workers generally.

[1] *Op. cit.*, p. 76.

With merchant seamen the problem can be seen at its most extreme. The main organizational problem facing seamen's unions arises out of the Merchant Shipping Acts. These restrict attempts at job regulation, and union activity, once seamen have signed articles.[1] Recruitment and the collection of dues must be done on shore unless management agrees to a check off. This means that it is impossible to prevent seamen getting in arrears, and consequently large sums must be extracted from them before they sign on.

It is not suggested that problems of turnover and contact are the only factors making for closed shop demands in any of these cases, but they are a significant part of the explanation of why the practice has been demanded in each instance.

(b) The Problem of Inter-Union Competition

A less important factor touching off some demands for the closed shop is the problem of inter-union competition. It is usually most extreme in the case of a breakaway union, where the original organization denies the breakaway's right to exist. Whenever, as in London Transport, an established union like the Transport and General Workers, faces a militant breakaway, like the National Transport Workers, which is systematically 'poaching', it is apt to demand the closed shop to eliminate and destroy this threat. Conversely, a union like the tiny Admiralty Employees opposed the closed shop—if only because its implementation on behalf of the unions with recognition rights in Admiralty Dockyards would mean the union's extinction.

But the breakaway difficulty is only the problem of inter-union competition at its most inflamed. There is also the problem of the well established 'bona fide' union which fails to observe the Bridlington Agreement and poaches members. In the past the General and Municipal Workers has alleged that this is the case in respect of the National Union of Public Employees in the Local Government field. Where practicable the closed shop is used as a weapon against such poaching. Other examples of the effect of inter-union competition are in engineering. Here stewards of the Transport and General

---

[1] The Act of 1894 imposed imprisonment and loss of pay for refusing to go to sea after being formally engaged and for 'combining with any of the men to disobey lawful commands' while at sea. Picketing was also made an offence; fines of £10 per seaman 'tampered with' and £20 for giving shelter to such seamen were prescribed.

Workers, the Engineers, and the Vehicle Builders, sometimes demand the closed shop, in part, because they cannot agree to eliminate competition. Consequently recruits can 'play one union off against another' and use inter-union rivalry as an excuse for remaining non-members. Those who do join can demand frequent transfers, and drop out of the union if they are refused. In this situation the closed shop can be employed to restrict and control competition. New entrants are given a choice on entrance, but must join one union or another and remain within it. If they drop out of their original union when refused a transfer they can be excluded as non-unionists.

(c) The Problem of Worker Indifference

Where workers are relatively indifferent to unionism (lacking the elementary solidarity, or group cohesion, to respond to attempts to organize them), there is usually nothing to be done; unless, as was seen in the case of the Co-operative movement, unions can obtain managerial assistance via the closed shop. Demands for the practice among unions organizing co-operative workers have sometimes been motivated by the feeling that *only* in this way could they solve their membership problems.

(2) PROBLEMS OF CONTROLLING THE LABOUR FORCE

Even if the problems listed above can be overcome, unions may still run into difficulties when employing their sanctions against employers and when trying to ensure that members act in a united and disciplined way. These problems are essentially those of controlling the labour force once it has been organized. There are three problems which must be mentioned here, because of their effect in giving rise to demands for the discipline function of the closed shop. The first concerns the imposition of unilateral regulations.

(a) The Problem of Enforcing Unilateral Regulations

When unions seek to regulate the job unilaterally, they are trying to ensure that workers observe rules of behaviour laid down by the union. The utility of the closed shop here is obvious: it ensures that the entire labour force is recruited, retained, and subjected to the discipline of the union while it remains on the job. In this way it adds to the internal strength of the union and enables it to wield more effective sanctions against employers. The importance of the practice in this respect can best be indicated by examples.

The musicians' union is, perhaps, most dependent on effective unilateral regulations. It has formal agreements with employers who hire musicians on a permanent basis, but most of its members work on a shifting or temporary basis, where the settled processes of collective bargaining are difficult to operate. Consequently the union relies on the publication of a pattern of rates and conditions constituting the 'union contract'. Members are told, in their rules. that they must 'observe not less than the minimum rates and conditions of employment which are from time to time adopted by the union'. They must not accept engagements of more than a week without obtaining the permission of their branch secretary, and consent may be withheld where 'the terms and conditions offered are not acceptable to the union'.[1] Non-conformity with the rules merits punishment, if necessary expulsion, but obviously unless expulsion involved exclusion from the job those who were undermining the union's attempts at unilateral regulation would be free to continue to do so. The need to enforce such regulations has been the main factor determining the attitude of musicians to the closed shop. From its foundation, the union has campaigned for the exclusion of non-unionists from the ranks of full-time professionals.

But musicians were not the first group to want the closed shop to enforce unilateral regulations. As the Webbs stressed, in *Industrial Democracy*, the traditional technique of job regulation used by the old craft unions presupposed a similarly comprehensive closed shop. The 'Strike in Detail', which they describe, is the nineteenth-century equivalent of the objectives set out in the Musicians' Rule Book. Where uniform price lists and customs were not respected, unions like the Flint Glass Makers would either not take work, or take it temporarily, after obtaining branch permission. The objective then would be to place members working in such a shop elsewhere, where the unions' unilateral regulations were tolerated. Thus:

As man after man leaves ... then it is the proud and haughty spirit of the oppressor is brought down and he feels the power he cannot see.[2]

But as the Webbs realized:

As a deliberate Trade Union policy, the Strike in Detail depends on the extent to which the union has secured the adhesion of all the competent men in the trade.[3]

Another group whose attitude has been conditioned by this problem are the dockers. Giving evidence to the Royal Commission of

---

[1] Musicians' Union Rule Book, Rule 14/3, 1957.
[2] *The Flint Glass Makers' Magazine*, July 1850, as quoted in the Webbs, *op. cit.*, p. 169.
[3] *Ibid.*

1891 a non-unionist stevedore complained of trade unionists refusing to work in conditions below those stipulated by their union, and refusing to allow non-unionists to undertake such work. Similarly the manager of the Surrey Commercial Dock Company protested that, as a result of union rules, men were unable to go from one job to another, and concluded:

a man who is a deal porter must do the work of a deal porter; a man who is a corn porter must work as a corn porter. . . . The consequence is that it often happens that when we are particularly busy there are a great quantity of wood porters who are standing idle, and who, under the old system which prevailed, would have been glad to avail themselves of the opportunity to work.[1]

The overtones of resentment in this quotation illustrate an aspect of the relationship between unilateral regulation and the closed shop which must be discussed. It has been seen that where unions still have to enforce the closed shop by unilateral regulation this is to some extent a sign of weakness, or insecurity. As union strength and determination on the issue of non-unionists comes to be accepted as a permanency, management accepts that it must operate with a working force that observes such customs and learns to tolerate them. This process occurs with unilateral regulations other than the closed shop. Managements grow to accept them as part of the recognized terms of employment. If they wish to change them they raise the issue with the unions, as a subject for bargaining and bilateral agreement. When this results in a negotiated change in a union rule, we may say it has passed out of the sphere of unilateral and into the sphere of bilateral regulation. An outstanding example is the case of the apprenticeship ratio in printing. In days when the unions were weak, they sought to impose the ratio unilaterally. When it became obvious they could be troublesome to employers who refused to recognize their right to do so, the printing employer offered to bargain over the question of adjusting the ratio. The result was a collective agreement bilaterally regulating what had previously been imposed by the union alone.

But it does not follow that the more bilateral regulation advances the less likely it is that unilateral regulations will continue. The regulation of terms of employment by union groups tends to grow in complexity and scope. The fact that aspects of the job that were once unilaterally regulated are now covered by agreements, does not mean that there does not exist, at any one time, a set of rules

[1] I.R.C. Q6121, p. 299.

which the group observes itself, for which management will take no
responsibility. Thus, although the unilateral regulations referred to
by the manager of the Surrey Docks are now recognized by the
N.D.L.B. this does not mean that dockers do not regulate many
aspects of their job unilaterally. Similarly, although many of the
previously disputed customs of printers are now recognized, this
does not mean that unilateral regulation is unimportant in the printing industry. As has been seen, the extent to which employers are
prepared to accept the movement of union rules and customs from
the sphere of unilateral regulation to the sphere of bilateral regulation, depends partly on the fact that they realize that the union *could*
maintain them unilaterally.[1] For this reason groups like the boilermakers deny that their rule books, which contain working rules that
employers now recognize, are out of date. They believe that they
still need these rules, and the ability to enforce them, if necessary
with the closed shop.

From the employers' point of view the impact of past unilateral
regulations is probably at its most all-pervasive among newsprint
workers organized in the labour supply shops of Natsopa, and
employed in the machine and publishing rooms of Fleet Street.
Here there are manning standards and output limitations that are
insisted upon by the union, which in the opinion of the recent Royal
Commission on the Press, both inflate the labour force, and give
rise to unnecessary overtime. In an attempt to decide how far these
regulations, which are nowadays often the subject of agreement,
result in the employment of excess labour, the Commission asked a
firm of industrial consultants, with considerable experience of printing, to investigate four national newspapers in London. The team
of investigators concluded that the papers had '53 per cent more
staff on the Production and Distribution side than is required'.[2]

(b) The Problem of Strike Solidarity

The threat of effective strike action is the main sanction behind
union attempts at job regulation, both unilaterally and bilaterally.
It may be required where unilateral regulation is non-existent or

[1] There are other considerations affecting employers. They may know they cannot resist
a practice, like the apprenticeship ratio of the boilermakers, yet not be prepared to recognize
it formally, or even bargain over its alteration. They may still think it to be in their interest
to continue to protest, in public, about the continued existence of the ratio.

[2] *Report of the Royal Commission on the Press*, 1961–62, H.M.S.O., Cmnd. 1811, p. 210.
Only slightly less restrictive on the employers concerned are the working rules of the 'bummarees' and other groups in London's Wholesale Markets—see S. Rottenburg, *op. cit.*

unimportant. It is suggested that if any group comes to rely, to a substantial extent, on the use of the strike, it is bound to demand the closed shop as soon as this is practicable. The relationship between the closed shop and strike action is one of the most important factors in explaining the closed shop pattern.

Nothing exposes the menace of non-unionism like a strike, nothing gives rise to bitterness like the spectacle of one's workmate walking through picket lines. It is for this reason, above all, that so many of the comprehensively closed groups—the dockers, the miners, the shipyard workers, and so on—are intolerant of non-unionists and sceptical of their consciences. But the relationship between strikes and the closed shop is complex. Basically there are two related problems, which may be termed the problem of *strike solidarity*, and the problem of *strike control*. They must be dealt with separately.

To ensure that a strike has the maximum effect, workers must withdraw their labour as a 'solid' mass, and remain on strike until it is decided to return equally 'solidly'. Non-unionists, and even members if they fear no reprisals, may refuse to strike, or may return to work before the strike is officially terminated. The relationship between the problem of strike solidarity and the closed shop can best be illustrated by a short account of the rise of the practice in mining.

(c) The Example of Coal Mining

British coal-miners have relied on the strike weapon more consistently, and to a greater extent than any other group. On average they were almost eight times as strike prone as the average British worker throughout the period 1911-45, and more than four times as many working days were lost in mining as in any other industry.[1] From their earliest days, organized groups of miners have also tried to obtain the closed shop. Page-Arnot, in his *History of the Scottish Miners*, quotes a remarkable record of the early association between the closed shop and strike action in the eighteenth century. It reads:

They have among them too a practice which makes any reformation of their manners difficult. They have among them what they call brotherings: It is a solemn oath, or engagement, to stand by each other. In the west-country, where this practice is universal, they have some *watchword* by sending round of which they can lay the *whole of the collieries in the country idle*. . . . If a collier from England,

[1] See Knowles, *op. cit.*, pp. 162-3, 203 and 207.

or from any other place, who is not of the brotherhood, comes among them, he is immediately obliged to enter into the Society, and take this oath, or they will not allow him to work. The case is that they are generally united and if the majority in the pit agree to make an *idle* day the rest must do the same.[1]

Yet mining strikes pre-date the creation of widespread closed shops, or even strong unions. In the early days non-unionists greatly outnumbered trade unionists, even among face workers. Surface workers were virtually unorganized. However, when unions began to grow, they were committed to a strike policy, and so it was necessary to devise ways of securing the co-operation of 'nons'.

The practice grew of consulting them on the advisability of strike action, and paying them out of union funds so long as they withdrew their labour along with union members. In 1889, for example, the newly formed Miners' Federation imposed a levy of 2d. a week on members to yield a strike benefit of 7s. a week for members and 5s. a week for 'nons'. Page-Arnot comments:

. . . it should be understood that throughout these early stages of the Federation, those who were called 'non-unionists' could generally be relied upon to act along with the trade unionists, even though they did not become financial members: in contrast to later stages when non-unionist had become synonymous with potential blackleg.[2]

But, necessary though this method of securing strike solidarity was, it had disadvantages. The non-members were not only a financial drain, but the knowledge of their existence acted as a drag on militancy. Many strikes were cancelled in deference to non-unionists. Thousands of pounds were paid to 'nons' who subsequently black-legged.[3] In time the attitude towards non-unionism hardened, and a recruiting drive began among surface workers and boys. When resistance was encountered demands for the closed shop began to grow.[4] After 1900 the number of recorded strikes over non-unionism roughly trebled, and by 1913 they accounted for about a third of all strikes.[5] As a result the level of unionization rose rapidly. By 1910 the Federation could claim to have organized 60 per cent of all wage earners; by 1914 the figure was nearer 70 per cent, and

[1] Allen and Unwin, 1955, p. 12.
[2] *The Miners*, Vol. 1, 1949, Allen & Unwin, p. 136.
[3] See Page-Arnot, *The Miners*, *op. cit.*, pp. 220, 261.
[4] The organization of surface workers was also stimulated by the fact that the general unions had gained a foothold in the pits by recruiting these groups. By 1894 they had begun to take action on their own account and their strikes had thrown face workers out of work. The Miners' Federation turned to the closed shop partly as a way of dealing with this inter-union competition.
[5] See Board of Trade (Labour Department) *Reports on Strikes and Lockouts*, 1893–1913.

during the war it rose still further.[1] Many of these workers were probably already in closed shops.

After the war unionization fell slightly, although the closed shop remained an issue, particularly in strike-prone South Wales. In 1926 the miners became involved in the most widespread and drawn-out strike in their history—and once again the issue of strike solidarity became crucial.

The employers locked out miners who would not accept wage-cuts from May 1. The great bulk of the labour force followed the lead of the Federation in rejecting these terms, and the ensuing strike remained 'solid' for the first three months; by the beginning of September less than 5 per cent of the membership of the Federation had returned to work. By the end of the month the figure had risen to 10 per cent. Shortly afterwards George Spencer, the Nottingham miners' leader, defied the Federation and negotiated a separate settlement. As a consequence most of the 25,000 Nottinghamshire trade unionists went back to the pits. By November almost a quarter of a million miners were at work—well over 25 per cent of the organized labour force.[2] At the end of the month the Federation sanctioned an official return on the owners' terms.

The effect of the defeat on the level of unionization did not register significantly until the returns for 1928. By that time the Federation, with two breakaways in existence, could not claim more than 60 per cent, in an industry with a smaller labour force than at any time since 1918. In 1929 and 1930 the level fell to around 55 per cent—not far from the 1890's level.[3] In four years the Federation's level of organization had fallen by roughly a third. It was not until the outbreak of the Second World War that the union really recovered.

A feature of the war-time period was the negotiated closed shop agreements outlined in Chapter 2.[4] Still more important were the widespread 'understandings' which grew up in many pits, and the various forms of semi-closed shop which also developed alongside the check off. Significantly these moves were accompanied by a rise in the number of strikes. Over half the 4,000 or so war-time strikes were in mining.

[1] See Page-Arnot, *The Miners*, op. cit., Vol. 2, p. 545.
[2] Page-Arnot, *The Miners*, op. cit., Vol. 2, p. 504.
[3] Page-Arnot, *The Miners*, op. cit., Vol. 2, p. 545.
[4] See p. 53.

I

The miners' story is illuminating in a number of ways. It shows how a group committed to strike action found it increasingly necessary to take action against non-unionism. As organization spread downwards to the lesser skilled, as union policy became more militant, the non-unionist came to be regarded more and more as an obvious source of weakness. Moreover, having made the closed shop their objective, the miners retained this intention in times of adversity, and disinterred it with even greater conviction after their humiliating defeat in 1926. But the example of the miners shows more than this. It also demonstrates that, although the need for strike solidarity may require the closed shop, too great a reliance on strikes, or too protracted and dogged strike action, can result in the breakdown of what closed shops there are, and cause a general decline in unionization. Although the closed shop acts as a ratchet under union membership, and this ratchet is extremely important to any group that uses the strike weapon, too much use of the weapon can break the ratchet itself. This point is important and more will be said about it below.

But there are other groups whose experience in relation to the closed shop and the problem of strike solidarity underscores these points and highlights certain others. More than any other factor the problem of strike solidarity helps to explain the rise of particular closed shops in the mainly open trades. Wherever, for example in chemicals or food manufacture, one comes across a factory with a number of closed shops, the chances are that this group is also more strike prone than average. Further inquiries usually reveal some incident, or series of incidents, connected with the needs of strike effectiveness, in which local leaders have come to see the need to eliminate non-unionism and to strengthen their disciplinary authority. This is also often the case in closed shop prone trades, such as clothing, or among unskilled workers in shipbuilding, and it is undoubtedly of greatest contemporary significance in engineering, where the closed shop is increasing at its fastest rate at the moment.

Of course, several other factors contribute towards demands for the closed shop in engineering; problems of turnover and contact are involved and, to a lesser extent these days, problems of enforcing unilateral regulations. Yet there is little doubt that nowadays the problem of strike solidarity is often more important. This can best be demonstrated by an account of the struggle to obtain the closed shop in a large car factory. This case study underscores the conclusions drawn from the coal-mining example, but it has lessons of its own.

(d) The Example of Car Manufacture

In common with most other car workers, the employees in this factory remained largely unorganized until the Second World War. During the war workers who were more union conscious drifted in from other parts of the country and unionization rose. Management joined the employers' association, and by the mid-1950's the three main unions organizing production workers claimed a membership between them of just under 50 per cent. At this time strikes were virtually unknown, and no action had ever been taken against non-unionists.

In 1956 the industry was affected by the credit squeeze, and by March most production workers were on a four-day week. One morning in June management announced that about 1,000 of the 7,000 or so production workers were to be given a week's pay in lieu of notice. After prolonged negotiation an official strike took place—long after the men dismissed had left the factory. Management claimed that only 15 per cent of the workers took part in this strike. The unions have never accepted these figures, but they were seriously shaken by the number of members and non-members who remained at work. As one shop steward remarked: 'What happened was a perfect example of how not to run a union.' After a week of bitterness the annual works holiday occurred and the dispute was settled meanwhile. No worker secured reinstatement, but there was some compensation and a promise to consult on future redundancy. One steward described this as 'the best way out of a bad business'. He commented: 'Of one thing we were certain—it was not going to happen again.'

Everybody interviewed on both sides agreed that the subsequent drive to obtain the closed shop was rooted in the stewards' experiences in this strike. Membership and prestige sank still further after the strike, but in time the union recovered ground and a recruiting drive began. As soon as the drive encountered a hard core of 'nonners' there was talk of strike action unless they agreed to join a union. The first strike to enforce a closed shop was in the trim shop. It was preceded by a ballot, lasted less than four hours, and was directed at two men; both of whom joined the union. Inspired by this success the joint shop stewards' committee decided to adopt it as a model. Short, sharp strikes would be called to 'protest' against particular non-unionists, after a decision to that effect had been taken by the workers concerned. During the next few weeks over a dozen different strikes took place in various parts of the factory, and the stewards instructed district officials to take up the whole question of non-unionism with top management. One afternoon in July the officials met management and demanded a post-entry shop. At the time of the meeting it was known that two more 'protest strikes' involving over 1,000 men were due for the following day. Faced with this threat management decided to act. They offered— as a compromise—a 'registration shop'—i.e. if the unions could prove a given shop or section was 100 per cent organized they would recognize a closed shop there in future. This offer was accepted, but the details of what was agreed were left vague. It was not clear how far management would put pressure on recalcitrants. The stewards agreed to 'recommend restraint', but it was unclear what this meant.

A period of comparative quiet followed. Stewards concentrated on recruitment and 'registering' 100 per cent areas. By the end of August they estimated that over 2,500 workers were covered by closed shops. This still left 4,500 manual workers in open shop areas and pressure began to mount for strike action. The stewards had already shown an increasing readiness to use strike action on other issues, and so, in an atmosphere of rising militance, a group under the chief steward of one of the general unions began to criticize the compromise of July and demand an all-out campaign for the closed shop. Eventually the joint shop stewards' committee passed a resolution saying they could 'no longer recommend restraint'.

The following week workers in one of the largest open shops struck to enforce a closed shop. Next day the chief steward's own shop, which he had never managed to qualify for registration, came out on strike. But there were differences about this stoppage. There was no preliminary shop floor meeting, no period of notice, and the chief steward took the decision to lead a walk-out on his own initiative. More important still, the strike was aimed at forcing forty workers into the union, and the chief steward announced that he was going to keep his members out until they had all either joined or been removed. Naturally this led to a charge that he had gone against the policy of the joint shop stewards' committee.

Nevertheless, the strike was effective and paralysed the factory. The district official of the union concerned urged a return to work, but the men demanded a mass meeting to discuss the issue of non-unionism. Three thousand workers attended this meeting and the case of the militants for an all-out campaign to enforce the closed shop was considered and rejected. Instead, the meeting recommended a return to work, and an application to the respective union executives to back an official strike.

Next day management complained publicly of rising unofficial strikes, threatened to discharge future offenders, and declared 'This state of affairs cannot be allowed to continue.' Yet despite several similar pronouncements, unofficial strikes have not noticeably diminished, although there are now relatively few to enforce the closed shop. Conversely, the unions have not managed substantially to alter the July settlement. After the return to work there were recriminations and altercations among the stewards, particularly when the union executives refused to agree to an official strike. This contributed to a decline in union effectiveness, but eventually interunion relations improved and another recruiting drive began. More departments were 'registered' and to-day over three-quarters of the manual labour force is covered by the closed shop. In time, too, management took a more accommodating view of the 1958 agreement. They are now willing to interview recalcitrants in highly organized but as yet unregistered areas, and have moved men to other departments to facilitate the registration of a particular section.

This example, drawn from the engineering industry, which could be paralleled many times over, reinforces the conclusions drawn from the miners' study. Once again the bitter humiliation and defeat of strike action due to insufficient solidarity, touched off and sustained a closed shop campaign pioneered and led by the men most affected—the workshop representatives. Determined to rely on their own strength and leadership, after their experience of taking action 'through procedure' in 1956 they turned to the closed shop sanctions as soon as they had the strength and power to do so. But, like the miners, they discovered that the closed shop is not a panacea. It could be enforced unilaterally, if the number to be coerced was small, and the strike required was not over long. By choosing the right time the employer could be forced to concede a measure of recognition. But it was also possible to push too hard and for subsequent recriminations to lead to disunity. Nevertheless, as with the miners, once obtained the practice functioned as a useful ratchet, and when disunity disappeared the ground lost was recovered.

What the study also demonstrates is the habit-forming effect of the closed shop. Alongside strikes to impose it, went other strikes for other purposes; the closed shop drive was not only a campaign for solidarity—it helped to engender it. Having learnt the technique of the 'protest strike' the workers have tended to use it more generally. Thus there can be no doubt that, although the achievement of the registration agreement was followed by a period of disunity, it represented a victory for the unions. They are immeasurably stronger than they were in 1956, and management knows this.

On the other hand, they cannot always get what they want. In an unstable industry like motor manufacture so much depends on the employers' impression of the future state of demand for his products. What the closed shop does is help to make the sanctions which the workers can impose in a strong market situation more effective— and thus more likely to succeed. It cannot compensate for the loss of bargaining power resulting from periods of overproduction and short-time working. This is another sense in which it is not a panacea.

(e) The Problem of Strike Control

In the section on the discipline function of the closed shop in Chapter 4 its help in ensuring obedience was explained, and reference was made to the action of the leaders of Bisakta. in 1947.[1] This was no isolated instance and in the case of this union and its forerunners the need to ensure the obedience of its members was one of the most important factors behind the closed shop drive. The knowledge that union leaders were prepared to use the practice in this way was also one of the main reasons why employers were prepared to recognize it. The obedience of members was important because union leaders wanted to control the use of the strike weapon, and show that theirs was not an irresponsible organization subject to sudden strike action as a response to rank and file pressure. For this reason the relationship between closed shop demands and the problem of strike control can best be explained by reference to this industry.

(f) The Example of Iron and Steel

In the early days of unions, labour relations in the industry were turbulent and bitter. Operating with a high degree of capitalization, high overheads and fuel costs, management was concerned to avoid the loss of production that a strike represented, particularly among those concerned with firing processes. Moreover, since theirs was

---

[1] See p. 104.

a trade where prices fluctuated sharply, they were also concerned to maintain a direct link between wages and prices. While unionization represented a threat to either of these principles employers were bound to fight it, if necessary by the systematic importation of blacklegs.

However, in the late 1860's leaders emerged ready to accept both conditions, in exchange for a measure of recognition. Fortunately there arose, at the same time, a number of outstanding employers who were ready to agree. Together these groups were a major factor in moulding the pattern of industrial relations that has endured ever since. They set up joint boards, settling wages on sliding scale principles, and resolving other differences. If both sides failed to agree, a dispute went to arbitration, and the decision was accepted as binding. Recognition of the unions was at first incomplete under this system. Formally the interests represented were employers and their workers. Unionists and non-unionists alike elected representatives to the boards, and sometimes these were not even union members. This withholding of formal recognition was designed to discourage the growth of union power and authority.

With the rise of the steel industry, and the Steel Smelters' union under John Hodge, demands for formal recognition became insistent. Hodge shared the dislike of other union leaders for strikes and accepted the system of arbitration they had developed, but he aimed at recruiting over a wider area than they did, and his members, who were mostly day-men, wished to abolish the contract system, and Sunday work, and obtain some control over conditions of promotion. Leading a unified and compact group, in a superior strategic position, Hodge was able to secure such concessions—though not without a struggle.[1]

The steelmasters continued to oppose demands for a board, on which union rather than works representatives were recognized, until 1905. In that year Hodge negotiated an important sliding scale agreement with the Ingot Makers which became something of a precedent. Under the agreement the relationship between wages and prices was made more regular and automatic, and in exchange for this concession the employers agreed to sign the agreement with the union rather than with the 'workmen concerned', though each branch had to ratify the compact.

The agreement was ratified, though not without resistance, and Hodge had to deal somewhat summarily with his opponents in the

[1] John Hodge, *Workman's Cottage to Windsor Castle*, Sampson Low, 1931.

branches. This was, however, no new development. There had always been opponents of the sliding scale, and unofficial strikes often took place over arbitration awards. Union leaders usually did their best to ensure a return of their own members in such cases, and if necessary they were prepared to expel them from the union and agree to their discharge. Indeed, it was a part of their case for the negotiation of agreements solely with union representatives that only 'responsible' leaders could combine a respect for collective decisions with an ability to ensure their observance by the rank and file. As Hodge's successor, Sir Arthur Pugh, wrote in his history of the Iron and Steel Unions, it was felt

In those days (that) it was especially essential that a trade union should demonstrate its ability to control the conduct of its members if it was to gain the confidence of the more progressive employers and avoid the all too ready censure of public opinion.[1]

At the annual meeting of the Midland Wages Board, in 1907, the operatives' secretary made a 'direct challenge to the employers on the union question'. He referred to the success of the 'Sheet Trade Board', where 90 per cent of the men were union members, and quoted from the report of a German delegation which had studied the work of the Conciliation Boards and decided that 'The higher the labour in any industry is paid and the better the organization is, the more perfect are the Conciliation Boards arranged by them (and) . . . the more smoothly and usefully do they work.[2]

In these and other ways union leaders sought to persuade employers that it was in their joint interest to confine worker representation to union officials backed by the disciplinary sanctions of the closed shop. By 1914 many employers were converted, and when Belgian refugees were introduced during the war they were 'expected to become members of the union'.[3] Nowadays, as was seen in Chapter 2, management throughout the industry assists in enforcing the closed shop. In return union leaders respect a procedure agreement which makes provision for binding arbitration, and the virtual elimination of the strike threat. To ensure they are able to honour this long-standing compromise, the leaders require, and if necessary use, the disciplinary functions of the closed shop.

[1] *Men of Steel*, Iron and Steel Trades Federation, 1951, p. 214. This remains the code of the union and Pugh's successor, Sir Lincoln Evans, expressed similar sentiments in the foreword to *Men of Steel* (p. xii).
[2] Pugh, *ibid.*   [3] Pugh, *op. cit.*, p. 74.

Other situations where union leaders have been prepared to exchange their right to strike for a reference to arbitration and the closed shop occur in the Scottish Baking trade, and the Exhibition industry.

It is not suggested that there are many groups where the need to secure strike control via the closed shop has been the most important factor making for demands for the practice, but the over-all effect of the problem in accounting for the closed shop pattern is discussed in detail in the next chapter.

(3) Problems of Organizing or Controlling the Alternative Labour Force

So far this chapter has considered problems engendering demands for the membership and discipline functions of the closed shop arising out of attempts to organize and control the labour force employed to do a particular job. But most jobs can to some extent be done by somebody else, and so there exists what may be termed an *alternative labour force*, which may be of three kinds: (1) other workers, engaged by the same employer but normally employed on other work; (2) unemployed workers; (3) workers who are prepared to leave existing jobs with other employers. If a sufficient quantity of any of these kinds of alternative labour is available to an employer, and he has an incentive to import it, it may be used as a substitute for union members. This will undermine the ability of the union to impose effective sanctions on employers—i.e. during a strike, when the alternative labour force may be imported as blacklegs—and may result in union members losing their jobs. It follows that the union must find some way of denying the employer access to the alternative labour force. The closed shop can assist here in one of two ways, but the alternatives mentioned in the section above on entry control must be faced;[1] either the membership and discipline functions of the post-entry shop can be used to organize as many as possible of the alternative labour force, and subject them to the control of the union, or the entry control function of the pre-entry shop can be used to restrict their access to the job.

The problem of the alternative labour force is seen at its most extreme among two contrasting groups: (1) unskilled workers, like merchant seamen and dockers; (2) craft groups, like the printers or the boilermakers. The reasons for this will be considered after an

[1] See p. 141.

account of the relationship between demands for the closed shop and the problem of the alternative labour force in these and other groups.

(a) Unskilled Groups

Seamen's unions have always been concerned with ways of controlling or excluding the periphery of casual labour that surrounds their trade. In their case this alternative labour force was partly foreign, and partly domestic, consisting both of the sailors of other nations and of the various mobile groups of unemployed that frequent dock areas. From the beginning of stable organization among seamen union leaders emphasized the need to restrict or exclude such casual workers. Havelock Wilson, for example, the founder of the National Sailor's and Firemen's Union, quoted as one of the union's objects:

To provide a better class of men for the Merchant Service, and to see that all members that are engaged through the union will be on board at the appointed time and in a sober condition.[1]

He regarded the bulk of the alternative labour force as unreliable 'riff-raff', largely unorganizable and a danger to decent seamen. To enable him to exclude such groups he wanted a labour supply shop. But the employers would not even agree to recognize Wilson's Union, and stressed their own right to engage labour as they pleased. In desperation he tried to impose his own closed shop by means of unilateral regulation at the point of hire. The struggle that ensued is of special interest as an instance of the crucial importance, in certain circumstances, of the size and availability of the alternative labour force. For this reason it is worth describing in detail.

In 1890 Wilson became associated with an officers' union, and announced that his members would not sail on ships manned by officers who were not members of this union. The employers replied by forming the Shipping Federation, which issued Federation Tickets to all seamen who undertook to accept engagements despite the fact that 'other members of the crew may or may not be members of any Seamen's union'. It was the intention of the employers to confine employment to holders of the Federation ticket. Wilson's members reacted by refusing to apply for Federation tickets, and refusing to sail with seamen who did.

[1] Wilson, op. cit., p. 127.

From this point until the outbreak of the First World War the industry was dominated by the attempts of both sides to secure a monopoly of the labour supply and a preference for those who held either the union or the Federation ticket. One leading official of the union has summarized the situation that developed:

The heart of the matter lay not only in the supply of crews where men and ships required them. From the men's point of view it lay in their ability to secure jobs. The tendency of the men was to favour the organization which could give them jobs; the interests of an organization were best served therefore in securing a monopoly of given jobs, because it captured the allegiance of the seamen.[1]

The position which evolved was something of a stalemate, with separate battles going to either side. The same writer sums it up like this:

If it was through the Federation chiefly that jobs could be secured the men took the Federation ticket. If the Union had the most business the men took the Union books and became members of the Union. In the past each organization had striven for mastery of this particular matter; now one would be on top, now the other.[2]

From the union's viewpoint the crux of the problem lay in the size and availability of the alternative labour force.

Whenever the union took unilateral action, to enforce its own ticket or for some other purpose, the Federation systematically recruited alternative labour. It chartered ships, filled them with lascar seamen, or unemployed labourers, and shipped them on board the anchored craft deserted by Wilsons' members. These men presented the union with a cruel dilemma. Since they were used to replace existing members, the question arose: how far should the union go in trying to recruit them, at least between strikes. The problem was most difficult with foreign seamen. Unless they could show that they had sailed on a British ship for four years they had to pay a £20 entrance fee. Wilson admitted that this was prohibitive and commented:

it was adopted with a view to keeping newcomers out . . . (but) the shipowners used it against us as being oppressive to the foreigners. Then, again, the men who had to pay the £20 to join were ever complaining how they had been swindled. It took us many years to get this matter righted, so that our system of protection was not a huge success.[3]

[1] Father Hopkins, C.B.E., *The National Service of the British Seamen*, Routledge, 1920, p. 69.
[2] *Ibid.*   [3] *Op. cit.*, p. 128.

In fact the union was divided about how far it wanted to sacrifice exclusiveness (and the measure of entry control it represented), for comprehensiveness (and the abandonment of entry control and job preference which such a policy implied). Doubtless the compromise reached was supposed to make room for the more stable foreign elements, without swamping the union. Nevertheless, the unwillingness of the union to open its doors to all on equal terms was an additional source of weakness.

The employers' difficulties were made much easier by the fact that most of their ships were not at sea at any one time, so that they were never faced with the need to replace the majority of their existing labour force in a sudden emergency. They were also helped by the fact that legally the union could only withdraw members who had signed off one ship and refrained from signing off another; if they did more than this their officials were liable to criminal prosecution. In desperation Wilson fell back on the only weapons remaining: the militant picket and the enlistment of aid from other organized groups.

The First World War gave the union a chance to opt for more peaceful methods. Losses at sea and the internment of foreign seamen created a shortage of labour. Both employers and government were forced to come to terms with the unions. In 1914 the Admiralty signed a national agreement with Wilson, in exchange for which he agreed to try to find seamen to man the merchant fleet under naval command. By 1917 the shortage was so acute that the government considered conscription. Wilson objected, and the idea was not pressed. Instead, unions and employers were asked to discuss a national wage scheme, and the problem of labour scarcity. In effect the Government offered Wilson assistance to obtain recognition from the employers; he replied by demanding the labour supply shop.

Even in wartime the Federation refused to accept this, and it required a strike in Liverpool to push the two sides into a compromise. A joint wages board was established, the unions undertook to 'attempt to enforce the observance of such agreements, and co-operate in preventing desertion'.[1] Most important of all, the two sides agreed to:

The creation of a single source of supply—to be jointly administered by the Shipping Federation and the Unions.[2]

---

[1] Under the American La Folette Act seamen of any nation could break their engagement in an American Port, and the American authorities would not co-operate in securing their return.   [2] Hopkins, *op. cit.*, p. 35.

The way that this scheme developed into a labour pool shop has been described in Chapter 2.[1] What has to be explained is why the war-time compromise lasted, and how far it represented a victory for the union.

At a meeting where they voiced their new-found mutual confidence both sides agreed to continue the war-time arrangement. Existing port consultants were informed that in the event of a dispute they should stress that the Sailors' and Firemen's Union, and the Federation, had agreed that

their members will abide by any decision of the District Board without resorting to a stoppage of work or a lock-out in the meantime.[2]

Action would be taken against those who refused to honour this agreement, and it might take the form of 'a replacement of the men if refusal be on their part'. By accepting this provision, and taking part in the disciplining of his own members, Wilson gave up the right to apply pressure by means of spontaneous local strikes, imposed at the point of hire. Naturally, this did not result in the total avoidance of all strikes. In 1922 Wilson agreed to a wage reduction, but this was resisted by the other major union recruiting stewards and caterers. Eventually they left the collective bargaining machinery, amalgamated with a small local union which had never been recognized and, as the Amalgamated Marine Workers, began poaching Wilson's members. This union's policy was similar to that of the Sailors' and Firemens' union before 1914, and it began fomenting local strikes at the point of hire. As a result Wilson and his officials were cast in the novel role of strike breakers, alongside officers of the Shipping Federation. One of Wilson's officials, Edward Tupper, wrote of this situation:

This was different from the old pre-war job; now I was striving every nerve to keep seamen to their agreements with shipowners. . . . It was a harder job for me, this holding men at work, than leading them to strike had been.[3]

As we have seen, the union leaders obtained their reward: a formal closed shop agreement for the whole of the lower deck. When this agreement was challenged in court the union and the Federation argued that only if *both* sides agreed to abide by decisions of the wages board could collective bargaining continue. They

---

[1] See p. 43.   [2] Hopkins, *op. cit.*, p. 159.
[3] Captain E. Tupper, *Seaman's Torch*, Hutchinson, p. 246.

appear to have convinced the court of this, for on pronouncing the agreement lawful the judge said that once a substantial proportion of seamen became members of the Marine Workers, instead of the Sailors' and Firemen, the employers could not continue to be bound by decisions of the board. 'In this case', he concluded, 'there would be a virtual end of the system of collective bargaining and strikes would almost certainly result'.[1]

At first sight this argument seems plausible. If the owners were to be faced with the militant unionism of pre-war days, and the constant overturn of nationally negotiated agreements by strikes at the point of hire, they might well have decided to end the system of national negotiations.

But did this mean that no future strikes could be justified, and that in effect Wilson had agreed to exchange recognition and the closed shop, for the use of the strike weapon? Did it mean that in future the closed shop would be used to crush strikes, rather than make them effective? In 1926 the union refused to participate in the General Strike, and officials who incited members to do so were restrained by an injunction and expelled from the union. In 1933 unofficial strikes against wage-cuts were dealt with by expulsions. In 1947 the union again co-operated with employers to break an unofficial strike, and most recently, in 1960, unofficial strikers were threatened with expulsion, while the union co-operated with employers to find workers to take their place.

Nevertheless, despite the fact that it has neither called nor recognized a strike since 1918, the union has not formally renounced the strike weapon. Writing in 1938, Tupper denied that the 'threat of strike action no longer really exists' and that the seaman's leaders had been 'nobbled and bribed into treachery'.[2] The truth seems to be not so much that the leaders have been 'nobbled' as that it is only recently that they have been in a position to disinter the strike weapon. Obviously their self-abnegation cannot be explained by the oft-repeated 'incompatibility' of collective bargaining with broken agreements. Of course collective bargaining involves a willingness to respect agreements, but in most industries there is a procedure agreement which permits strike action when other methods of settlement are exhausted. The question is: why has the

---

[1] Reynolds *v*. Shipping Federation Ltd., (1924). 1 Ch., p. 35. See p. 209 below, for an account of the effect of this decision on the status of the closed shop in law.
[2] *Op. cit.*, p. 263.

National Union of Seamen[1] not sought to obtain such an agreement?[2] Again the answer lies in the availability of an alternative labour force throughout the inter-war years.

The end of the war saw the end of the shortage of seamen and a consequent decline in the union's bargaining strength. Who can doubt that if the union decided to fight in 1922, or 1933, or at some other time, the Federation would have systematically imported blacklegs? While there was an alternative labour force they would always be under pressure to use it during a strike. Union leaders would then be back where they were in 1914; without the closed shop, and facing problems of subscription collection, strike finance, membership control and the renewed hostility of the owners.

During the Second World War strikes were illegal, and remained so until 1951. Since then the Seamen's Union has been free to call a strike of all its members at the point of hire.[3] With full employment and the present good relations between the union and other unions, both at home and abroad, it might be difficult for employers to muster an alternative labour force of much size. Still, a union that has not used the strike weapon for over forty years does not break its established practices lightly.

Whether on balance it would be in the members' interests if this happened is impossible to say. What is clear is that so far the achievement of the closed shop has not resulted in a complete victory for either side. There probably is something in the complaint that in the past, under the umbrella of the managerially upheld closed shop, the union grew soft and lost its sense of urgency in pressing for the redress of seamen's grievances. Employers must have known that if they rejected the union's claims there was little chance of an official strike. Nevertheless, it must not be assumed that this is a case against the closed shop. As we have seen the problem of turnover and contact, together with the problem of the alternative labour force, make some form of closed shop an organizational necessity for seamen. Until recently there were grounds for believing that the only stable type open to them was a managerially

---

[1] The present title of Wilson's Union.

[2] It should be noted that a union like Bisakta, who can also be said to have exchanged the free use of the strike for managerial acceptance of the closed shop, can force their employers to a form of independent arbitration which is binding. All the Constitution of the National Maritime Board stipulates is that *both* sides must agree to refer a dispute to an 'Independent Person' and his 'opinion or recommendation shall not be binding upon either organization'. (*National Maritime Year Book*, 1958, p. 134.)

[3] Such a strike could not involve the majority of union members for some time—since they would be at sea or under articles on shore.

upheld one, involving the suspension of strikes. If this is no longer the case, but the union still acts as if it is, this is more a criticism of it than the closed shop.

If the union changed its policy and called an official strike, this would only succeed if it did not endanger the closed shop itself. In other words the practice remains an organizational necessity, but it may be possible to obtain it at a lower price.

In most other unskilled groups, the choice between exclusiveness and comprehensiveness was clear from the beginning. Dockers, for example, always desired exclusiveness and entry control, for reasons analogous to seamen, and because of variations in the demand for their labour. Largely because they did not suffer from the unique organizational disadvantages of seamen they succeeded in imposing their own form of pre-entry shop at the point of hire long before the achievement of decasualization in 1940. Consequently dockers employed by the National Dock Labour Board now exert a degree of entry control which goes beyond that of seamen. It has been suggested that when this is coupled with unilateral regulations and customary methods of working, which the employer is forced to accept even though they prevent him from making the most efficient use of the labour he has, workers are able to maintain an artificial labour shortage, resulting in excessive overtime and other payments.[1]

Similar charges have been made about the labour supply shops of newspaper workers, and about those that exist in London's wholesale markets. In both cases relatively unskilled workers have chosen exclusiveness, rather than comprehensiveness, and have achieved their objectives.[2]

Elsewhere among unskilled workers it has usually been the reverse—i.e. they have wanted the closed shop to widen their area of recruitment and have been content with the post-entry shop. As E. J. Hobsbawm has put it:

The theory in the mind of the founders of the general unions of 1889 (and of their predecessors) was fairly simple. The 'labourer', mobile, helpless, shifting from one trade to another was incapable of using the orthodox tactics of craft unionism. Possessing 'merely the general value of labour' he could not, like the 'skilled man' buttress a certain scarcity value by various restrictive methods, thus 'keeping up

[1] See *Ocean Shipowners' Tally Clerks*, Report of a Ministry of Labour Committee of Inquiry, H.M.S.O., 1960.
[2] The question of how far the closed shop furthers these ends among such groups is discussed in more detail in Chapter 10.

his price'. His only chance therefore was to recruit into one gigantic union all those who could possibly blackleg on him—in the last analysis every 'unskilled' man, woman or juvenile in the country; and thus create a vast closed shop.[1]

Unions such as the National Union of Gasworkers and General Labourers of Great Britain and Ireland (founded in 1889) thought in terms of comprehensiveness. Their leader, Will Thorne, told the Royal Commission:

If we should confine ourselves to one particular industry, such as gasworks alone, and if those other people in various parts of the country are let go unorganized, then, if we had a dispute with one of the gas companies, these men would be brought up to be put in our places.[2]

But the grandiose objective of the universal union or 'ticket' was not attained. The genuine floating or mobile worker was difficult to organize. Those unions which survived depended far more on their foothold in certain industries and large works, than on their ability to recruit indiscriminately. Indeed, Hobsbawm suggests that in this period the philosophy of comprehensiveness, as expressed in the phrase 'one man one ticket',

found an increasingly lukewarm reception from the champions of the alternative tactic, which we may call 'one ticket one job'; the local job monopoly.[3]

He distinguishes three stages of general union tactics: 'the old-fashioned general unionism of 1889–92; the cautious, limited and conservative "sectional" unionism of 1892–1910; and the revolutionary urge for amalgamation . . . which arose out of the expansions of 1911–20'. He concludes that whereas the second period tended towards exclusiveness: 'Both the first and the third aimed at the organization of all "unskilled" workers',[4] and the recruitment of as many as possible of the alternative labour force.

Since 1920, it appears from Chapter 2, most unskilled groups, apart from those mentioned above and a few others like fishermen, have tended to respond to the problem of the alternative labour force by continuing to seek comprehensiveness rather than exclusiveness; they have thus been content to demand the post-entry rather than the pre-entry shop.

Since the Second World War the problem itself has declined in importance because the arrival of full employment meant that an

---

[1] 'General Labour Unions in Britain, 1889–1914', *Economic History Review*, Vol. 1, Nos. 2/3, 1949, p. 125.
[2] Quoted by Hobsbawm, *ibid.*   [3] Hobsbawm, *op. cit.*, p. 134.
[4] Hobsbawm, *op. cit.*, p. 135.

K

obvious alternative labour force, in the form of the unemployed, was not available. Employers who desire to import substitute labour during a strike are mainly forced to attract it from other employers; this is difficult, particularly when it is known that the workers on strike will object to the strike breakers when they return. Because of this the problem of the alternative labour force is no longer a crucial factor making for demands for the closed shop among the lesser skilled—except in the cases noted above where entry control has been practised over a period and it is felt that the opportunities and security of employment it makes possible is worth preserving.

(b) Skilled Groups

It is also worth considering how the problem of the alternative labour force affects closed shop demands among more skilled groups from an historical angle. In their *Industrial Democracy* the Webbs described how the apprenticeship ratio and the exclusion of 'illegal men' functioned as the pivot of eighteenth-century trade unions. They thought these features were transitory. They believed that technology was creating 'circumstances' so complex and fluid that it passes the wit of man to define the 'right to a trade'. Also a 'perpetual revolutionizing process' was at work, ineluctably breaking down what might be termed the *skill gap* between the craftsman, the machine-minder, or helper, and the labourer, so that alternative classes of workers were 'brought in to execute some portion of the operation'. Since these developments were 'precisely the conditions which are typical of most of the industries of the present century' the Webbs could see no future for a policy of restrictionism and exclusion.[1]

As was seen in Chapter 2, they were right in their prophecies concerning the outcome of many of the struggles they observed. In clothing, unions that refused to recruit women were superseded by those that did. In the boot and shoe trade the old cordwainers were swallowed up by the newer comprehensive boot and shoe operatives. The most that is demanded in these industries nowadays is the post-entry shop. Similarly, in building, the unions that survived were forced to modify their policies, drop their apprenticeship qualifications and attempts to impose a ratio. But it was also noted that in two major industries at least the old craft tradition is

[1] *Op. cit.*, p. 479.

very much alive—i.e. printing and shipbuilding, and elsewhere isolated pockets of the old craft system have survived—for example in the small-scale metal-using trades. It is necessary to consider how it is that, in a minority of cases, the Webbs' prognostications were wrong.

Before this can be done, however, the problem of the alternative labour force as it arises among skilled groups must be analysed further. In one sense the Webbs were right; the opportunity for skilled workers to affect entry control arises out of the existence of a recognized *skill gap*. If members' jobs need a special skill, requiring a period of training, then, if craft unions can secure the recruitment of all the men with that skill, they have a labour monopoly and immediately, at any rate, there is no alternative labour force. But there are three ways in which such a monopoly can be undermined. First, the number being trained may grow faster than the demand for the skill or for the full employment of those already trained. If this happens there arises a group of unemployed craftsmen; an alternative labour force that the union must organize and control. Secondly, for various reasons usually connected with technological developments, other skilled groups may claim the work of the group; if they are successful there arises a new alternative labour force which may, in time, replace the union's members. Thirdly, and in the long run most important of all, technological developments, as the Webbs suggested, may undermine the skill gap. The periphery of semi-skilled and unskilled labour that surrounds the skilled group will then lay claim to the work previously done by the group. Indeed, sometimes new methods of production may render the old skill useless.

The closed shop can be used to fight each of these developments. In the first instance it will be allied to an apprenticeship ratio; members will refuse to work with those who have not been admitted to the unon, and this will be closed to non-accredited apprentices. In the second place members will not work alongside members of another union claiming the right to the job, and will punish or expel those who do. In the third place members will refuse to work alongside any worker, not a member of the union, engaged on work which is considered a union monopoly, and, if necessary, the union will strike against employers who use non-members for such work.

But if it is not strong enough to make such sanctions work, the union may change its tactics. Unaccredited trainees employed in shops where ratios are not observed may have to be admitted to the union in order to control them. Agreements may have to be reached whereby rival skilled unions are granted limited recruitment rights; if this is impossible all attempts to retain the job monopoly may have to be abandoned (in which case the job monopoly need not disappear, but may merely be taken over by another group). Most important of all, entry restrictions may have to be abandoned altogether in an effort to retain a hold on the industry.

Thus the choice between exclusiveness and comprehensiveness faces craft unions in more complex forms than lesser skilled groups. Ideally they want to eliminate rather than exclude the alternative labour force; actually they may be forced to admit varying proportions of this force, at various times. This may assist existing members, but need not always do so. It may presage the end of all entry control, or may merely entail an alteration in its forms, or a postponement of its attainment. This can best be made clear by a short account of the experiences of the printing and ship building unions.

(c) The Examples of Printing and Shipbuilding

Craft unions in both trades have pursued entry control via the closed shop with tenacity yet flexibility. Occasionally yielding to the pressure of events, they have not lost sight of their traditional objectives. The history of the Typographical Association in this respect is fortunately well documented in A. E. Musson's history of the union.[1] It bore the brunt of two 'industrial revolutions', both of which threatened its craft status. The first began in the second half of the nineteenth century, and arose out of the proliferation of printing firms outside the traditional centres of organization. This mainly affected the apprenticeship ratio. It had been difficult to impose this even where the union was strong, and in 1853 the union recognized this when it allowed 'illegal men' to join 'with a view to bringing the influence of united effort to bear in the localities hitherto without the pale of the Association'.[2] But many branches resisted this, regarding the ratio with 'a kind of superstitious veneration, as an ancient palladium against all ills, against unemployment, low wages, "illegal men" and incompetents'.[3] By 1890 the Webbs observed that 'a very considerable proportion' of compositors had

---

[1] The Typographical Association, Oxford University Press, 1954.
[2] Musson, op. cit., p. 117.   [3] Musson, op. cit., p. 214.

undergone no period of training at all, but had 'picked up' the trade, while working at the full market rate. They continued:

As in the country districts any number of boys are, in fact, learning to be compositors, and eventually drifting into the towns, the unions are in a dilemma. If they rigidly maintain their apprenticeship rules, and decline to admit these 'illegal men' they find themselves foiled in their negotiations with the employers by the presence of a steadily growing crowd of non-union men indisposed to defer to an organization from which they are excluded.[1]

However, in the years which followed, printing experienced another 'industrial revolution' and the union's success in dealing with this enabled them to make up lost ground.

The revolution concerned the introduction of mechanical composition and printing machines, and the pace was set in newspapers, where the unions were strongest. Union leaders decided not to oppose these developments, which would ultimately benefit the expanding industry by lowering costs, but decided instead that the new machines 'must be exclusively worked by Journeymen and duly recognized Apprentices, such Apprentices to be reckoned in the total number allowed to each office'. Indeed, they 'applied to the composing machines all the old regulations restricting output with the aim of preventing undue displacement of hand compositors'.[2] To combat these and other constrictions the Linotype Company decided to develop its own alternative labour force; they established schools to train non-apprenticed workers in operating their machines. Faced with this threat the unions wisely conceded ground; they offered to remove various restrictions and, most importantly, began to recruit members among the schools of the Linotype Company. Musson comments:

... by thus bending instead of being broken the T.A. was enabled, on the whole, to keep the working of composing machines in the hands of its own members and to exercise a salutary control over working conditions during this period of industrial revolution in the printing trade.[3]

By 1898 this flexibility had its justification when the Linotype Users' Association agreed that 'All skilled operators were to be members of the T.A.' as part of a general settlement of the machine question which produced 'order out of local chaos' and ended the 'constant guerilla warfare' of the previous ten years.[4] This agreement

---

[1] *Industrial Democracy, op. cit.*, p. 468.   [2] Musson, *op. cit.*, p. 224.
[3] *Op. cit.*, p. 232.   [4] Musson, *op. cit.*, p. 233.

created an important precedent. When, subsequently, the new Monotype machine was introduced into general printing, it was also possible to insist that union members should operate the keyboard as craftsmen. A similar revolution in the press room was met with the same tactics. Moreover, says Musson, although many of the new men had served no apprenticeship, once through the door they wanted it closed to others; they joined the time-served craftsmen in demanding the re-introduction of apprenticeship ratios as soon as the union was strong enough to impose them. It was this development, unforeseen by the Webbs, that enabled the T.A. and other unions to have the best of both worlds; to combine periodic use of the policy of the 'open door' with the long-term pursuit of entry control and craft status.

By 1902 their success was recognized when the newly established Federation of Master Printers initiated national negotiations on the vexed issue of the apprenticeship ratio. Conferences dragged on, but in 1911 modifications of existing unilaterally enforced rules were negotiated as part of a general settlement on wages and conditions. This agreement represented the final triumph of craft union-ism; from that day apprentice limitation was accepted as a matter of bilateral rather than unilateral regulation. By bending, instead of breaking, the unions made it worth the employers' while to negotiate. Helped by the knowledge that theirs was an expanding market, where over-all costs were falling, employers accepted the case for the skill gap, and entry control, for the sake of industrial peace; in short the costs of concession were less than the costs of resistance.

The inevitable result is a growing complaint, among employers and others, that nowadays many so-called craftsmen are only required for semi-skilled work, which is repetitive and simple.[1] It is said they make little use of what they are supposed to learn, and that their training is overlong. Another complaint, from the excluded semi-skilled workers, is that the rigid application of entry control means that long after they have actually bridged the skill gap—and could do the work of the so-called craftsman—they must remain his assistant, or the assistant of his newly-apprenticed succes-sor. The extent to which the closed shop gives rise to practices of this sort, and their justification, is a matter considered further

[1] I.e. distributing type, minding folding-machines, feeding nipping presses, putting metal into a melting-pot, lifting plates, feeding the linotype machine with metal, etc.

below.[1] At the moment these developments are of importance as a means of emphasizing one final point.

Although the opportunity for any skilled group to obtain a job monopoly by means of entry control and the pre-entry shop depends, in the first instance, on the existence of a *real* skill gap, and although any development undermining the reality of the gap is a threat to the groups job monopoly, the group itself may rebut the threat, even if the skill gap continues to narrow until it disappears. If it can match employer power sufficiently, and for long enough, any group can win recognition, however reluctant, for the *notion* of a skill gap. So long as this continues, and the craft qualification shop operates, we may speak of the existence of a group job monopoly; only now it will be founded on a *national* rather than a *real* skill gap. It is unnecessary, at this stage, to decide how far printers and others rest their claims on what are now purely notional skill gaps—but this matter is considered further in a later chapter.

The printers' example shows how unions may surmount two threats to their job monopolies—the proliferation of trainees, and technological developments. They have not been over much bothered by the third kind of threat; disputes over the right to certain jobs. To explain this we must look at the struggle of the shipyard unions.

Craft unions in shipyards were never threatened by the growth of small-scale production in centres outside their influence. On the contrary, the major technical innovation of the nineteenth century, the substitution of metal for wood, positively strengthened the hold of the most powerful union, the boilermakers, since it was carried on almost exclusively in gigantic establishments belonging to a distinct class of employers. It was in these establishments that the union was at its strongest. The threat to job monopolies, arising out of technical change, was a blurring of established craft boundaries. As a consequence, plumbers laid claim to the work of brass-workers, who quarrelled with boilermakers, who fought with ship-wrights, who disputed with carpenters. Although many individuals suffered, the unions survived, for once again technical innovation was accompanied by expansion and increasing specialization. Luxury liners, special purpose refrigerator ships, colliers and oil-tankers, all demanded new specialisms and ever more complex fitting-out operations. Apart from the traditional craftsmen required to construct the hull there arose, at the end of the nineteenth century,

[1] See pp. 241–4.

a growing demand for fitters, metal workers, joiners, plumbers, heating engineers, smiths, painters and various other specialists.

The demarcation disputes that arose, though fierce and a source of annoyance to employers, were as much a product of the expansion of craft opportunities as threats to established job monopolies. It was the industry's misfortune to be at the meeting-ground of many well-organized craft unions, and to offer an expanding range of new jobs at a time when many old-established jobs were declining. Naturally, the unions concerned tried to gain in one direction what they lost in another.

As with the printers, the employers had decided by the end of the century that they could not break the grip of the unions; instead they too fell back on attempts to negotiate the boundaries of craft monopolies. Essentially, as in the case of the printers, this represented an acceptance of the claims made by the craft unions. Yet once again the maintenance of craft status was not possible without a measure of flexibility on the union side. The nature of the jobs performed by their members have changed extensively over the last fifty years. So long as they could retain their craft monopolies the unions have not resisted this, and have encouraged their members to acquire the new skills. In slumps, when their power was weakest, they have been prepared to accept wage cuts; in periods of rapid expansion—such as during two world wars—they have accepted non-apprenticed dilutees, though they have insisted that these new entrants should be accorded craft status, and have never abandoned their objective of the closed shop and the reimposition of the apprenticeship ratio.[1] In this way they have prevented employers from being driven to the point where they felt it worthwhile launching an all-out attack on their craft monopolies. Naturally, there has been a greater concern for the maintenance of the ratio among groups like the boilermakers and shipwrights, whose skills are virtually confined to the industry, for there has been an extremely unstable demand for their services. As Gertrude Williams rightly states:

The years between the wars were disastrous in this industry, which was one of those with the highest and most continuous rates of unemployment; the percentage of unemployment never fell below 21 per cent during the period from 1924–38

---

[1] Of course unions like the boilermakers have recruited outside the boundaries of their craft, mainly among craftsmen's mates and assistants. But, as was stressed in Chapter 2, workers of this sort are not supposed to inherit the jobs of the apprenticed craftsmen.

and at one time rose as high as 62 per cent. In some districts as many as two-thirds of the men ostensibly attached to the industry were out of work for years at a time.[1]

War brought full employment, but the unions remained concerned about the possibility of this happening again, and the unemployment of the last few years has sharply reinforced their fears.

Finally, the craft unions in shipbuilding, like their counterparts in print, are often charged with defending the notion of notional rather than real skill monopolies. There are said to be a great variety of simple tasks performed by so-called craftsmen, which could just as easily be done by the lesser skilled, who are prevented from progressing to this sort of work. Also jobs that could easily be done by one man are divided up among numerous craftsmen, who each perform one simple operation.[2] Employers argue that this adds to costs, and even leads to a loss of markets.[3]

(d) Exclusiveness versus Comprehensiveness

We may now summarize the effect of the problem of the alternative labour force on the rise of the closed shop, both in unskilled and skilled groups.

If there is an easily available pool of unemployed, unorganized labour willing to work below union conditions, employers of unskilled labour demanding union conditions have an incentive to use it. If the organized workers are on strike, and the employer handles perishable goods, or is particularly vulnerable to strike action for some other reason, the incentive may be irresistible. The larger the pool the more casual or seasonal their employment opportunities, and the more they are forced to rely on strike action, the more organized workers will seek to deny employers access to this labour force. It is to be noted that all these conditions apply to both merchant seamen and dockers.

---

[1] *Recruitment to the Skilled Trades*, Routledge and Kegan Paul, 1957, p. 73.

[2] For example, in the fitting of a portlight seven craftsmen are usually required: a shipwright to mark the position of the light, a burner to cut the opening, a caulker to dress it, a driller to drill and fit the frame, a brass finisher to fit the hinged glass frame, a driller to fit the deadlight, and a joiner to fit the deadlight hook to the linings of the steel deck-head. Even to fix a door-stop five 'skilled' men are needed. A joiner marks the position of the stop, a driller drills the hole, a caulker and mechanic fit the bolt, and a painter touches up the job.

[3] In this respect employers in ship building refer to the Admiralty shipyards where much of the work done by 'craftsmen' boilermakers is, in fact, performed by semi-skilled workers, and to the position which operates among shipyard workers in continental shipyards, where labour is much more easily transferable. See *The Economics of Shipbuilding*, by J. R. Parkinson, Cambridge University Press, 1960.

The incentives operating on employers of *skilled* labour are different. Before they feel it is necessary to import alternative labour, two conditions must be met. First, there must be a pool of sufficiently skilled men (either the assistants of the original craftsmen, or others trained in similar techniques) willing to transfer to this work. Second, the original craftsmen must be demanding or enjoying wages and conditions which the employer regards as unjustifiably high, partly because of limitations on entry and partly because of restrictive methods of working. The more valuable the wages and conditions are to the group, and the more they fear the consequences of losing them, the more they will feel it essential to deny the employer access to alternative labour. These conditions apply to printers and shipyard workers.

Both groups are in the same position in that the alternative labour force represents an opportunity to the employer and a threat to the union; they differ in that if the closed shop is to be used in either case to *exclude* this labour it must take a different form. Unskilled groups must restrict access by forcing employers to accept their right either to supply labour or to obtain some form of preference for their members in competition with others. If they do not have the strength, or cannot make it worth the employers' while to grant such a concession, they must recruit and control as many as possible of the alternative labour force by means of the post-entry shop. Skilled groups, on the other hand, must restrict the use of untrained labour by forcing employers to recognize a skill gap, and must then control the supply of skilled labour. A crucial factor determining whether or not they are successful is the pace and form taken by technological change. If, as in shipbuilding, change is comparatively moderate, and assists unionization, the task may be easy, particularly if the industry is expanding and increasing its need for specialisms. Yet, even if change takes a form tending to undermine unionization, as with printers, it may still be possible to 'bend rather than break' to admit the nominally skilled and subsequently re-adopt the policy of exclusiveness: if not, then as in the case of the unskilled, the group must campaign for a comprehensive post-entry shop.

It is worth noting that this is what has happened in the engineering industry, and explains that industry's present domination by the post-entry shop. Engineering has been influenced more than most industries by technological change, which has had a perpetually disruptive effect on craft monopolies.[1] Many of the most important

---

[1] See J. B. Jefferys, *The Story of the Engineers*, Lawrence and Wishart Ltd., 1945.

disputes were caused largely by the attempts of craft unions to defend these monopolies, and to prevent the promotion of the lesser skilled. But by the end of the First World War they had largely abandoned the task and the most important union, the Engineers, decided in favour of the post-entry shop. By 1912, a minority of the union recognized the logic of events and argued that:

instead of wasting time and energy in putting forward sentimental reasons why tradesmen should be allowed to man certain tools, we should make the conditions of entry into our Society easier . . . and so get all the workers in the engineering industry, both skilled and semi-skilled, into the A.S.E.[1]

Following the rise of the general labour unions, and the re-introduction of dilutees during the Second World War, the union began to concentrate more and more on the comprehensively based post-entry shop, and the wholesale recruitment of the lesser skilled.

Other unions in other trades who have been forced to make a similar decision include the Vehicle Builders, and the Union of Building Trade Workers.

But whether the aim was exclusiveness or comprehensiveness, the need to deal with the problem of the alternative labour force has been a powerful factor making for closed shop demands among all the groups mentioned in this section and among craft unions generally.

(4) THE INFLUENCE OF GROUP MORALITY AND THE CLOSED SHOP TRADITION

Although most closed shop demands arise from attempts to over-come specific problems concerned with the organization, control or exclusion of workers, once a group achieves the closed shop, or regards it as a part of its traditional objectives, the passage of time tends to reinforce allegiance to the practice. Non-unionism is looked on with growing disfavour, even when the consequences of relaxing the closed shop's sanctions, in terms of the effect on the group's bargaining position, would be negligible.

This influence affecting the maintenance of the practice in an industry or trade long dominated by it may be termed the effect of a *closed shop tradition*. The effect of this tradition is seen when the existence of the closed shop is explained as the effect of 'good trade union principles' or the by-product of 'working-class solidarity'.

[1] Jefferys, *op. cit.*, p. 157. In 1920 the A.S.E. amalgamated with a number of smaller unions and became known as the A.E.U.

When influences of this sort maintain group hostility towards non-unionists there were invariably important problems that the closed shop was required to solve, at some time in the past. The closed shop tradition, once established, must be regarded as an independent factor. In such groups one can accept at face value the explanation of workers who say that their actions are based on the feeling that the toleration of non-unionism is 'morally' wrong. Independent of the effect of non-unionism on their bargaining position, indeed in spite of its unimportance, they feel that workers benefiting from the results of union job regulation 'ought' to be made to contribute to the union by joining it. If such workers will not voluntarily accept their common obligations, union members 'ought' to force them to do so. If this belief is general we may say the enforcement of the closed shop has become part of the collective code or group morality.

The most obvious example of a group morality which ensures a continued opposition to non-unionism is in general printing. Skilled groups may argue that employers only recognize their right to bargain over apprenticeship ratios because they know that these could be imposed unilaterally via the closed shop, but among the broad mass of members of the Printing and Bookbinding workers no such issues arise. Nowadays there are few difficulties of turnover and contact for any of the unions in the industry, and strikes are comparatively infrequent.[1] Yet despite the fact that the sanctions of the closed shop are not often utilized, and appear to perform only minor functions, the unions would scout any suggestion that they should be relaxed. It is difficult to believe that much would happen if they did. Suppose the odd recruit who resisted joining a union in a medium-sized provincial printing house were left alone; suppose the existing member who wanted to lapse because of some personal dispute were allowed to do so? No union official seriously contends this would cause a chain reaction; yet the majority of printers would regard these suggestions as far more outrageous, not to say immoral, than most other union groups—many of whom are in far greater need of the closed shop than they are.

The next chapter contains an attempt to assess the importance of the closed shop tradition in maintaining hostility towards non-unionism in other groups.

---

[1] Of course there are occasional national strikes in printing. The unions are proud of their record of solidarity in these strikes, and convinced that the gains achieved as a result would not have been possible without such a demonstration of strength. To the extent that they believe that national strike solidarity is still dependent on the closed shop sanctions, the practice is not without some contemporary significance to them.

(5) The Attitude of Unions and their Officials to the Closed Shop

This chapter has tended to assume that unions are institutional monoliths—composed of people with the same priorities, problems and attitudes to the closed shop at every level. This over-simplification now needs to be qualified.

Because closed shop demands largely originate in attempts to overcome specific problems the extent to which union officials are directly concerned with these problems, and feel responsible for solving them, affects the attitude which they, and the union, take towards the practice. The more the union and its officers are affected the more they are in favour of action to obtain and enforce it.

In general, the further one travels towards the top of the union hierarchy the less likely it is that officers will be particularly concerned to encourage the closed shop—especially if this may result in 'unofficial' strikes. For example, the ex-general secretary of one of the largest non-craft unions informed the writer that 'taking the broad view' he did not believe in 'forcing men into a union'—though he did subscribe to the maintenance of existing closed shops, particularly when directed against a breakaway organization, and admitted that his members have 'the right to refuse to work with non-unionists'. Other national officials of the same union were very much conditioned in their attitudes by the industries they organized, i.e. by their experience of the advantages of the closed shop and the difficulty of organizing effectively without it.

On the other hand, several district officials of this union interviewed were prepared to argue the case for the closed shop in more uncompromising terms—though they stressed the trouble that unofficial strikes to impose the practice might cause them. Generally speaking, H. A. Clegg's choice of the group most likely to be in favour of agressive action to obtain the practice appears to be correct. In his study of the General and Municipal workers he wrote:

In fact, local militants are far more ready to be excited about working with a non-unionist than are union officers, and officers are content to leave them to settle this question for themselves. Only if a dispute threatens or breaks out does the officer intervene to try to get a formal agreement in the union's favour, or some compromise which his members will accept. Even then, as we have seen, permission for a strike to enforce the closed shop may be refused.[1]

[1] *General Union*, Blackwells, 1954, p. 258.

Allowing for the fact that the General and Municipal Workers is a union with relatively little closed shop tradition, organizing in open or mainly open trades, this is a picture which, with adjustments, could be applied to most other unions. Usually it is at shop steward or branch secretary level that the advantages of the closed shop are most directly felt. When, as in engineering, the practice is advancing rapidly, it is usually largely as a result of initiatives taken by leadership at this level. Not that this implies that in this matter the rank and file can be 'ordered into battle' irrespective of their own feelings. As the example of the closed shop drive at the motor-car factory described above indicated, rank and file attitudes and willingness to respond to leadership initiative, are always important and sometimes crucial.

(6) THE ARGUMENT SO FAR

It has been argued in the last three chapters that the closed shop pattern cannot be explained simply by reference to its relative disadvantages to employers, or in terms of union solidarity. It should be viewed as a device which unions want to assist in dealing with particular problems concerned with organizing, controlling or excluding different categories of workers. By helping to overcome such problems it adds to the effectiveness of the sanctions unions impose on employers and so aids them in their task of job regulation. The determination and resolution behind most demands for the practice depends on the extent to which unions feel that they face problems that are insoluble without its aid, just as the nature of the problems determine the type of closed shop demanded. If there are no such problems, or workers are unaware of them, closed shop demands are not likely to arise; unless, of course, past problems have given rise to a closed shop tradition. But no matter how necessary the closed shop may be, the crucial factor which finally determines whether or not most groups obtain the practice is whether or not they can muster sufficient power, without its aid, to impose it unilaterally, or make it worth the employers' while to concede it.[1]

Similar considerations govern the maintenance of the practice. So long as unity and solidarity are preserved; so long as technological or market developments do not result in an erosion of the union's bargaining position it will endure and in time probably

---

[1] The exception here is the employer-initiated closed shop. This apparent paradox is discussed further in the next chapter.

become part of the unquestioned assumptions of both sides of industry. But the development of such a situation, and in the last analysis, its continuance, depends on the fact that it is appreciated that, if challenged, the great majority of unionists would defend the closed shop. If they or their leaders allow membership to fall sufficiently, the closed shop concession may be withdrawn, or it may be impossible to impose it unilaterally any longer. If strikes are called too often, or last too long, members may return to work or drop out of the union, and the closed shop may be powerless to stop them; indeed, it may itself collapse.

In short, although the closed shop arises and is maintained because it solves pressing and immediate problems it cannot guarantee that no future problems arise. Even unions with a closed shop tradition are helped, or hindered, or in extreme cases destroyed by such general factors as a change in the demand for labour, or the quality of their leadership. The closed shop is an extremely useful and sometimes necessary device; it is not an organizational panacea.

These considerations are important, both in explaining the closed shop pattern and in relation to the question of the justification of the closed shop, which is considered in the second part of this book.

CHAPTER 6

AN EXPLANATION OF THE CLOSED SHOP PATTERN

THE last two chapters were concerned with the advantages which unions gain from the closed shop and the circumstances in which they feel that they need these advantages. In this chapter an attempt will be made to use what has been discovered to provide an explanation for the closed shop pattern which was described in Chapter 2.

(1) LIMITATIONS ON UNION POWER

The manifest inability of large groups of British workers to develop even a moderate degree of union strength without the aid of the closed shop is the most obvious factor explaining its absence in many trades. The fact that trade union organization is unknown, or almost unknown, among most non-manual groups employed in private industry, and throughout many service trades such as catering, laundering, hairdressing and domestic service, means that no question of the closed shop can arise in their case.

Similarly, the low level of unionization among agricultural workers, as well as semi-skilled and unskilled workers employed in trades such as civil engineering, food and soft drinks, leather and fur manufacture, toys, and the great bulk of distribution firms outside the co-op, means that these are bound to remain more or less open trades.

Within sections of the mainly open trades which are affected by the closed shop, a contrast can also be drawn between, say, the gas industry, where closed shop demands are largely confined to the more militant and highly organized sections, such as the retort house, as against the more effectively unionized electricity generation and supply industry, where demands have been more widespread, despite the fact that neither can be regarded as a closed shop prone industry.

But perhaps the relationship between union power without the aid of the closed shop, and the subsequent rise of effective demands for the practice, can be seen even more clearly in closed shop prone trades. Correlations between the general state of union strength and

148

the existence of determined closed shop demands were, in fact, specifically mentioned in a number of cases in previous chapters—for example among building, clothing and engineering workers. Even among non-manual groups there are examples of this correlation. It was noted that in entertainment while the musicians were strong enough to impose a closed shop throughout their membership, other artist groups were not yet in a position to do this really effectively outside the London area.

Nor is this all. The correlation is also of importance in providing part of the explanation for the regional variations noted in Chapter 2. The most obvious example here is that of the Scottish Bakers, where a long history of group militance, and the advantages of organizing in two relatively compact areas, gave the union a chance to demand the closed shop more effectively on a scale not possible elsewhere. But this is only one example of the correlation. Most unions maintain that they are generally more highly organized, and find it easier to retain members, in places like the north-east coast and South Wales.

Yet as was seen in Chapter 4, no explanation of the closed shop pattern simply in terms of union strength can account for the forms which it takes, or for the fact that not all groups demand the practice with equal force as the level of unionization rises; it also provides no explanation for the paradox of those groups—listed in Chapter 2—where unions *have* managed to secure a high level of union membership without becoming closed shop prone. To account for these features it is necessary to consider how far the various groups involved have been affected by the factors listed in the previous chapter. Two separate tasks are involved here. First, the trades where the closed shop is prevalent must be classified and considered according to the particular combination of factors which have brought about the rise of the closed shop in their case. Second, the rather special position of the exceptions listed in Chapter 2 must be examined.

(2) GROUPS WHERE THE CLOSED SHOP IS PREVELANT

Six different groups need to be distinguished. They are:

(a) Skilled 'craftsmen', where the need has usually been for the craft qualification shop;

(b) Lesser skilled trades, where other forms of pre-entry shop have been an important union objective;

L

(c) The great majority of remaining trades affected by the closed shop, in which the most that has usually been required has been the post-entry shop;

(d) Process workers employed in the iron and steel industry;

(e) Workers in entertainment affected by the closed shop;

(f) Workers covered by the employer-initiated closed shop.

An account must be given of the factors affecting each one of these groups.

(a) Craftsmen

In the case of all the craft unions organizing among this group of workers—for example in printing, shipbuilding, iron foundries, and so on—the problem of enforcing unilateral regulations has invariably been of considerable historical importance. Also of some significance, among unions recruiting isolated craftsmen employed on maintenance work, for example the boilermakers, has been the problem of membership contact. But by far the most important factor operating in all trades has been the problem of the alternative labour force. Whenever a craft group wishes to protect its skill monopoly and raise job security by restricting entry to the trade, some form of craft qualification shop, however modified and diluted it may be in practice, becomes a natural objective.

(b) Lesser skilled Pre-entry Groups

In this category are all those lesser skilled trades where the labour supply or labour pool shop operates, or is attempted—i.e. seamen, dockers, wholesale market workers, film and television technicians, semi-skilled newsprint workers, fishermen, and so on.

Once again, one of the major factors throughout the group has been the problem of an alternative labour force. In particular the seamen, dockers and fishermen have wanted to limit the access to the job among the periphery of casual labour surrounding the trade. Faced with a shifting labour demand, and little or no job security, the imposition of a union membership qualification at the point of hire has appeared to be a crucial organizational necessity if any stable organization was to be built up. However, the factors operating upon this group are more varied than those described in the case of the skilled group.

The seamen, for example, have been very much influenced by the additional problem of how to contact their members and extract subscriptions, while the dockers have been more affected by the problem of strike solidarity, and the need to enforce unilateral regulations. The main unions remaining, in newsprint, wholesale marketing and films and television, have been affected by somewhat different factors. In each case the trade concerned has, in the past, been subject to large fluctuations in labour demand, which were particularly severe among wholesale market workers before unionization. In newsprint there was the additional need to control the distribution of opportunities for casual work. By supplying the employers' wants in this regard through the union office it was possible to maximize overall employment opportunities for existing members. In time, as casual employment has become steadily more remunerative, and full employment more accepted, there has even emerged in London and Manchester a group of workers known as 'regular casuals'. They work for two or three days a week on a number of newspapers and magazines in turn. All their engagements, together with the remaining extra-employment opportunities that are shared out among the bulk of union members, depend on the continued maintenance of the labour supply shops.

Also of importance among unions organizing newsprint employees and wholesale market workers has been the desire to enforce and gain acceptance for the unilateral regulations and working customs of both groups, and what began as defensive devices to raise job security have become ways of ensuring a continued supply of well-paid jobs and ample overtime opportunities.[1]

In the film industry the problem has mainly been that until the rise of television a succession of booms and slumps made the union organizing camera crews and other technicians particularly concerned with job security. Lacking any recognized training scheme or apprenticeship system, they tried to limit access to the trade in any way they could, and a labour supply shop seemed the obvious method.[2] After quickly establishing the principle of the post-entry shop, the union during the war registered as a labour agency, and, at a time when experienced technicians were short, producers discovered that their only chance of obtaining them was through the union.

The two groups listed so far contain about a sixth of all workers covered by the closed shop. What both groups have in common is that the workers within them felt that they needed the closed shop mainly in order to follow the policy of exclusiveness, in some form or another. That is why they required the pre-entry shop. But the

[1] See p. 114 above.
[2] Subsequently a recognized training scheme was accepted for the more skilled technicians.

particular form this took in each case was also related to the specific organizational needs of each group. In the case of the first group the closed shop took the form of the craft qualification shop, with its absence of control over the movement of trained labour, because once the skill gap was recognized, and training restricted, there was no organizational need to control the movement of properly qualified men from job to job. On the other hand, in the case of the second group there was no question of a recognized skill gap, and no chance of limiting the number of trainees via an apprenticeship ratio. It was therefore essential to control entry at the one place at which this was possible—the point of hire. This involved either a labour supply or a labour pool shop.

But perhaps the best example of the connection between the problems which the closed shop is required to solve and the form it takes, occurs among skilled craftsmen in newsprint. It will be remembered that in this trade the unions operates *both* the craft qualification shop *and* labour supply shops. The first is needed to maintain the skill gap and restrict apprentices, while the second is imposed to deal with the special problems of casual labour.

(c) The Post-Entry Trades

The third group of workers that needs to be considered is much larger and more difficult to define. It consists of the great majority of the remaining workers affected by the closed shop, with the exception of iron and steel process workers and those covered by employer-initiated closed shops. What all these workers have in common is that in each case the most important factors affecting them have been related to either: (*a*) problems of turnover and contact, or (*b*) the problem of strike solidarity. These problems have not always arisen in the same form or to the same degree, and there have often been other comparatively minor influences at work; nevertheless, the groups have enough in common from the viewpoint of the functions which the closed shop performs for them, to be grouped together.

The turnover problems of the more important trades involved— e.g. building workers, engineering workers, were fully discussed in Chapter 5 above, as were the contact problems of other trades, such as road haulage workers and miners. Also concerned with these problems are the unions organizing among semi-skilled and unskilled groups in trades such as clothing, food manufacture, tobacco, textiles, pottery, and small-scale metal using. In all these cases, the main method of obtaining subscriptions is by means of stewards collecting from workers on the job, supplemented, in the case of cotton and pottery workers, by methods of house to house collection.

The great bulk of union dues are now collected in the workshop, as a matter of course. Some unions, like the Transport and General Workers, or the General and Municipal, provide for this in their rules, and appoint paid collectors. Others, like the Engineers, rely on 'volunteers', who are for the most part shop stewards. In practice this makes little difference to the proportion of stewards involved in collecting. Clegg, Killick, and Adams, in a recent survey of steward behaviour, discovered that shop stewards did 'almost as much collecting in a union which makes no provision for it, does not pay for it and in which this practice is of doubtful legality'. They found that 68 per cent of the Engineers' stewards collected subscriptions, as against 76 per cent of the Transport Workers' stewards, and 74 per cent of stewards belonging to the General and Municipal.[1] Summarizing their conclusions on methods of subscription collection they wrote:

It is a reasonable inference that the organization of production workers in modern manufacturing industry demands collection by stewards, and that shop stewards are willing to add collection to their other duties without payment by the union. How else could the Engineers collect contributions in a large factory in which they organize hundreds or even thousands of members who certainly cannot be persuaded to attend branch meetings regularly.[2]

But the difficulty of workplace collection is that the system is apt to collapse from time to time, as stewards resign, or leave the job, or merely lose interest in what is basically a dull and repetitive chore. This immediately leads to the problem of collecting members' arrears, as soon as the system can be re-introduced.

Whenever the collecting system is apt to break down, or is difficult to operate without occasional lapsing, there will be a tendency for the more committed and union conscious stewards to feel the need of a closed shop—particularly if they are also affected by the problem of strike solidarity.

Both influences have clearly combined to make the practice necessary in one important group—coalminers. The relationship between miners and the problem of strike effectiveness has been

---

[1] *Trade Union Officers*, Blackwells, 1960, p. 160.   [2] *Op. cit.*, p. 161.

described earlier, but it should be stressed that conditions of work at the coal face and among underground workers generally, make the collection of dues at work particularly difficult. Largely because of this, miners' unions have always laid particular stress on the impor- tance of attendance at lodge meetings. But it is readily accepted by miners' officials that the great majority of miners cannot be prevailed upon to attend the lodge with regularity—even if the present pattern of shift-work would allow them to do so. As a result they have, in the past, made use of house to house collectors, and in Durham the practice has arisen of erecting collecting booths, on company property, near the pay office. Even before nationalization these methods were often supplemented by demands for the check off, which was conceded in some pits. Naturally, in circumstances such as this the membership function of the closed shop, when allied to a check off, is particularly advantageous.

In road transport these problems are at their most difficult among workers employed by private road hauliers, where strikes are more common, and labour turnover is high. As a result, whenever the Transport and General Workers' union, which has a monopoly of organizing rights among drivers and mates, achieves any real strength in a firm, its members generally make moves towards a closed shop. The practice is for members to recruit to 100 per cent or near 100 per cent level, without openly demanding the practice. Union officials are then contacted and asked to negotiate what is termed 'recognition of the 100 per cent shop'. This means manage- ment agrees to screen new applicants and to use its influence on lapsers. Eventually it may be asked to discharge those who refuse to remain in compliance.

Among the 20,000 or so manual workers employed to drive and service the fleets of the nationalized concern of British Road Services, the need for the closed shop is less pressing and so less in demand. On the whole, turnover is less rapid than it is in the private sector of the trade, and the company itself is more prepared to 'encourage' union membership and provide facilities for subscription collection. Formally B.R.S. stress that they would not agree to discharge men simply because their membership had lapsed. Union officials, particularly below national level, assert that while this may be generally true there have been cases of men moved from one job to another to avoid trouble; they also stress that management does all it can to discourage non-unionism and to help in eradicating lapsing.

This attitude often results in a semi-closed shop situation. Lower levels of management inform non-unionists that individual grievances should be funnelled through union representatives. Managers agree to interview those who resist these and similar pressures to 'persuade' them to join and so avoid further difficulty. They also make use of 'screening' to see that workers realize that they may be expected to join the union if they are engaged.

The contrast between the public and private sector of the road haulage industry can be summarized by saying that although it is *less* likely that a worker in private road haulage will be in a union, since the bulk of the smaller private contractors have so far resisted unionization, it is much *more* likely that if he is he will be in a closed shop. Private road haulage can thus be said to be more closed shop prone than public road haulage, and the reason can be found in the fact that in the latter case the closed shop is not so necessary.

Similar contrasts can be found among road passenger transport workers. Once again there is more likelihood of *demands* for the closed shop arising within the 100,000 or so workers employed in the privately owned passenger transport trade, as against the 85,000 or so workers employed in municipally owned passenger transport. However, there have been two other influences at work among passenger transport workers, which must be taken into account. Many of the workers are employed either by the London Transport Executive or by Labour controlled local authorities.

In the case of the L.T.E., as was described in Chapter 5,[1] there was the additional problem of breakaway unionism, which gave rise to the demand for the closed shop. In the case of Labour controlled local authorities there are a few examples of the employer-initiated closed shop. These exceptions apart, it remains true that the remaining workers in the public sector of the passenger transport industry are less closed shop prone than their counterparts in the private sector, and for similar reasons.

Another relatively minor factor affecting a large section of workers in this group is the effect of a closed shop tradition. It is to be remembered that several comprehensively closed groups, such as newsprint workers, and workers in the shipyards and the docks, are surrounded by examples of the practice among workers not normally much affected by it—for example, there are closed shops among proof-readers and teleprinter operators, or among tally clerks in the docks, or draughtsmen employed in the offices of

---

[1] See p. 110 above.

shipyard firms. These are, in fact, merely the most obvious examples of the effect of a closed shop tradition. There are several other groups of manual workers whose attitude towards non-unionists has been affected by their close proximity to long established comprehensively closed trades. Each of these groups is itself in need of the closed shop, in that in each case it brings with it important advantages; nevertheless an extra force is given to demands for the practice as a result of the experience and attitudes of others.

In printing the pace in organization and job regulation was made by the skilled groups. The lesser skilled, when they came to organize, grew up in an industry dominated by the closed shop tradition. The same can be said of similar groups in shipbuilding and iron and steel. The effect of the closed shop tradition in trades such as this was threefold. First, there already existed groups that were well organized. In some cases, for example in iron and steel, where recruitment was undertaken by the same union, this meant that expansion could proceed from a stable base. Second, even where this was not so, it meant that as unionization arose among the lesser skilled the advantages of the closed shop were fully appreciated, while the degree of tolerance accorded to non-unionists was low. When faced with problems of turnover and contact the organizers of the lesser skilled in these industries were encouraged to turn to the closed shop, and were sometimes able to use the 'borrowed strength' of workers already imbued with a closed shop tradition to achieve this aim. Third, as was noted in Chapter 3, where a closed shop tradition exists on any wide scale in an industry employers come to accept as normal, and even inevitable, demands for the exclusion of non-unionists. This means that they are less likely to resist demands for further extensions of the closed shop.

Finally, mention must be made of the historical effect of the problem of the alternative labour force among the trades now being discussed. It is not suggested that in their case the problem is of as much contemporary significance as it is among either of the earlier groups considered—i.e. the skilled craft trades, and the lesser skilled pre-entry trades, whose need for the entry control function of the closed shop were described in detail in Chapter 5.

Nevertheless, as was also explained in that chapter, it was originally a part of the objectives of many of the unions organizing among what have been defined above as the 'post-entry trades' to secure comprehensive closed shops over as wide an area as possible, partly to be able to control the alternative labour force which could be used to undermine bargaining power in times of strike action. Full employment has considerably alleviated this problem, however, and it is not suggested that to-day fear of the use to be made of the alternative labour force is an important motive behind closed shop drives among this group of trades.

(d) Process Workers in Iron and Steel

The next group which needs to be considered are the process workers in iron and steel. This group has been subjected to a rather special set of influences, and on the face of it does not appear to be, nowadays, much in need of the closed shop apart from the continued necessity, from the union leadership's point of view, of securing maximum strike control. However, in the past strikes to obtain recognition were quite common in the industry, and other strikes were sometimes held where employers would not agree to join the local Wages Board and submit to its arbitration provisions. The systematic importation of blacklegs, and the discharge of union members or ringleaders, was common in circumstances of this sort. To-day there are virtually no problems of turnover and contact, at least among the higher levels of the promotion ladder, if only because mobility of labour is virtually non-existent. This was not always so, however, particularly in the days before the union managed to get a method of promotion accepted which is based largely on seniority. Before that date it was a constant complaint that men were passed over, or even discharged, in order to make room for a more 'acceptable' worker, who may have been a non-unionist. Since there was no recognized 'transferable' skill this meant that the man displaced had to return to the status of labourer. Because of this the union was much concerned with the problem of job security, and the control of promotion was one of the ways in which it tried to improve the position. Nevertheless, it seems doubtful if any of these features was crucial in determining the attitude of union officials and giving rise to their demand for the closed shop. Basically they seem to have been most affected by the advantages of striking a bargain with employers over the issue of strike control. No doubt in this matter they were not unmindful of the fact that the securing of the closed shop would help them to extend their organization among the labouring groups.

But perhaps the comprehensive nature of the closed shop among process workers in iron and steel is best regarded as an example of what a union can do, once it is effectively organized, in an industry where strikes are particularly feared by the employer. In the days when the unions could be denied formal recognition it was at first difficult to recruit and retain a high level of membership; the closed shop would at that time have been invaluable, but the unions were naturally not able to enforce it. Later union strength increased and the employers were willing to recognize the practice as soon as they were convinced that the result would be fewer rather than more strikes.

(e) Entertainment Workers

As has been said, musicians and other artists affected by the post-entry shop have been mainly influenced by the problem of enforcing their own unilateral regulations, since theirs is a profession in which the settled habits of bilateral regulation (or collective bargaining as it is usually called) are the exception rather than the rule. Since there is no universally recognized system of training in any of these trades, and very considerable variations in demand, there is little job security and frequent unemployment, even to-day.

Indeed, there is no doubt that the bargaining power of this group of workers as a whole would benefit very much from some form of job-entry control and the exclusion of some part of the alternative labour force. However, unlike the film production workers, performers have never been able to secure this. The main reason seems to be that, in their case, the employer has always put particular stress on his right to hire who he wanted. Because of this, any attempt to obtain even a moderate degree of job preference for existing members of the profession would be fiercely resented, and fought hard. No system of preference can work unless it is generally accepted that for most types of work required one worker is as good as another. In the case of musicians, or actors, or sopranos, this is strenuously denied. Consequently, even the well-organized Musicians' Union has had to be content with a post-entry shop, and sometimes has to allow outstanding soloists or conductors, who refuse to maintain their union membership, to contract out. This is because if these artists are in sufficient demand their presence on the platform is indispensable, in that without them management would not be interested in engaging the other players.

The only form of entry control the Musicians' Union has been able to impose affects ordinary musicians who are new entrants to this country. Their rule book stipulates that entry to the union is open to any person engaged to play in a full-time orchestra, unless he has previously been expelled or is a 'foreign musician who has not been continuously resident in Great Britain or Northern Ireland for at least twelve months prior to his application'.[1] Foreign musicians who remain for more than a year may then apply for admission, but permission of the Executive Council is required.

In practice this rule is only used to assist in preventing the wholesale importation of orchestras from abroad. Individual musicians, who settle in this country, have little difficulty in getting into the union, particularly if they are outstanding performers whose services are in demand. Any individual whose employment makes it more likely that others will be employed is not likely to have his application to join the union refused. Once again the closed shop is required to protect union members; if its rigid application would harm their interests, then it is waived.

(f) Employer-Initiated Closed Shops

Finally, we come to the apparently paradoxical position of those groups where pressure for the closed shop originates with employers. Their situation seems to contradict what has been written about the need for union power without the aid of the closed shop and the essentially negative attitude of employers. However, properly understood, the workers covered by employer-initiated closed shops are not really exceptions to these rules, for in each case their remains a sense in which the demand for the closed shop still comes from trade unionists—although not from trade unionists on the job.

As was seen in the case of the Oxford Co-operative Society, moves to initiate the closed shop which come from employers occur when trade unionists, or their associates, such as Labour councillors, either become employers or get into positions where they can influence the employment policies of other organizations. To some extent they are influenced at this point by respect for the closed shop tradition, that is to say they believe in the 'rightness' of the closed shop and consider that just as it would be 'wrong' to work with a man who refused to join a trade union, so it would be equally 'wrong' to employ him. It is mainly for this reason that the full-time officials and office staff of British trade unions are expected to become and remain members of either the union that employs them or a suitable and 'bona fide' organization like the Clerical and Administrative Workers. Similarly, all full-time Labour Party

[1] Rules of the Musicians' Union, Rule 2, page 5, 1957.

agents are required to join the National Union of Labour Organizers and Election Agents.

But there are other considerations. It has long been a part of trade union policy to foster the spread of 'fair practices' and 'decent conditions' for all workers. Their concern with the promotion of 'fair wages clauses' and other forms of industrial legislation are indications of this. The rationale behind such activities is partly that in this way industrial norms acceptable to the unions gain acceptance as general standards. Obviously in their role as employers of labour trade unionists also want to encourage such norms by observing them themselves. By refusing to accept the toleration of non-unionism, as well as by recognizing the right of their employees to join unions and obtain union conditions, trade unionists serving on local authorities and co-operative management committees argue that again they are helping to set standards. In addition, by forcing union membership upon such comparatively reluctant volunteers as shop assistants and local government employees, they help to raise the general level of union finance.

In short, drives to obtain the practice among these groups are influenced by factors not unlike those that give rise to the practice elsewhere. The closed shop is still required, at least in part, to raise the level of union power and influence.

(3) The Relative Importance of the Closed Shop in Different Trades

Although the closed shop assists all the groups discussed above, it is impossible to measure the precise extent to which each trade or group would be weakened if, for some reason, they were prevented from making use of the closed shop. It is particularly difficult to decide in advance and in each case to what extent a group would merely be unable to secure further advances in wages and conditions, and how far in addition it would be unable to sustain a viable system of job regulation. That is to say how far, in the terms discussed in Chapter 4, they would be able to develop and maintain sufficient collective strength to:

(a) ensure continued recognition by employers, and the right to participate in bilateral job regulation;
(b) take effective action if individual employers did not observe negotiated agreements;
(c) enforce their own unilateral regulations if recognition could not be secured.[1]

[1] See the section on Job Regulation and Union Sanction, at p. 95 above.

However, in the case of some groups, notably seamen and musicians, it seems incontestable that none of these things would be possible without the closed shop; a viable system of job regulation necessitates the attainment of the practice in one form or another. Similarly, in the case of distributive workers, and many of the less well organized groups like the builders labourers, high and stable levels of unionization seem to depend on the closed shop, which is required to maintain the limited degree of strength which those groups have secured.

With many other groups the effect of removing the closed shop is not so easy to calculate in advance. The right of craft groups like the boilermakers to their job monopolies depends on the existence of the craft qualification shop, just as the job preferences of the lesser skilled groups who operate the labour supply shops depends on its continued operation. Still, it is difficult to say how far the conditions of employment of both these groups would deteriorate, in the long run, if either of them could no longer operate the closed shop in its existing form. It is even more difficult to estimate, in any objective way, to what extent the closed shop upholds the bargaining position of each one of the trades listed above, most of whom have had to be content with the post-entry shop.[1] Probably groups such as those in passenger transport, or publicly owned road haulage, would be affected least, which is why demands for the practice among this group are comparatively weak. And this brings us to a final issue which must be considered before this chapter ends.

(4) Well-organized Groups in which the Closed Shop is not Prevalent

It will be remembered that the most important of these were:

(1) Non-industrial Civil Servants.
(2) Teachers and other non-manual groups employed by local authorities.
(3) Sections of the Industrial Civil Service.
(4) Firemen.
(5) Footplate workers on the Railways.
(6) Clerical and Administrative workers in Nationalized Industries.
(7) Electricity workers employed by nationalized undertakings.
(8) Boot and Shoe Operatives.

[1] Nevertheless, it is necessary to try to come to some general conclusions on these matters if one wishes to consider the question of the continued justifiability of the closed shop, and the case for reforming its position in law. For this reason the final chapter of this book, which contains a statement of the writers' own attitude towards the contemporary justifiability of the closed shop, begins with a personal assessment of the consequences of denying unions the right to demand and obtain it.

As was mentioned in Chapter 2, four of these groups are employed by government authorities, three by nationalized industries and only one by private employers. Three of them are non-manual groups.

The explanation for this part of the pattern should by now be obvious. It has been possible to organize and control the workers in these groups without the need to overcome the problems set out in Chapter 5. The unions responsible have either developed methods of job regulation which do not require the closed shop, or at least it has appeared that its attainment would not result in substantial advantages. This can best be illustrated by the case of the Civil Service unions.

The most obvious problems which have not bothered unions organizing civil servants are those of strike solidarity and control. Since the first staff unions were founded in the 1850's withdrawals of labour have been extremely rare, and usually unsuccessful. As one student of union organization among Post Office workers wrote of an early strike in the department:

The postmen's strike was a horrible failure. It perhaps never could have succeeded for the men were backing an enterprise with almost limitless resources while their resources were strictly limited. The monopoly position of the Department and its intimate connection with the well-being of the public made a strike policy among postmen unlikely to meet with success or popular support.[1]

In the early days of organization strikes were sometimes threatened, even within the non-industrial civil service, but it soon became apparent that alternative methods of job regulation were more likely to succeed. The unions discovered that more could be effected by making 'representations' to the Department, circulating petitions, and, most important of all, giving evidence before Parliamentary and other committees of investigation into civil service pay and conditions.

After the First World War, relationships between the civil service unions and their respective Government Departments were put on a permanent and satisfactory footing by Government acceptance of what came to be known as the 'Whitley System'. In effect this implied full recognition and the right to independent arbitration. But Whitleyism has come to mean more than this. In the words of the General Secretary of one civil service union, it 'broadened the

---

[1] The History of Employment in the British Post Office, by Leo Martinuzzi, unpublished B.Litt. thesis, Oxford, 1952.

scope of joint negotiation and consultation beyond anything previously contemplated by the unions themselves'.[1] Moreover, under
the system, as it operated until very recently, either side could
demand access to the Civil Service Arbitration Tribunal over pay
disputes and the Treasury honoured awards of the Tribunal in full.
Formally the Government continued to reserve the right to refuse
arbitration because it remained legally 'responsible to Parliament for
the administration of the public service and cannot relieve itself of
that responsibility'.[2] But in practice access to the Tribunal was only
refused on one major issue—equal pay. This became the subject of
a highly successful agitation in the post-war years under the leadership
of the civil service unions.

More important still, since the coming of Whitleyism there have
been two vitally important Royal Commissions on the principles
governing civil service pay, and the unions have had the opportunity
of presenting detailed evidence before these Commissions.[3] As a
consequence of this development, more or less agreed principles
emerged governing civil service pay which linked the rate of
remuneration to what was happening in outside industry. Consequently it became increasingly unlikely that basic disagreements
would arise. Both sides had an accepted frame of reference to argue
within, and if they disagreed about the specific application of the
principles laid down to the case in hand they could always refer the
matter to the Civil Service Arbitration Tribunal for binding decision.

The result has been that, for the most part, civil service unions
have regarded the threat of arbitration as a much more effective
threat than that of strike action. Indeed, the specifically civil service
staff associations have little or no experience of strikes, while many
state openly that they have 'no strike policy'. By this they mean
that a use of Parliamentary pressure, extra-parliamentary agitation,
and the threat of reference to a tribunal whose awards are customarily
accepted by the employer in full, is considered incompatible with
the use of the strike weapon. Strike action might jeopardize these
techniques, alienate Parliamentary and public opinion, and cause the
Treasury to set aside its commitment to mutually binding arbitration.
To the extent that this is believed, one can say the civil service unions
have come to view their traditional techniques of job regulation

[1] Douglas Houghton, General Secretary of the Association of H.M. Inspectors of Taxes,
quoted in R. V. Humphreys, *Clerical Unions in the Civil Service*, Blackwells, 1958, p. 102.
[2] *Staff Relations in the Civil Service*, H.M.S.O., 1955, p. 112.
[3] See Report of the Royal (Tomlin) Commission, 1930–31, and Report of the Royal
Priestley) Commission, 1953–55.

as ruling out a refusal to work in principle; if this is so, then clearly they also rule out a refusal to work with non-unionists.

Unfortunately it is impossible to say how far these traditional assumptions have been permanently affected by the unusual behaviour of the Government during the 1961 'Pay Pause'. It will be remembered that during the first few months of the pause the Treasury withdrew from the scope of arbitration the date at which awards of the Civil Service Tribunal should take effect. This meant that when the Tribunal decided that a particular union's members should be paid more than the Government had offered, they did not receive the excess until after the end of the first phase of the Pay Pause. Moreover, even then there was to be no question of retrospective payments.

Even more important, perhaps, in the long run, was a passage in the Government's White Paper 'Incomes Policy—the Next Step', published at the beginning of the second phase of the Pay Pause. This seemed to indicate that the Government was re-examining its longer term commitment to the principle that civil service pay should be linked to comparable movements in private industry. For although it admitted that 'comparisons will still have a part to play', it went on to add, ominously, that 'in the immediate future more regard will have to be given to general economic considerations'.

Civil service unions may have to re-examine their absolute preference for arbitration rather than strike action, if it were to turn out that this phrase means that future governments will reserve the right to reject arbitration awards, based on comparisons with outside industry, whenever they are out of line with some overall maximum figure which the Government's advisers think is all that the country can afford. For the unions would be unwilling to admit that it was fair and just to import such a principle into the determination of civil service wage rates, and would argue that it made nonsense of their traditional right to 'independent' arbitration.

Already the actions of the Government during the Pay Pause have produced a number of untypically militant acts on the part of several unions. The Civil Service Clerical Association, for example, were preparing a 'work to rule', when the first phase of the Pay Pause ended. The Union of Post Office Workers actually carried out a work to rule, and the Post Office Engineering Union imposed both a work to rule and an overtime ban.

It is interesting to speculate how far the Post Office Engineers' customary toleration of the few non-unionists that refuse to join their organization would survive many more developments of this kind. Already one can observe a hardening of rank and file attitudes. For example, following the union's overtime ban, which was supported by something like 95 per cent of the membership, there were demands from a number of branches that individuals who broke the ban should be punished by the union. More recently the union suggested to the Post Office that in future wage increases obtained as a result of union action should not be paid to non-unionists. It is not suggested that developments of this sort, in the present situation, are likely to give rise to demands for the closed shop, but if the actions of the Treasury ever forced the union to consider seriously the possibility of adopting a regular strike policy there is no doubt that more demands of this sort would arise from the more militant London branches.

However, at the moment of writing the civil service unions as a whole can be said to be still overwhelmingly committed to a rejection of the strike weapon, as any regular part of their armoury, and while this remains the case there does not appear to be any substantial advantage to be gained from the closed shop. They appear to be able to solve their other problems without its aid.

For example, the problems of turnover and contact which so often afflict other unions are virtually non-existent over a wide area of the civil service. In the non-industrial civil service 79·6 per cent of workers are established, and the great majority will remain in the job or office they are attached to for the rest of their working life. In the industrial civil service the figure is rather lower, i.e. 49·2 per cent, but what this implies is that workers have to wait rather longer before they are taken 'onto establishment'. Labour turn-over is still comparatively low, certainly when compared with many groups on similar work outside the civil service. Nor is this all, for civil service unions enjoy even more striking advantages over the great majority of their counterparts in private industry in contacting their members. It is impossible to measure the differential here, but those in a position to know most about it, i.e. the officers of unions organizing similar grades inside and outside the civil service, stress the considerable difference in attitude towards the performance of union duties during working hours. Moreover, active members of unions like the Post Office Engineers, or the Civil Service Clerical Association, maintain that they are virtually free to take whatever time they need to perform their union duties, as they put it 'in the Department's time'. Certainly there are few restrictions placed on

M

the collection of subscriptions during working hours, and individuals have informed the writer that in their experience time is usually allowed to seek to persuade reluctant new entrants to join the union.

Moreover, consider the comparative absence among civil service groups of the problem of the alternative labour force. Since most workers are established, and even fewer are discharged on grounds of redundancy, this problem has been almost totally absent, at least since the unions became well organized. Nowadays there are very detailed negotiations over such issues as educational qualifications, examinations, and so on, so that if any union wishes to protect or raise the 'status' of the work done by its members it has an avenue of negotiation open to it. In the Post Office, for example, there is an Engineering Practices Committee, which considers the effect on job security and earnings of changes in methods of working which management wants to initiate. In the opinion of Mr. A. A. Brewer, the full-time official of the Post Office Engineers responsible for these matters, the effective working of this committee is one of the main reasons why new technological developments have not been resisted by workers in the Post Office factories. It is submitted that the establishment of such committees may also be a reason for the absence of unilateral regulation among even non-industrial civil servants. Printers are an exception—but then they have a closed shop, and the practice is not quite unknown among other craft groups like the shipwrights. In the Post Office, however, one of the main objectives of the Engineering Practices Committee is to remove objections to change, and thus help to minimize the need for the unilateral regulation of such things as output, manning, and so on. Indeed, up to the present, only two of the problems listed as giving rise to closed shop demands have affected civil service workers to any marked extent. They are: the effect of a closed shop tradition and the influence of inter-union competition.

The consequences of the first of these is easily estimated. It largely accounts for the situation in the Stationery Office, and is of importance in explaining the position among skilled groups like the shipwrights. It is also of some relevance in accounting for the presence of closed shop and semi-closed shop pressures among skilled engineering workers in places like Woolwich Arsenal, and in the Post Office factories it explains the rather more hostile attitude towards non-unionism adopted by the Amalgamated Engineering Union as against the Post Office Engineers.

The effect of competition—or rather its absence—is more difficult to explain. Breakaway trade unionism is not unknown in the civil service, and in the past it has been quite common.[1] Yet it has not led to demands for the closed shop. This is mainly because the unions concerned have felt it easier to keep the breakaway union outside the established machinery of negotiation, rather than to demand a closed shop.

Faced with a breakaway an established union can demand that the new organization be denied recognition and threaten to withdraw from the Whitley machinery if it is recognized. Moreover, since the seats allotted to each union on the staff side of the Whitley machinery are settled by agreement between the unions themselves, they can always combine together to keep out secessionist organizations. Tactics of this sort have been regarded as more effective than demands for a closed shop, and they have usually been successful. Official representatives have not wanted to upset established unions by supporting breakaway organizations, and have generally gone out of their way to prevent an all-out clash of the sort that might lead to a closed shop demand.[2]

But, as was mentioned in Chapter 3, in the case of the civil service there is one additional factor at work; those responsible for staff relations in the civil service go out of their way to stress that as instruments of H.M.G. they could not and would never agree to anything in the nature of a closed shop. As was seen, this is not absolutely and unreservedly true, but what is true is that there is a very real resistance to anything which looks like official recognition. There are three reasons for this. First, there is the conviction that the principles of Whitleyism presuppose 'voluntary trade unionism'. One is invariably informed that this has always been the 'Treasury view' on the matter, and that government policy has always been to resist demands for the closed shop for this reason. Secondly, and more vaguely, one has the feeling, talking to official side representatives, that they are particularly sensitive to the effect of public opinion. The Government, they suggest, would be subject to much hostile criticism if it were seen to be supporting coercion of the kind the closed shop is said to represent.

[1] See *Breakaway Unions and the Small Trade Union*, by Shirley W. Lerner, Allen and Unwin, 1961, Chap. 4.
[2] A well-documented example here is the dispute between the P.O.E.U. and two post-war breakaways, set out in Lerner, *op. cit.* at p. 144.

This concern for adverse publicity shades over into the third reason advanced by officials; the consequences of recognizing a right to the closed shop in fields like the civil service where there is only one employer. Finally, there is the very practical objection that the high percentage of 'established' civil servants would make the implementation of a formal closed shop policy almost impossible.

Taken together these arguments represent an attitude towards the closed shop which is strong enough to constitute a marked difference to that of employers in general elsewhere. When it is remembered that the state, not being a commercial concern, is in a better position to stand by such principles in the face of union pressure, it is not surprising that throughout the area of state employment the closed shop is the exception to the rule, even among groups affected by the closed shop tradition. Indeed, some union leaders responsible for the organization of state employees take the view that at the moment even a successful campaign for the closed shop would not be worth the price.

Aware that they often need to appeal over the heads of the Departments to Parliament and the public, they are particularly sensitive to the effects of such a demand on public opinion themselves. Nor is this all. There is a sense in which one feels that many of the present union leaders would be embarrassed if it were offered to them by Departments. In negotiations and public announcements they often refer to the fact that 'voluntarily' and 'without pressure' they have reached a certain level of unionization. This is advanced as an indication of the strength of their influence among the staff, and even, at times, of the very justifiability of the case they are advancing. It is often argued that the high level of unionization is to some extent the consequence of deeply felt grievances, or at the least that it is one sign that the unions have the staff behind them in their demands. It was considerations of this sort that caused a leading civil service union official to state:

If we were offered the closed shop we would probably turn it down—it would do us more harm than good.

This remark was echoed by a national official of the Fire Brigades' Union, who when asked why his union did not campaign for the closed shop replied: 'because there is nothing in it for us.' Similar views are advanced by officials of the teachers' unions, and by those organizing other non-manual groups employed by local authorities and administrative groups in nationalized industries.

In all these groups there is no strike tradition, no difficult problems of turnover and contact, no examples of unilateral regulation, and no fear of an alternative labour force. Job security is high and the few non-unionists who exist do not appear to be a significant threat to union power. Lacking any closed shop tradition there is no reason why such groups should not be tolerant of the few non-unionists that are left.

Similar considerations apply to two of the remaining three groups —electricity workers in public employment and footplate workers on the railways; in each case the closed shop would bring few advantages. Both groups have few problems of turnover and contact, there is an exceptional continuity of employment, and the facilities to collect dues and maintain contact with members are exceptionally good.[1] Unilateral regulations are unimportant and breakaway unionism is not a problem. It is true that there is inter-union competition among footplate men, between the National Union of Railwaymen and the Association of Locomotive Engineers and Firemen, but this has not resulted in attempts to obtain the closed shop, as was the case in London Transport, because the unions are too evenly matched.[2] Job security is high among both groups and there is no awareness of the problem of the alternative labour force. Strikes are not entirely ruled out in either group, but both groups threaten strike action more often than they withdraw labour, and in recent years national wage negotiations have often proceeded against strike threats that do not actually materialize. Moreover, if a national strike did take place in either industry, the crucial issue would be to secure the immediate paralysis of the transport or electrical supply system as a whole. If this could be done it is unlikely that the strike would last for long.[3] The essential issue, in this respect, is not the extent to which railwaymen or electricians withdraw their labour *in toto*, so much as the ability of their unions to pull out a number of key grades—e.g. signalmen on the railways, and certain key maintenance groups in electricity generation. Thus, in explaining why these two well-organized groups are not closed shop prone it is essential to realize that it is not merely that they

[1] There are problems of turnover among certain groups of manual workers employed by British Railways, but not among engine drivers, motormen and firemen, who constitute the footplate grades. See below.

[2] The N.U.R. claims over 30 per cent of drivers, motormen, firemen and cleaners employed by British Railways, almost all the rest are members of the A.S.L.E.F.

[3] The only strike of any length on the railways since the war was the national strike of the A.S.L.E.F. in 1955. This lasted sixteen days. The main reason was that the N.U.R. was not a party to the dispute, and footplate men organized by the N.U.R. remained at work.

seldom have to strike, but also that even if they did, the problem of maintaining strike effectiveness would not take a form likely to generate demands for the closed shop.

Indeed, the only factor likely to give rise to the closed shop which is present to any degree among publically employed electricity workers and footplatemen is a closed shop tradition among members of the Electrical Trades' Union who have worked in the private sector of the electrical contracting industry—which is closed shop prone. The main reason why this factor has not resulted in more widespread demands for the closed shop is that when trouble over non-unionists does arise in the public sector there are unusually effective pressures, of a semi-closed shop sort, which are generally sufficient to deal with the problem. Indeed, in electricity the effectiveness of pressures which stop short of the closed shop are an important factor in explaining the absence of closed shop demands in this group. For this reason it is worth describing briefly how they operate.

In 1947 the National Joint Industrial Council for manual workers in the publically owned sector of the industry adopted what has become known as 'Minute 297' dealing with the issue of 'non-unionism'. The subject arose because some local authorities with formal closed shop agreements had electricity undertakings which had been taken over by the newly formed Central Electricity Board. The question therefore arose as to whether the C.E.B. could agree to go beyond the mere publication of a statement 'encouraging' workers to join their respective unions, and whether they were willing to honour their predecessors' obligations on the question of union membership.

The C.E.B. refused either to recognize existing closed shops or to extend them. What they did accept was a procedure whereby the reluctant non-unionist is seen first by a full-time official of one of the unions—usually either the General and Municipal Workers or the Electrical Trades Union—during working hours. If he still refuses to join he will be interviewed by his local manager, who explains that the Board 'prefers' workers to be union members, and outlines the procedure for dealing with non-unionists. This means that if the recalcitrant still proves obstinate his case can be brought before higher management and leading union representatives on the Works Committee. Further interviews may then take place, and if necessary the problem will be referred to the District Council. Finally, if he persists, the recalcitrant is told that he will be the subject of a discussion at national level; a full report of his case will come before the National Joint Council.

There are no provisions for bringing the reluctant non-unionist or persistent lapser face to face with the entire council, and no private interview takes place with the Chairman. But unless the man agrees to join at some stage the whole dispute may be referred back to the District Council concerned for further discussions. In practice this is not necessary. Ninety-nine per cent of non-unionists agree to join before national level is reached; only two or three cases a year reach the N.J.I.C., though a considerably larger number succumb at district level. Clearly, although management means what it says when it states that this is not an undercover closed shop, and it is not the practice to threaten men with dismissal unless they do agree, the very knowledge that such a procedure exists, and can be invoked by the union, acts as an important social pressure making for the maintenance of membership. When it is supplemented, as it often is, by strong social pressures operated by the workmen themselves, one can say that something akin to a semi-closed shop exists over large areas of publicly owned electricity generation and supply which operates as a substitute for the membership function of the closed shop.

But the reluctance of the Central Electricity Board either to recognize or extend the closed shop in 1947 highlights one final factor which should be mentioned in connection with all the groups employed by nationalized industries and listed above. The state's fears of public criticism, if it were known to be supporting the closed shop, has also been reflected in the attitude of nationalized industries. Fears of this sort were one reason why the N.C.B. would not agree to any formal extension of the closed shop, and they undoubtedly conditioned the attitude of the Central Electricity Board. Of course this sensitiveness to possible criticism has not proved an absolute bar even to the formal closed shop—witness the case of London Transport—but it has resulted in a reluctance to concede, unless forced to do so.

At the moment, concern over public reactions to any concession on the part of the employer in a nationalized industry is also a major factor preventing the extension of even the semi-closed shop to manual workers other than footplatemen employed by British Railways. The National Union of Railwaymen, who recruit among this group, have recently experienced increasing difficulties in maintaining a stable level of unionization among workers in places like stations and goods yards, largely because of the rapidly rising rate of labour turnover in these areas. This development, coupled with a 20 per cent decline in total membership over the last decade, due mainly to the effects of the railway modernization programme, has produced a demand for help from the British Transport Commission in raising the level of unionization.

So far the British Transport Commission has refused all requests for anything in the nature of a closed shop or even a check off. The furthest they have been prepared to go is to agree to post a notice calling attention to the 'benefits' of trade unionism.

The union's response to this rebuff has so far been extremely mild. There has been no move to demand strike action, or to put further pressure on the employer. These are sure signs that at the moment of writing at least even those workers on the railways who could now be said to be in need of the closed shop are not yet ready to look on it as an objective worth fighting for. Given the present attitude of their employers they cannot expect any substantial concessions unless and until they do.[1]

The last group which needs to be discussed is boot and shoe operatives. Their position is slightly different and it is rather more difficult to explain why they have not become more closed shop prone. It is true that nowadays they do not rely on unilateral regulation, that they have no problems of inter-union competition, and are not bothered by fears of an alternative labour force. However, there is a normal rate of turnover among many of their lesser skilled grades,[2] and although the union is offered reasonable facilities for contacting members one might have expected more demands for the closed shop based on the need for its membership functions. This apparent paradox is all the more marked when one considers the history of the union. It was not always easy to persuade the boot and shoe operatives to join the union and George Sedgewick, union agent in 1878, presented a report on the 'state of the union'

[1] Of course the bulk of the N.U.R.'s membership employed in engineering workshops owned by British Railways are subject to the usual form of engineering closed shop, and there are strong pressures enforcing membership in the more militant parts of the country— such as Manchester. However, in the past, and these exceptions apart, the N.U.R. has never developed any closed shop tradition.

[2] Many of whom are women. Just over 50 per cent of the union's total membership are women.

in which he stressed the unwillingness of certain groups. In some cases, he wrote:

a certain amount of pressure had to be brought to bear before men could be brought into the Union. The class of men just named are by no means willing unionists, and lose no opportunity of withdrawing their connection with us the moment the pressure . . . is removed.[1]

Once recognition was obtained and the union began regular bargaining over piece rates and other important matters, this problem declined in importance at least within the Northampton area—where most of the larger employers were members of the employers' federation, and parties to its agreements. But the reluctance of boot and shoe operatives to join the union in traditional 'black-spots' like London, and in those new areas into which the industry was moving, where trade unionism was sometimes non-existent and always difficult to develop, remained a source of weakness. Indeed, the inability of the union to organize such groups came, in time, to undermine their ability to extract concessions from federation employers. As the numbers of non-unionized firms grew, employers dropped out of the employers' federation, so that by the 1930's it accounted for little more than a half of total production in the industry. Moreover, not all those who remained within the federation observed its agreements, and the union appeared to be too weak to enforce them. In 1934 the Federation gave notice of its desire to terminate the National Agreement, stating,

The wide non-observance of the National Agreement . . . which has gone on for so long unchecked to any effective extent, has created an intolerable position for federated manufacturers. Firms of long standing and good repute are being driven out of business and there is considerable insecurity and uneasiness amongst several firms whose position at one time was unassailable.[2]

In fact the union was able to persuade the Federation not to terminate the national agreement, but it was not until it was able to raise the level of organization in the 'black-spots' and the great majority of employers joined the Federation during the war that its position was secure. To-day federation coverage is almost complete, national agreements are universally observed, and unionization is above the 90 per cent level. The remarkable thing is that all this has been achieved without the use of the membership functions of the closed shop.

[1] *A History of the National Union of Boot and Shoe Operatives*, 1874–1957, by Alan Fox, Blackwells, 1958, p. 41.   [2] Fox, *op. cit.*, p. 513.

There appear to be two reasons for this. The first, and most important, is that from the inception of the union it has been led by moderate men, who sought to create a system of mutually binding arbitration which effectively ruled out the strike weapon. They soon persuaded the larger employers of the Northampton area who were members of the employers' federation to accept this system.[1] Consequently, a strike tradition has never developed within the industry, and, within the area covered by the employers' federation, there has not been an official strike since the dispute of 1895.[2]

Secondly, because employers who were members of the Federation wanted to see the National Agreement universally observed, they genuinely wished to foster union growth. As Fox puts it:

The belief that a powerful Union could help to bring 'stability' to the industry (i.e. help to limit the forms through which competition worked) by imposing on all employers a uniform labour code, was now an established article of Federation faith.[3]

The effect of this was that federation members were encouraged to do everything to facilitate the achievement of '100 per cent membership' in their factories, and as long ago as 1914 the Federation itself formally accepted the 'desirability of all boot and shoe operatives becoming members of the National Union'.[3]

This policy combined with the no strike tradition, has influenced the union in two ways. Firstly, inside the Federation area drives to eliminate non-unionism usually dealt with the problem of recalcitrants by the pressures of the semi-closed shop, supplemented, where necessary, by managerial 'persuasion'. If this did not always result in the total elimination of all non-unionism the union did not

---

[1] It is notable that although union leaders 'sold' arbitration as an alternative to strikes, there was no subsequent demand for the closed shop to ensure the obedience of union members, as in iron and steel. There are two reasons for this: (1) boot and shoe operatives have been much more willing to accept the results of arbitration, and were less in need of restraint if it went against them; (2) the high degree of autonomy granted to branches, who had their own funds, made it more difficult for leaders of the union to impose discipline, even if they had had the closed shop at their disposal. Fox, *op. cit.*, p. 209.

[2] Under the terms of settlement signed after that dispute local boards of conciliation and arbitration were created, and provision was made for a mutually binding settlement. Under the terms of a further agreement, signed in 1910, a monetary penalty may be imposed in the event of a strike or lock-out lasting beyond three days. See Fox, *op. cit.*, Chap. 22.

[3] Fox, *op. cit.*, p. 446. In the 1920's the Federation joined with the union in campaigning for the legal enforceability of the national agreement throughout the whole industry. This attempt failed, but, of course, the passage of Order 1305, some twenty years later, in effect gave the industry what it wanted; under its provisions the union could bring any employer before the National Arbitration Tribunal and compel them to pay the terms laid down in the National Agreement. This naturally stimulated the growth of the Federation, since employers felt that if they had to pay federation wages they might as well assist in their determination.

worry—at least it has not been sufficiently concerned to demand the closed shop to deal with those non-unionists that remained. Secondly, and more importantly, outside the Federation area, among the largely unorganized groups whose owners were not yet members of the Federation, the union concentrated on forcing the employer to recognize the union and join the Federation; the assumption has been that if this could be done then a high and stable level of organization would soon be reached without the need to demand the closed shop. Thus, although the union has been prepared occasionally to strike for recognition and the observance of the National Agreement, it has not found it necessary to go on and demand the closed shop.[1]

(5) SUMMARY

The argument of the last four chapters can be summarized thus:

It is only by separating a number of related but different questions that one can arrive at an acceptable explanation of why the closed shop arises to the extent that it does, in the forms that it takes. Crucial to this explanation is an appreciation of the advantages it makes possible and the problems it helps to solve. To the extent that unions are influenced by the various factors which give rise to these problems, they tend to demand the closed shop as the level of their strength rises. Apart from the area of state employment on the one hand, and labour movement employment on the other, employers generally merely react to such demands according to how far they feel that they have more to lose from resisting rather than conceding what is demanded.

It will be argued in the next part of this thesis that these conclusions are crucial to a discussion of the many issues of justification which need to be considered.

---

[1] See Fox, *op. cit.*, pp. 287, 377, 436, 450 and 527, for details of official strikes against non-federation employers with the object of securing recognition and National Agreement rates. In 1921 co-operation between the Federation and the union to secure the enforcement of the National Agreement took the extreme form of financial assistance from the Federation in a strike against a Chesham employer who decided, simultaneously, to secède from the Federation and throw off the National Agreement (Fox, *op. cit.*, p. 450).

PART TWO
JUSTIFICATION

'After God had finished the rattlesnake, the toad, and the vampire, He had some awful "substance" left, with which He made a Scab. A Scab is a two-legged animal with a corkscrew soul, a water sogged brain, and a combination backbone made of jelly and glue. Where other people have their hearts he carries a tumour of rotten principles. When the Scab comes down the street honest men turn their backs, and angels weep tears in heaven, and the devil shuts the gate of Hell to keep him out. No man has a right to Scab as long as there is a pool of water deep enough to drown his body in, or a rope long enough to hang his carcase with. Judas Iscariot was a gentleman compared with a Scab, for, after betraying his Master, he had enough character to hang himself.'

From the *Johannesburg Strikers' Herald*; quoted by Captain E. Tupper in *Seamen's Torch, op. cit.*, p. 82.

CHAPTER 7

THE ISSUES INVOLVED

(1) INTRODUCTORY

IN the first part of this study the closed shop was described and analysed; this part deals with arguments advanced for its justification, together with objections raised against it. It contains:

1. An account of the attitude of the law towards the closed shop.
2. A consideration of recent suggestions for modifying the existing degree of legal immunity.
3. Conclusions concerning the contemporary justification of the practice and suggested measures of reform.

While it is not necessary to attempt a legal history of the closed shop, no account of the present position is comprehensible without reference to the general issues of labour law as they have been considered in the past by Parliament and the Courts. Moreover, this historical debate was not conducted on narrowly legalistic grounds. It raised questions of public interest, individual freedom, and economic efficiency. Indeed a review of the legal controversies surrounding the closed shop serves as the best introduction to a consideration of the wider issues involved in its justification. An account of the arguments used raises most of the main arguments for and against the practice. The single major exception is what may be termed the *common obligation argument*.

This form of justification is based on somewhat different grounds from most other arguments. It will therefore be discussed separately.

(2) THE COMMON OBLIGATION ARGUMENT

The argument is almost as old as the closed shop itself.[1] A recent T.U.C. publication stated it thus:

. . . the position of the non-unionist cannot be justified either on grounds of principle or expediency, The liberty of the individual is not an absolute and unqualified right. It is subject to restrictions for social ends which admit of no compromise. . . . Stability, order and regularity in the conduct of industry depend upon the proper functioning of trade unions, and upon recognition of the fact that no man or woman is entitled to benefit from the work of trade unions without acceptance of the obligations of trade union membership. In the view of the

---

[1] See, for example, the Webbs' *History of Trade Unionism*, Longmans Green, 1920, p. 296.

General Council, recognition of such obligations are incumbent not only upon individual workers, but upon management and employers.[1]

Three propositions are advanced here: (1) no man is entitled to benefit from the work of an association unless he contributes towards its advance; (2) unionists justifiably object to non-unionists' refusal to accept their common obligation in this respect; (3) it is therefore the duty of employers to accede to union demands for the enforcement of such obligations, where they are not accepted by the individuals concerned. The implication is that if unionists seek to force management's hand by a refusal to work, this is justified. In the words of Arthur Deakin to the 1952 T.U.C.: 'We challenge the suggestion that workers should be free to join a union or stay outside, and shall continue to assert with the utmost vigour the right of trade unionists to say whether or not they will work alongside non-unionists.'[2]

This argument is the most common form of justification used by trade unionists to defend the closed shop. The writer has listened to it in a multiplicity of forms, and the crucial initial proposition has received a wealth of embroidery. As might be expected the best short statement of what it involves came from a working printer:

The non-unionist benefits directly from the collective action of his colleagues through the results of collective bargaining. On what principle of freedom does he take all these things, pocket the increased wages, enjoy the increased leisure, while contributing nothing.

We can all enjoy street lighting, street paving, public parks, a water supply, the collection of dust and waste from our houses, municipal libraries, swimming pools and other advantages, but we are in turn required to contribute our share to the cost of the provision of these amenities, and there is no hanky panky about it.

Does the Government disapprove when a County Council says to a householder 'You must pay your rates however strongly you may object'. Would the member who says we must preserve the freedom of the individual at all costs have the boldness to declare in Parliament that the individual is free to please himself whether he pays rates or not?[3]

Several objections can be raised against this argument. First, trade unionists themselves do not accept unreservedly the proposition that no man should benefit from the work of a group to which he neither belongs nor supports. Numerous associations—i.e. the Oxford Preservation Trust, the Friends of Abingdon, the British Empire Cancer Campaign, the Marriage Guidance Council, etc.— do work of which they may approve and from which they benefit

---

[1] 'The Closed Shop', T.U.C. *Annual Report*, 1946, p. 256.
[2] T.U.C. *Annual Report*, 1952, p. 80.
[3] Chairman's Letter, *Bulletin of the Oxford Branch of the N.U.P.B.W.*, August 1957.

without them feeling an obligation to contribute towards the up-
keep of such bodies. If, after an incident in which an individual has
benefited in a substantial way, he feels like making a contribution,
most people, including trade unionists, would regard this as a
voluntary and private act. Few have suggested that if an individual
does not act in this way he ought to be compelled to do so. Thus
there is a recognizable field of voluntary group action which results
in benefits to those who neither belong to the group nor share in its
obligations. In this field the onus of deciding whether to make a
contribution is generally regarded as falling on the individual concerned. The question therefore arises: why cannot the benefits
which arise out of union action be so regarded? Asked this question
unionists deny that their benefits are comparable with the minor,
indirect and altogether less tangible ones which, they say, result
from the activities of the associations listed above.[1] They claim
that their benefits are more analogous to those provided by the
state—via taxation and rates, and consequently assert that a similar
measure of compulsion is justified.

But the analogy with the state is an unprofitable one. Given that
unions are not precisely like the Oxford Preservation Trust, they
are even less like sovereign states. They are not expected to perform
the same sort of duties or to provide benefits of a similar scope.
Consequently, they cannot hope for, do not need, and have never
desired the range of penalties that a modern state requires.[2] In fact,
there are so many differences between the state and trade unions
that the analogy would only be worth considering if it could be
shown that, whatever the other differences between them, in the
enforcement of membership and financial obligations the state and
unions were on a par. But this is not the case. I do not know of any
state which has left it to those living within its boundaries to choose
whether or not they shall pay taxes. Indeed, it is very difficult to
imagine a state being able to function in such circumstances. On

---

[1] In this respect the writer remembers asking a group of North Staffordshire Miners how
they could reconcile their enjoyment of the views of Oxford from the top of Boar's Hill
with their refusal to subscribe to the Oxford Preservation Trust, which helps to preserve the
views. Their answer was that the benefits of the N.U.M. were not to be compared with such
fripperies.
[2] For example, British unions do not usually wish to see collective agreements legally
enforceable. As Kahn-Freund has said: 'They are devised to yield "rights" and "duties" but
not in the legal sense; they are intended, as it is sometimes put, to be "binding in honour"
only, or (which amounts to very much the same thing) to be enforceable through social but
not through legal sanctions' (*The System of Industrial Relations in Great Britain*, ed. by Flanders
and Clegg, Blackwells, 1954, p. 58).

N

the other hand, as earlier chapters have shown, there are many trade unions who manage to function without the sanctions of the closed shop, and the great majority do, at least in respect of some of their members. What has to be shown is why it is that other members ought not to be expected to show such tolerance, and this cannot be done by means of an analogy with the state.

Moreover, even if the analogy were sound it may still be objected that states do sometimes allow individuals to benefit from activities they do not help to support. Those who, in wartime, accept a common obligation to defend the state admit that some individual may contract out on grounds of conscience. Why not accept that men may have a similar objection to joining a union?[1] It may be objected that there can be no comparison between the pacifist's genuine revulsion against shedding blood, and the average non-unionist's desire to avoid paying subscriptions—but this is just the point. Argument by analogy in a matter of this sort can always be met with the objection that there is an insufficient similarity to support the conclusion that what is justifiable in one case is justifiable in the other.

It would be possible to explore further the degree to which trade unions operating a closed shop are analogous to other groups in society, from bowls clubs to sovereign states, but it is suggested that this analysis by analogy causes more confusion than it resolves. The real issue is *not* whether unions should be allowed to use the functions of the closed shop because they are in some way like other associations, or whether union contributions are analogous to income-tax. The issue is how far, *as trade unions*, they should be permitted to pursue an objective like the closed shop in whatever way they wish, irrespective of the social and economic consequences.

To consider this question is a much more fruitful starting point than any attempt to proceed by way of analogies. As we have seen, the closed shop is an important and sometimes essential device which adds considerably to the power of unions to coerce and restrict the freedom of action of both employers and employees. All power of this sort is used to certain ends, and has certain consequences.

[1] A number of religious groups, like the Plymouth Brethren, maintain that their religion forbids them joining a union, just as it prevents them from fighting. Some unionists are in favour of allowing these men to remain outside the union, though some insist that they leave the job, and some that they pay an equivalent amount to a 'good cause'. In practice few trade unionists would allow such men to refuse the benefits which negotiations make possible, for fear that this would put a premium on the employment of non-unionists and undermine the rates they wish to see operate throughout industry.

Three questions may therefore be asked in relation to any association which uses power in this way:

(1) How far may one approve of the purposes for which the power is used?

(2) To what extent is it needed to further such purposes—i.e. are there any less draconic ways of pursuing the same ends?

(3) Do any other undesirable consequences follow from its use in this way which outweigh one's approval of the original purposes for which power has been acquired?

A practice like the closed shop must be justifiable on all three grounds. One must approve of the purposes for which it is acquired; it should be clear that on balance it is necessary to achieve such purposes; and it must not result in disadvantageous consequences which outweigh its advantages. A major weakness of the common obligation argument is that it does not address itself to such issues. It is exclusively concerned with basing a right to coerce on a feeling of resentment that others are evading their share of a common burden.

One may question whether the burden itself is necessary or desirable; one may admit that it is both necessary and desirable, and even that it ought to be shared by all; one may still question whether it is right to impose it by coercion. One may agree that in general it is right, yet object to certain ways in which coercion is enforced. One may merely object to some of the secondary consequences of accepting the practice, and wish to suggest ways of avoiding them. To raise issues of this sort is to leave the confines of the common obligation argument and to enter the broader fields of public policy and individual freedom that have concerned those who have had to define the attitude of the law to the practice.

There are two final points to be made against the common obligation argument. It is not merely that it does not attempt to cover a number of important issues germane to the problem; it also says nothing about the use of the exclusion sanction to secure the obedience of existing members. It is concerned with justifying action taken to force men into the union; it is not concerned with justifying the rules and penalties unions operate to ensure group discipline. This is a problem which the courts have been concerned with, and they have defined the limits of legally justifiable expulsion from a union operating a closed shop. Finally, the common obligation argument also fails to consider another use of the exclusion sanction —that directed against non-members when the pre-entry shop is used to effect entry control. The common obligation argument states why trade unionists feel they are justified in threatening workers with exclusion unless they agree to join the union; it does not say why they feel justified in refusing to admit those who *are* willing to join. Once again the law has had to consider issues of this sort.

One concludes that the common obligation argument cannot be accepted as in any sense a complete or satisfactory defence of the closed shop. Based upon a natural enough feeling of resentment it fails to deal with many relevant questions, and falls back upon a misleading use of analogy when challenged. Yet it will be suggested, at the conclusion of this work, that when supplemented and modified by other arguments and considerations the argument itself need not be entirely left out of account. There is a germ of truth in the notion of the common obligation argument, but in the form advanced by most trade unionists it cannot form the basis of an acceptable justification for the closed shop.

CHAPTER 8

THE RIGHT TO EXCLUDE NON-MEMBERS FROM THE JOB

TO explain, criticize and evaluate the existing legal position of the closed shop it is necessary to distinguish between a number of issues. A distinction must first be made between the right to exclude non-members, and the right to exclude ex-members, who have been expelled from the union. The legal position of these two groups is not the same and they must be explained separately before it is possible to consider criticisms of the present position, and proposals for reform. This chapter is therefore solely concerned with the removal of restrictions on the right to exclude non-members from the job. The following chapter deals with the position of ex-members, and subsequent chapters consider suggestions for a reform of the present position in respect of both groups.

This chapter is divided into three sections. The first deals with the removal of criminal liability; the second concerns civil liability; and a final section summarizes the existing position and the assumptions on which it is based.

(1) THE REMOVAL OF CRIMINAL LIABILITY

(a) Legal Justifiability

The activities of British unions have had to pass a series of legal tests which it is convenient to consider under three heads. First, although the purpose of unions is generally considered to consist in 'maintaining and improving the conditions of their (members) working lives'[1] they pursue this purpose via a number of proximate objectives, or devices. Between 1800 and 1824 combination for any purpose or objective was illegal, but for the most part the law has objected to combination for more specific purposes—e.g. to oppose machinery, restrict numbers, and so on. One such illegal objective has been the aim of excluding non-members from the job. Secondly, objection has been taken to certain customary methods of pursuing union objectives. Again between 1800 and 1824 the method of the

---

[1] The History of Trade Unionism, *op. cit.*, p. 1.

strike, whatever its purpose, was illegal, but for the most part objection has been taken to one or another of the ancillary activities involved in strikes; i.e. the issuing of threats, the bribing of blacklegs, the persuasion of others to strike, and other activities loosely described as picketing. Finally, it may be lawful to pursue certain objectives using particular methods, unless this results in particular consequences, e.g. a breach of the strikers' contract of employment. One such consequence has been the cancellation of a non-members' contract of employment as a result of union pressure.

Before a form of union activity is legally justifiable it must have escaped liability on all three counts: the objective itself, the methods used to effect it, and the consequences of using such methods in a particular case must all be perfectly lawful. The forms that legal liability take are two: the one criminal, the other civil. The main object of this section is to outline the arguments and statutes which led to the removal of criminal liability from the closed shop. Because this process was intimately bound up with the general removal of criminal liability from union activities, and because it is another object of this chapter to provide material for a discussion of the wider issues involved, this account will not be confined to the narrow issue of the closed shop itself. Nonetheless, other matters are only introduced in so far as they are relevant to this central theme.

(b) The Royal Commission of 1867

From the earliest combination acts, and the statutes regulating wages and conditions which they accompanied, the courts were able to penalize combinations aimed at circumnavigating such legislation. Attempts to exclude non-unionists, alleged to be so motivated, could be struck at as a criminal conspiracy. In 1824 and 1825 existing legislation was repealed and in 1825 a statute passed which expressly legalized combinations for limited purposes. The intention was to allow common law liability to continue to operate against combinations and agreements not expressly legalized by the Act. As a result it was thought, in 1867, that the closed shop sanctions were illegal. Together with other union objectives it was actionable as a conspiracy in restraint of trade.[1]

---

[1] This was the opinion of the legislature when passing the 1825 Act, and there were common law dicta to that effect based on the case of R. v. Starling (1665), 1 Sid. 174. In fact this view was subsequently challenged in R. v. Stainer (1870), L.R.I.C.C.R. 230 and 'authoritatively disproved' in the case of the Mogul S.S. Co. v. McGregor, Gow and Co. ((1892), A.C. 25). See R. W. Hedges and A. Winterbottom, The Legal History of Trade Unionism, 1930, Longmans Green, Chap. 5.

This was the position when the issue of trade unions and the law was considered by the Royal Commission on Trade Unions.

(c) The Reforms Proposed by the Majority Report

The majority report of the Commission had three main objectives: to grant legal protection to unions whose objectives were approved of; to ensure that other unions with other objects were still liable; to create a framework of laws which induced or compelled unions to function as voluntary associations—in the sense in which that phrase was understood by the commissioners. Although the arguments of the majority report and their recommendations were partly superseded by the third dissenting or minority report, they constitute a classic statement of the extreme case against the closed shop and are therefore of importance to this study.

On the general right to combine the commissioners argued 'providing the combination to be perfectly voluntary and that full liberty be left to all other workmen to undertake the work which the parties combining have refused, and that no obstruction be placed in the way of the employer resorting elsewhere in search of a supply of labour, there is no ground of justice or of policy for withholding such a right to workmen'.[1] Indeed, since bargains over wages and conditions result from a struggle in which the employer has the advantage that he can more easily afford to hold out, workmen need some compensating advantage and 'it is to redress this inequality that the power of combining is justified by the promotion of trade unions'.[2] But 'upon the same principle' special care should be taken to ensure that equal rights are secured by those workmen who desire to keep out of the combinations. Indeed, 'it is the more important that the law should protect the non-unionist workman in his right freely to dispose of his labour as he thinks fit, because standing alone, he is the less able to protect himself'. Thus the law must recognize the right of the individual labourer to dispose of his labour, and the right of the employer to dispose of his productive powers, for,

the interest of the public will be best consulted by allowing each of these parties to do what he thinks best for himself without further interest of the law than may be necessary to protect the rights of others.[3]

[1] *Eleventh and Final Report of the Royal Commission on Trade Unions*, H.M.S.O., 1869, Vol. 1, p. xx.   [2] *Ibid.*   [3] *Op. cit.*, p. xxi.

The general principle enunciated here may be termed that of collective protection through voluntarism. Workmen may combine to advance their trading interests, but not to coerce others to combine with them, or to use their power to deny employers the right to do without them. Such action transgresses the non-joiner or employer's right to advance *his* interest in the way *he* thinks fit.

From this formula virtually all the detailed recommendations of the majority report are derived. Unions should not be regarded as unlawful, because their objects may be regarded as in restraint of trade; provided that unionists are still liable to be sued in respect of any damage they cause, union agreements are not legally binding, and nothing is done to make lawful 'any combination to refuse work with any particular person, with intent to prevent the employment of such person'.[1] Similarly, when proposing registration facilities which would afford unions protection for their funds, the commissioners argued that the privileges of registration should be denied to unions seeking to limit apprentices, prevent the introduction of machinery, engage in sympathetic strikes or try,

To prevent any workman from taking a sub-contract, or working by the piece, or working in common with men not members of the union.[2]

These provisions were the incentives with which the majority wished to supplement the penalties they saw operating through the existing picketing laws, common law liability for damages, and proposals for a statutory specification of the continued illegality of combinations whose purpose it was to prevent the employment of particular persons. Both incentives and penalties aimed at enforcing a pattern of behaviour on trade unions—rigid voluntarism. Only while they remained within this pattern would they be given legal encouragement and freedom from liability. The argument that only narrowly defined and non-coercive union activity is justified did not end with the publication of the majority report. But it is arguable that if one takes into account the draft report of James Booth, which accompanied the majority's findings, the crucial issues involved have never been more clearly expressed.

In Booth's report the majority's economic objections to the closed shop and other coercive activities were developed. Such practices forced up costs, caused capital to leave the trade, and markets to be lost abroad. Also, they restricted the efforts of the more productive

---

[1] *Op. cit.*, p. xxiii.   [2] *Op. cit.*, p. xxiv.

and hardworking men—many of whom had been forced to submit to them via the closed shop threat. In the end they would lead to a decline in the level of employment. Booth even dealt with the assertion that economically the trade unionist left at work was better off under the union's cramping rules than he would be driving his own bargain. The supporters of this argument, he wrote, assumed that the supremacy of competition required permanently low wages. But even if this were true, it was better that 'the masses should get low wages than that they should starve'. For profits could not be made without relatively cheap labour; short hours and high wages, if pushed far enough, could only end 'in the impoverishment and ultimately the ruin of the great mass of the people'.[1]

Taken together these two reports constitute the nub of the extreme case against the closed shop. It has two aspects, one libertarian and one economic. The practice is condemned, along with other examples of what Booth called 'the tyranny of Labour' in that it interferes with the freedom of the individual worker and employer. It also assists both directly and indirectly in the enforcement of other coercive devices, which have various economic ill-effects. Such activities may add temporarily to the economic welfare of those who employ them, but they cannot hope to add permanently to the welfare of any group. If persisted in they seriously affect the welfare of all. It follows that unions who undertake such activities may be justifiably penalized.

The Webbs called the majority report 'inconclusive and somewhat inconsistent', because while of the opinion that 'combination could be of no value to workmen' it 'nevertheless recommended the legalization of unions under certain conditions'.[2] This is not quite fair. The majority argued that combination was necessary to match employer bargaining power; but they did not want unions to attain so much power that they were able to 'tyrannize' both employers and workers who stood out against them. This is not to say that the argument they advanced was not capable of serious criticism as was shown in the minority report of Harrison, Hughes and Lichfield.

(d) The Argument of the Minority Report

The report itself was a short document, merely summarizing the detailed statement drafted by Harrison and appended to it. It opposed a legal framework of inducements and penalties to delimit

---

[1] *Op. cit.*, p. cx.   [2] *History of Trade Unions, op. cit.*, p. 269.

the scope of justifiable union activity, suggesting that there was no case for special laws relating to the employment of labour and personal molestation by workmen during a trade dispute. It suggested setting aside the effects of common law liability for conspiracy and a declaration making it lawful for unions to negotiate agreements,

with respect to the persons by whom, or the mode in which any work is to be done or is not to be done, and with respect to any terms or conditions under which any work or employment may or may not be carried on.[1]

Thus, to the majority's declaration in favour of voluntarism, the minority opposed the suggestion that the disputed practices, including the closed shop, should be legalized. To the libertarian arguments of the majority Harrison replied that workmen had a right to agree among themselves the terms on which they would work, so long as they did not break the ordinary laws of the country. Workers needed to combine to match employer power—so much was conceded by the majority—but existing conspiracy laws and limitations on picketing struck disproportionately at the base of union strength. The penalties of the 1825 Act relating to threats, intimidation, and so on, not only ensured that acts were unlawful which would be quite legal in other circumstances, they applied sanctions which, in practice, only restricted trade unions. Employers could circulate black-lists, coerce buyers, threaten tenants with eviction, and so on, but if unions sought to coerce non-unionists they were legally liable. In practice, they argued, the state did not attempt to suppress the restrictive activities of employers; only the legal restrictions effectively limiting the coercive activities of unions remained. This was unfair and anomalous. No logical distinction could be made between justifiable attempts to raise wages, lower hours, and so on, as against unjustifiable attempts to exclude obnoxious foremen, or non-unionists, or to change a works rule. In one sense all acts of individuals, and all concerted acts, 'interfere and put pressure on others'.[2] The mill-owner who closes his mill puts pressure on workmen; a group of owners who do likewise put pressure on a town. In these and countless other ways acts producing harm, and performed with that intent, were tolerated by law and opinion; indeed, it was often argued that it was as a result of this process that wealth was accumulated via the working of the market mechanism. Why, then, regard the introduction of a new machine beggaring

---

[1] *Op. cit.*, p. xxx.   [2] *Op. cit.*, p. lxii.

thousands as 'meritorious' and the workman's use of union power as criminal? Why, when workmen in the pursuit of their trading interest cause harm, did 'opinion and law in their present form take alarm'?

The report concluded that there were no justifiable grounds for penalizing one group rather than the other. All attempts to draw a line between the justifiable activities of voluntarism and the un- justifiable coercive practices of unions were arbitrary and unfair. There was,

no logical halting place between the old system of compulsion and that of entire freedom.[1]

To speak of 'not interfering with the rights of others' was to use 'language too vague to be effectual, in which there lurks a serious fallacy'.[2]

Having considered the libertarian aspects of the majority case Harrison dealt with Booth's economic arguments. Considering the economic consequences of the closed shop and related coercive practices he made use of four arguments. First, most of the practices complained of, including the closed shop, output limitations, and opposition to the introduction of machinery, were discredited and dying out. Second, even where they existed, they were usually mere defensive actions against attempts of employers to launch attacks on union standards. Third, other groups resorted to them as well—i.e. the professions.[3] Fourth, in any case, since they advanced the interests of those involved this in itself was a justification.

The last point seems to be the most fundamental. If it could be shown that the closed shop added to union power, and that unions ought to be free to advance their interests more or less irrespective of the effects of this on other groups, then it would not be necessary to show that the practices complained of were unimportant, or a mere defence mechanism. It would not even be necessary to prove that other groups were as guilty.

At times the minority report came near to implying just this. They proclaimed that unions had the right to use any weapons needed to match employer power, so long as they did not commit crimes of violence, etc. But in this part of their report they seem less sure of their ground. They go out of their way to try to minimize

---

[1] Op. cit., p. lxi.　　　[2] Ibid.
[3] As Chapter 2 shows, in respect of the closed shop there is truth in this assertion (see p. 75 above).

the extent and importance of the disputed practices, and in particular they dismiss the closed shop as a waning phenomenon which will gradually disappear. There could be three reasons for this. It may be that they did not appreciate how far the closed shop actually assists union power, or they may have thought it advisable to minimize its importance. Alternatively (and there is no reason to suppose that the commissioners must have been motivated by only one of these reasons) they may have been doubtful themselves of the complete justifiability of the practice, as it then operated, and so have tended, understandably, to accept too readily the view that it was on the wane.

(e) Voluntary versus Non-Voluntary Trade Union Regulation: the terms of the closed shop debate

It is now possible to summarize the issues dividing the two groups on the Commission. Both agreed that the weak bargaining position of workmen justified the right to combine; both agreed that even within the existing pattern of liability unions indulged in coercive action which restricted the liberty of others and might be economically restrictive. The majority argued that on grounds of public policy, and to protect the rights of non-members and employers, activity beyond the confines of voluntarism must be penalized. The minority replied that this would lead to unfair and unjustifiable restrictions on union power. They suggested the removal of legal liability from all customary union activities. The only liability they would accept was based upon a narrow interpretation of individual rights which allowed unionists to be prosecuted for a number of what might be termed 'non-trading offences'—i.e. offering violence, and so on.[1] It is worth making three brief comments on these two positions.

Firstly, much of the argument rests on partly unresolvable or highly disputable issues. For example, both agree that labour has the right to combine to match employer power, but disagree about what constitutes parity. The minority consider that the illogical restrictions imposed in the name of voluntarism will not allow unions to develop a sufficient parity of power; the majority clearly fear the consequences of such widespread freedom, partly because, in their opinion, sufficient parity is attainable without it. It is not easy to

---

[1] In fact neither group really considered questions of civil liability, but this seems a fair enough interpretation of the general degree of immunity which the minority were claiming for trade unions.

see how to settle a question of this sort, or what is the nature of the evidence required. Because of this it is possible to accept what might be termed the *matching power* argument in justification of union action without necessarily agreeing about the degree of legal immunity required.

But the area of dispute is wider than this. Most of the economic arguments involved are almost as difficult to resolve. It would be tempting to assert that this was due to the primitive state of economic analysis at the time, if one could believe that there had emerged, since the report, a generally accepted account of the economic effects of the various forms of union activity discussed.[1] But if there are difficulties in settling such relatively factual issues, it is even more difficult to settle debates which involve matters of individual liberty and civil rights—yet these are clearly in dispute.

Who is to decide what rights the minority have to arrange their terms of employment, and how far the majority is justified in circumscribing these rights in what it assumes to be its own interest? Who is to say where the rights of the worker, intent on advancing his trading interests, conflict with the right of the employer to manage his business as he thinks fit? And what of the rights of the public in all this—how are these to be interpreted, and who is to prescribe them? The Commissioners were adept in advancing arguments in support of their own interpretation of these issues, but it was hardly to be expected that they would arrive at universally acceptable solutions. No final and generally acceptable solution is possible in issues of this sort; it is, by its very nature, a debate which continues.

Secondly, it is possible to assess the general logic of the position adopted by the two sides. The majority were right to stress the unsatisfactory nature of the distinction which the minority sought to draw between the so-called uniquely coercive activities of unions and those which were in some way 'voluntary'. As the Webbs pointed out:

There is a certain sense in which every regulation, whether imposed by law or public custom, laid down by the employer or insisted upon by the trade union, may be said to restrict entrance to an occupation. It is inherent in any rule that its enforcement incidentally excludes those who, for one reason or another, cannot or will not conform to it.[2]

Moreover, as they also saw, it is the intention of unions that this should be so. If unions manage, unilaterally or bilaterally, to regulate

---

[1] See Chap. 10 below at p. 236.   [2] *Industrial Democracy, op. cit.*, p. 704.

the terms of their members' employment they almost invariably insist that their regulations are adopted as 'common rules' in the trade, and imposed on unionist and non-unionist alike. In addition they use the strike weapon to advance union objectives, and this is by its nature a coercive weapon affecting not only non-unionists and employers but the public at large. It is therefore not possible to argue that there is a sphere of voluntary regulation, clearly and uniquely divided from the so-called coercive activities of unions. What is at issue are two things: first, should unions be allowed to use coercion at all; second, is there *any* valid distinction to be drawn between one use of coercion or another. The first question must be answered in the affirmative unless one is to outlaw collective regulation in any form. The second received a rather peculiar answer from the Webbs themselves, which is worth considering at this point.

Curiously enough, the Webbs, while realizing the illogicality of much of the majority's argument, sought to show that there was something in their fears concerning the economic effects of one union objective—entry control via the closed shop. They accepted that if the device were the *only* means by which wages could be maintained at anything above subsistence level it would be preferable to 'perfect competition' because

it has the economic advantage of fencing-off particular families, grades, or classes from the general degradation, and thus preserving to the community, in these privileged groups, a store of industrial relations, a high level of specialized skill, and a degree of physical health and general intelligence unattainable at a bare subsistence wage.[1]

But they also argued that it 'lowers the level of productive efficiency all round' by causing a misuse of resources, a restriction of production and a raising of costs. Yet the same may surely be the case with any other object of union regulation. As Booth argued, wages may be forced up to a point where markets are lost. Lower hours or other conditions imposed by unions may deplete production and profit and affect the competitive position of the industry—indeed, arguments of this sort are proverbial in the armoury of employers.[2]

The Webbs thought this unlikely in respect of wage regulation because they believed the stimulus of high wages lead employers

---

[1] *Industrial Democracy, op. cit.*, p. 712.

[2] e.g. the Shipbuilding and Engineering employers, who have used exactly these arguments to explain why they could not agree to the union's demands, before each one of the post-war Courts of Inquiry into wage disputes in these industries. (See *Court of Inquiry Reports*, H.M.S.O., 1948, 1954, and 1957.)

to concentrate more on efficiency.[1] But this is to say that the union's job is to raise obstacles and the employer's job to overcome them. Unions provide the stimulus and employers the initiative making for industrial innovation and efficiency. If this is so with regard to wages why is it not so with regard to other union demands? If the efficient employer is stimulated by additions to his wage bill, or reductions in hours, why is he not stimulated by the fact that unions restrict entry via the closed shop? Given that all successful union demands may add to an employer's costs, or lower his immediate level of efficiency, why should it be assumed that the compensating influence of employer stimulus will only work with wages? In fact, it is obvious that *any* union demand may, in any particular case, either stimulate or depress any particular employer. What is difficult to establish, in advance, is why it is *of necessity* bound to do one or the other.

It may of course be argued, as the Webbs went on to assert, that if the stimulus effect of a wage rise does not produce sufficient increase in efficiency prices, prices will rise, demand will decline, and fewer union members will be needed. Consequently, unions will see that wages must be lowered, and in any case will not be able to prevent this. One objection to this argument is, of course, that in practice this 'self-regulating mechanism' gets stuck; but there is a more obvious *a priori* objection, when the argument is used to demonstrate the relative harmlessness of union regulation of wages. It acquires plausibility because it is assumed that the real cost of labour is forced up, causing a rise in costs and a fall in demand. But *all* interferences in managerial functions, such as restrictions on machinery utilization, and the insistence on skill gaps, may result in rising real labour costs. This, after all, is the nub of the case against them. If it is assumed that a self regulatory mechanism motivated by a rise in real labour costs *prevents* wages being forced up to the point where they damage competitive power, this *should* happen with other equally deleterious regulations. Unions ought to perceive their disadvantages too, and if they do not the consequent weakening of their power *vis-à-vis* the employer will make it possible for employers to insist on the abandonment of such practices. But it is assumed that restrictions like entry-control *can* be maintained without touching off the self regulatory mechanism, then why should this not be the case in respect of other subjects of union regulation?

---

[1] An argument still used by unions and pro-Labour economists. See Chap. 10.

In fact, as recent investigations into the effects of union regulations show, it is exceedingly difficult, in general and in the abstract, to decide what are the economic effects of particular union devices, including the closed shop's entry control functions.[1] Employers may find it easier to overcome the effects of a wage rise by introducing new methods, if they are not restricted in other ways, but this is not the point; the point is that *all* union regulation may, in some instances, result in a rise in costs and this may or may not have effects on the prosperity of the industry. Just as we cannot draw a line between the objects of union regulation on coercive and non-coercive grounds, so no absolute distinction can be made in terms of relative economic harmlessness.

But if there is doubt about the validity of the line drawn by the majority commission does it follow that, in the absence of satisfactory evidence of the total amount of coercion and economic damage caused by one form of union regulation or another, unions should be given the benefit of the doubt and all forms of union activity legalized?

One argument in favour of this is that in practice the line suggested is disproportionately disadvantageous to certain groups. As has been seen, the methods of job regulation adopted by a group are largely a function of the problems they face. Civil service groups do not need the strike weapon; other groups have no need for entry-control, and even those who demand the post-entry closed shop do not all need it to the same extent. Any general ban on particular union objectives, such as the closed shop, does not weaken union power to the same extent everywhere; it tends to bear most heavily on those groups who can least afford to do without the device.[2] If for no other reason, the illogical distinction of the majority report seems unfair, and to that extent unjustifiable.

Yet even the minority were concerned about the possible effects of unlimited legalization, and it is arguable that while there is no case for outlawing, by general fiat, a whole range of union objectives in the way suggested, there may be a case for circumscribing the limits of legal immunity in a less drastic way. This was the view

---

[1] See, for example, F. Zweig, *Productivity and Trade Unions*, Blackwells, 1951; J. R. Parkinson, *The Economics of Ship-building*, C.U.P., 1960; *Royal Commission on the Press*, 1961–62, H.M.S.O., Cmnd. 1811.

[2] i.e. seamen, musicians, distributive workers, etc.

taken by the courts in the field of civil liability after 1867. Their activities in this respect are considered in the next section.[1]

One third and final comment should be made at this point. It must not be assumed that there was nothing behind the distinctions drawn by the majority. Most of the disputed activities were, for the most part, upheld by unilateral regulation, and it has often seemed plausible to suggest that there is something particularly unjustifiable about this. But, as has been said, the continued importance of unilateral methods, particularly when related to the closed shop, can be an index of union weakness rather than strength. The really strong union is able to sign an agreement on such things, or at least gain a tacit acceptance from employers. Compulsion of the individual does not cease when this happens; it becomes more effective. The extent to which a job is unilaterally regulated depends on a host of factors: tradition, personal predilection, and so on. The assumption that unilateral regulations are especially coercive, or even economically costly, seems to depend on no stronger assumption than that bilateral regulations are necessarily the result of a good-humoured and mutually satisfactory compromise. It is assumed that every collective agreement results from a draw and not a surrender. Even if this were so the difference is one which does not affect employees; from their viewpoint it is immaterial whether union objectives are upheld by means of a threatened strike or the signature of the employer to an agreement. If anything, the latter is more effective.

But whether upheld unilaterally or bilaterally the closed shop is in some ways a unique objective of union regulation representing an attempt to widen the frontiers of union control. Its entry control function may enable those on the job to wield an absolute veto over entrance in their own interests. The closed shop is not the only way of securing entry control, and the absence of entry control by the union is not an absence of control but regulation solely by the employer. Yet in practice entry control via the closed shop may add an additional contingency not previously operating on the applicant. To the list of conditions laid down by the employer, partly the result of union regulation, there is added the additional condition of obtaining entry to or selection by the union. When this is used, to accord an absolute preference to existing members,

[1] It can also be argued that while it is unfair to outlaw the closed shop by general *fiat*, there is a case for investigating particular complaints against its actual effects in specific industries. Suggestions of this sort are considered in Chap. 10.

O

or a total restriction on entry to the non-apprenticed, obviously
there is more involved than a mere transference of regulatory
authority. A situation arises in which, in the Webbs' words, there
is a

direct exclusion of specified classes of persons, whether they conform or not, by
regulations totally prohibiting their entrance.[1]

There is also the effect of the disciplinary function. All union
regulations are potentially coercive, but most of them are more or
less directly related to specific work conditions. Where there is a
closed shop the contents of the union rule book are added to the
workplace regulations, since exclusion from the job may follow if
any union rule or order is infringed. Union rules are only marginally
concerned with workplace practices; they mainly concern two other
issues: (1) the payment of dues; (2) enforcing strike action and loyalty
to union leadership. Thus, while the closed shop is not uniquely
coercive, it does result in a widening of the range of coercion by
adding to the effective conditions of employment. Both the exclusion of entire classes of worker, and the widening of the range of
compulsion may be defended on the general grounds that they help
to advance the interests of the group by making it more able to match
employer power, but, as has been seen, this is only apt to settle the
argument only for those who do not object to such practices in the
first place. The conclusion is that while the distinction between
unjustifiable and justifiable practices advanced by the majority
cannot be defended as it stands, the conclusions of the minority do
not follow unreservedly and may be open to objection on a number
of grounds. These matters will be raised later in this study. At the
moment it is necessary to state the results of the Royal Commission,
and the developments which followed.

(f) The Results of the Royal Commission

The Trade Union Act of 1871[2] was passed as a result of the Royal
Commission and instituted a system of voluntary registration, which
conferred on unions a special legal status. It was made clear that
members would not be liable for criminal conspiracy because their
objectives were in unlawful restraint of trade. Agreements or trusts
of trade unions were made legal and valid, but limitations were
placed on the extent of civil legality. So far the legislation arising

---

[1] *Industrial Democracy, op. cit.*, p. 705.   [2] 34 & 35 Vict., *c.* 31.

which is anomalous in more than one respect'.[1] Yet the Lord Chancellor denied the validity of drawing a distinction between an act of this sort when done by one man or by a number of men. He argued that it would be a most peculiar position if Allen were to be deemed not liable simply because he had shown that he had acted alone and without the approval of the chairman and secretary of the boilermakers' union.

There are obviously important differences of interpretation here, echoing the contrasting views of the minority and majority reports. On one hand it is argued that there is a right to employ one's labour as one wishes, and interference in such a right requires justification. Defence of legitimate trading interests may count as such a justification. On the other hand, it is said that motive is irrelevant; it can neither waive liability nor serve as its root. What matters is whether the law recognizes such a right. The implication is that it does not. On the contrary one judge puts forward the right of others to decide 'where and with whom they should work'. On the relevancy of combination there is also division of opinion. Some imply that the irrelevance of motive to a case of this sort does not affect the issue of conspiracy; but one judge denies that the absence of combination alters the case in question.

There seems no reason to wonder at the subsequent debate which arose as to what was settled by this case. At the moment, however, it was interpreted as implying the legality of excluding non-members even when combination could be proved. This was maintained by Mr. Justice Darling in the case of Huttley v. Simmons.[2]

Quinn v. Leatham

In this case an action was brought against trade unionists for wrongful interference in the plaintiff's business. The defendants, members of an Irish butchers' union, refused to work with non-members and upon meat supplied by firms employing non-members. In conformity with these customs they demanded the discharge of the non-unionists in the plaintiff's employ. He refused, and offered, instead, to 'pay all fines, debts, and demands against them'. He also asked the union to admit them. The defendants replied that this was no longer acceptable. The men must be forced 'to walk the

---

[1] Ibid., p. 124.
[2] (1897) 14 T.L.R. 150. In this connection the judge also quoted an Irish case (Kearney v. Lloyd (1890), L.R. Ir. 268), in which it was held that civil conspiracy could only lie when the act complained of would have been actionable without combination.

streets for twelve months', presumably as a punishment for refusing to join the union earlier. When the plaintiff refused the defendants approached one of his customers and asked him to cease buying from the plaintiff until the men were discharged. The customer refused and was threatened with a strike of union members in *his* employ. At this point the customer gave way. The defendants also circulated black lists which resulted in the loss of another customer to the plaintiff. They also induced one of the plaintiff's employees to leave, in breach of his contract of employment. The plaintiff thereupon brought an action for malicious conspiracy to procure breaches of contract and to coerce his employees to leave him. The lower courts found for the plaintiff and the defendants appealed to the Lords. By a unanimous decision the House of Lords dismissed the appeal. In doing so they substantially undermined the protection which appeared to be afforded to the closed shop by Allen *v.* Flood, and set aside the application of that judgment in the case of Huttley *v.* Simmons.

Giving judgment the Lord Chancellor said that since the plaintiffs had satisfied the jury that the defendants had conspired maliciously to injure them they must be granted a remedy or 'it could hardly be said that our jurisprudence was that of a civilized community'.[1] Moreover, he added, before Allen *v.* Flood no one would have doubted that liability would lie. But, he continued, a case must only be regarded as an 'authority for what it actually decides', and not necessarily for a 'proposition that may seem to follow logically from it'. In the Allen case the court had assumed that no unlawful threats had been made, and 'that there was no case of conspiracy or even combination'.[2] Quinn *v.* Leathem was different. Here there were both unlawful threats *and* conspiracy, 'so that loss of business and interference with the plaintiff's legal rights are abundantly proved'.

As N. A. Citrine says

This decision had the effect of making one law for the individual and another for a combination of individuals. It rendered illegal any combination to effect any purpose which a Court considered 'unjustifiable' or not in pursuit of the legitimate interests of those combining.[3]

The result is that the issue of whether combination can be proved is relevant to the degree of liability involved in enforcing a closed shop.

[1] (1901) A.C. 506.   [2] L.R. p. 507.   [3] Citrine, *op. cit.*, p. 16.

A combination to act so as to injure another is a conspiracy, and as such illegal unless the motive is one which the court will accept. Since, in practice, closed shop demands are usually the result of collective action the issue of the motive presumed to inspire them is crucial to their position in common law. In the Quinn case it was assumed that the motive was malice. Yet it may be argued that, as one writer has put it, the court, in considering the defendants' motives

took as clear evidence that their sole purpose was revenge against the non-union men, through injury to the plaintiff, the defendants' refusal of the plaintiffs' offer to pay all fines and dues if they would admit the non-union men. Yet if, as seems clear, they had, up to the point of declining to admit the non-unionists, a legitimate trade interest in their indirect measures of pressure on Leathem by pressure on Munce—a just cause an excuse in Bowen's concept—how can it be said that the interest stopped there? It might be most harmful to union bargaining power to let it be known that non-unionists could always, after years of non-membership, get all the advantages of membership *ex post facto* by paying fines and dues. Correct and just or not, that would certainly be a view the defendants might have taken without any desire as such.[1]

Moreover, as the writer does not appear to have noticed, the trading defence was accepted in the Mogul case, although in that case too an application to join the association was refused. It was one of the major objects of the combination to keep outsiders from enjoying the benefits made possible by collective action. Indeed, it is worth noting that even in Allen's case there was no question of allowing the shipwrights to join the boilermakers' union; what was in dispute, and what is involved in the full legal justification of the closed shop, is the right to exclude non-members—not the narrower right to exclude only those who refuse to become members. No doubt this is the major cause of exclusions, but in its pre-entry form the closed shop requires the wider form of immunity. At any rate, it is necessary to remember that in each of these three cases there was no question of allowing the defendants into the association, and so it is a little difficult to ground liability in one of them on the presumed existence of motive proved by reference to this fact.

There followed a whole series of cases decided against trade unions on similar grounds, many of which involved attempts to uphold or enforce the closed shop. Moreover, between the years 1901–6 other cases were decided in which the trading interest defence was successfully pleaded by employers.[2] After 1901 the growing

---

[1] *The Province and Function of Law*, by Julius Stone, Stevens, 1947, p. 617.
[2] For a summary of the more important cases of this period see G. R. Askwith's evidence to the Royal Commission on Trade Disputes and Trade Combinations, Minutes of Evidence, H.M.S.O., London, 1906, Cmd. 2826, pp. 1–57.

vulnerability of trade unions to legal action was made much more punitive as a result of the Taff Vale case,[1] and in 1903 another Royal Commission sat to consider the legal position of the unions. In an extremely thorough and balanced account of developments since 1871, which he gave before that body, G. R. Askwith, then official arbitrator for the Board of Trade, referred to the conflicting spate of dicta which could be extracted from these cases as follows:

if the actual decisions of these cases alone are taken, possibly some general rules may be deduced from them. If the decisions and the *obiter dicta* are all to be taken together as making the law, there cannot be much doubt that there is much entanglement which must be a great difficulty for even a clever man after study to attempt to work out.[2]

Askwith argued that despite the Mogul decision indicating that combinations to defend trading interests were not liable for a civil action for damages, the law had taken the view that combinations to prevent others from working were liable. Despite Lord Watson's dictum, in Allen v. Flood, that 'The Law of England does not take into account motive as constituting an element of civil wrong', the House of Lords, in Quinn v. Leathem, brought out 'from the armoury of the law, this doctrine of conspiracy', in order to re-establish trade union liability. The position was that though it had been long accepted that both individuals and groups acting in concert were liable for malicious damage, 'Allen v. Flood upset the idea of a malicious wrong being actionable *per se*, or requiring justification, and said that if an act is done in the exercise of a legal right it does not require justification'. As a result the judges, in the Quinn case, 'not having malicious wrong to fall back on, put forward conspiracy to injure, even if, as done by individuals, the acts did not amount to actionable wrongs'. To this end they made use of the ancient doctrine of conspiracy, arguing that additional liability could be rooted in the mere fact of combination. Furthermore, said Askwith, they 'did not define justification' but 'sent the parties to law to find out'.[3] This led to a most unfair situation for,

I think I am right in saying that at any rate I do not remember any single case in which upon the grounds of advancement of the interests of labour the men have won, and there have been a great many cases before the courts. . . .[4]

Indeed, according to some of the dicta expressed, 'If workmen combine to do anything the object of which would be to interfere

[1] Taff Vale Co. *v.* A.S.R.S. (1901) A.C. 426. This case decided that registered unions could be sued as quasi-corporate bodies for the wrongful acts of officers acting within the scope of their authority.
[2] *Op. cit.*, p. 12.   [3] *Op. cit.*, p. 14.   [4] *Op. cit.*, p. 19.

with the employer in regulating his business', this was an act of conspiracy, yet judges had repeatedly asserted that, as Lord Shand had remarked in the Allen case, competition in labour was 'in all essentials analogous to competition in trade, and to which the same principles must apply'.[1]

(b) The 1906 Act and After

The Principles of the Act

After the publication of the Royal Commission's Report the Trade Disputes Act of 1906 was passed. Introducing the Bill the Attorney General said that as a result of judicial action a scope had been put on the law of conspiracy 'so loose and so wide, that it is impossible to indicate beforehand what may be the legal character of the conduct of these organizations'.[2] Legality turned upon the random fact of whether or not combination could be proved. Thus a trade unionist could object to a non-unionist for any reason he wished, while if he combined with others to object he might be liable for damages. This impossible situation could only be remedied, said the Minister, by removing conspiracy as the gist of the offence in all trade disputes. In effect the Attorney General's object was to remove both motive and numbers as considerations determining the legality of normal union action. This was the intention of sections one and three of the Act. As these sections are still important in determining the attitude of the law towards the closed shop, they must be described in detail.

Section one removed the effect of conspiracy liability for trade disputes. Just as the 1875 Act was presumed to have dealt with criminal liability this section removed civil liability unless 'the act done, if done without any such agreement or combination would be actionable'.[3] Section three dealt with the situation which had arisen as a result of a series of cases where unions had been denied the trading interest defence and had been successfully sued for procuring a breach of contract or inducing others not to enter into contracts.[4] The section was deliberately couched in the widest possible terms so as to legalize all the likely consequences expected to

[1] Op. cit., p. 16.
[2] Hansard, H.M.S.O., March 28th, 1906, Col. 1295.
[3] Op. cit., s. 1.
[4] e.g. Bowen v. Hall (1881) 6 Q.B.D. 333; Temperton v. Russell (1893) 1 Q.B. 435.

arise during the prosecution of union objectives by customary methods. It stated that:

An act done by a person in contemplation or furtherance of a trade dispute shall not be actionable on the grounds only that it induces some other person to break a contract of employment or that it is an interference with trade, business, or employment of some other person, or with the right of some other person to dispose of his capital or his labour as he wills.[1]

The presumed effect of this section was that so long as those on strike refrained from striking in breach of their own contracts of employment *no* action could be taken against them.[2] Even if they did strike in breach of their own contracts no action would be entertained against the union officials who may have ordered them out.[3]

Section five contained the all-important definition of what was to count as a trade dispute for the purposes of both the 1875 and 1906 Acts. Once again the intention was to provide as wide a definition as possible. The relevant part of the section reads:

the expression 'trade dispute' means any dispute between employers and workmen, or between workmen and workmen, which is connected with the employment or non-employment, or with the terms of employment, or with the conditions of labour, of any person, and the expression 'workmen' means all persons employed in trade or industry, whether or not in the employment of the employer with whom a trade dispute arises.[4]

The layman might be excused if he concluded, in 1906, that this definition covered every eventuality—as indeed it was meant to do. Certainly it appeared to include disputes concerning the employment or non-employment of workmen who were non-members of the required union. In 1912 this view was confirmed when, in the case of Gaskell *v.* Lancashire and Cheshire Miners Federation,[5] the definition in Section five was held to cover a threatened strike to secure the dismissal of members of another union, causing them to be discharged in breach of their contract of employment. This was

---

[1] *Op. cit.*, s. 3.

[2] Section Two of the Act legalized peaceful persuasion and attendance during trade disputes. Strikers were still liable for such offences as trespass, unlawful obstruction, breaches of the peace, and so on, but in effect the object aimed at was that of the minority report of 1867; there were to be no *special* liabilities directed at trade unionists while engaged in a defence of their trading interests. Indeed, under the act special immunities were conferred on the unions as such. Section Four prohibited all actions for tort against trade unions.

[3] See below for a general description of the way the act has been interpreted since 1906.

[4] *Op. cit.*, s. 5.   [5] (1912) 28 T.L.R. 518.

upheld in the important case of Hodges *v*. Webb,[1] where it was
finally established that a closed shop strike was covered by the 1906
Act. Finally, in White *v*. Riley, an action for conspiracy to injure
in a closed shop case was dismissed not merely by reference to the
1906 Act, but also by reference to the common law doctrine of
action in defence of trading interests. For this reason White *v*. Riley
is a leading case, and needs to be examined in more detail.

Common Law Acceptance of the Closed Shop

As in the Gaskell case, in White *v*. Riley the defendant was a
member of a union—but not of the necessary sort. He was prepared
to become a member of the specified union if he could remain a
member of his own union as well.[2] The Master of the Rolls said he
could find no evidence of personal feelings. If the workmen 'had
been influenced by bad motives towards the respondents', he said,
'then according to the law which has been generally accepted by
the courts below, they would each and all of them have incurred
responsibility'. In fact, they had 'merely followed the course which
they thought would be most conducive to their own interests'.
Thus 'it was unnecessary to decide whether there was any dispute
between employers and workmen within the meaning of the act'.

With White *v*. Riley the balance of common law impartiality
was restored. The defence which was acceptable in the Mogul case,
but unacceptable in Quinn *v*. Leathem, was again accepted. Three
years later this decision was upheld in another important closed shop
case—Reynolds *v*. the Shipping Federation.[3] This concerned a
closed shop agreement, arrived at between the Shipping Federation
and the Sailors' and Firemen's Union.[4] Reynolds, an ex-member of
the union, obtained a provisional berth, but was afterwards informed
that because of the pre-entry closed shop agreement he must rejoin
the union and pay his arrears. He refused: his provisional engagement was cancelled, and he brought an action for malicious conspiracy. Counsel argued that while it was established that workmen
could leave an employer engaging non-unionists, it had not been

---

[1] (1920) 2 Ch. 70. In the case of Valentine *v*. Hyde ((1919), 2 Ch. 129) Astbury J. decided
that attempts to exclude non-members by threats of a strike were not 'directly' connected
with the employment or non-employment of any person and thus not covered by the act,
but this decision was criticized in Hodges *v*. Webb and finally over ruled in White *v*. Riley
(1921), 1. Ch. 1).

[2] This was also the case in Valentine *v*. Hyde.

[3] (1924) 1. Ch. 28.   [4] See p. 44 above.

decided that 'an association of employers and trade unionists can combine to agree that the employers belonging to the association will not employ men who do not belong to the union'.[1] The defence rested partly on the trading interest plea, and partly on a citation of the 1906 Act.

In dismissing the case the judge relied entirely on common law principles. He claimed that the case could be distinguished from Quinn v. Leathem[2] in 'at least two vital respects'. First, the agreement or combination was not directed at a particular individual, but at 'such individuals as might not from time to time satisfy a qualification which was within the reach of anyone who desired employment'; i.e. it was directed at 'a class and that a class to which anyone at any time might cease to belong'. Second, 'the motive of the exclusion was not a malicious desire to inflict loss on any other individual, or class of individuals, but a desire to advance the business interests of the employers and employees alike'.[3]

The first of these two distinctions is again open to objection. It is true that in this case entry to the union was offered throughout, whereas it was withdrawn at a certain stage in the Quinn case. But, if the judge sought to draw a distinction between Reynolds and Leathem in this respect he was hardly entitled to imply, as he did, that this fact brought the Reynolds' case closer to Mogul. For, as was mentioned, in the latter case there was no question of allowing the excluded trader into the association at any time. The fact that the judge accepted that the defendants were motivated by the need to defend their trading interests in this case is bound to give rise to doubts about the possibility of reconciling the original decision in Quinn v. Leathem with either the Mogul or the Reynolds case. It is difficult not to agree with Professor Kahn-Freund who had written of the compatibility of Mogul and Quinn: 'Much ink has been spilled in an attempt to "reconcile" these two decisions of the House of Lords, but the fact is that they are irreconcilable except in terms of an analysis of "extra-legal" judicial motives.'[4]

Whatever the reason, subsequent decisions have upheld this position. Indeed, in a most important and clarifying case, Crofter Hand

---

[1] Op. cit., p. 31.
[2] And Temperton v. Russell, op. cit., another case of malicious conspiracy, decided against trade unionists.   [3] Op. cit., p. 39.
[4] Kahn-Freund, op. cit., p. 117. Professor Kahn-Freund says of the contrast between the Reynold's case and Quinn: '(this is) . . . a far cry from Quinn v. Leathem, and a symptom of the transformation of judicial attitudes as a result of the First World War'. (Op. cit., p. 118.)

Woven Harris Tweed *v.* Veitch, decided in 1942 by the House of Lords,[1] common law immunity for the closed shop was extended to cover a situation presumed to be not dealt with by the 1906 Act, as it had been interpreted.[2]

In this case producers of yarn on the island of Lewis were approached by officials of the Transport and General Workers' Union and asked for a wage increase and the closed shop. The producers replied that these demands were impossible and a wage-cut more likely because of the 'cut throat' competition of merchants who imported cheap yarn from the mainland. The union then offered to assist in establishing minimum export prices, suggesting joint action against those who would not accept a price agreement. The employers refused, and tried, unsuccessfully, to negotiate an agreement themselves. The union then offered to instruct their members in the docks to refuse to handle the competitors' supplies or products in exchange for a closed shop agreement. The employers agreed and a successful boycott resulted in damage to the competitors who brought an action for malicious conspiracy. The defenders did not plead the 1906 Act, but relied on the trading interest defence.

The House of Lords, in deciding unanimously for the union officials, gave voice to a body of *dicta* as interesting, and in its way as important, as any summarized so far. They argued that the defenders were not liable because their 'predominant' motive was the defence of trading interests. In other words, there might be elements of malice in their motivation, but so long as the overriding motive was not malicious, liability would not lie. Moreover, the trading interests involved did not need to be identical; all that was necessary, according to Lord Wright, was that there should be a 'sufficient identity'. This was provided by the shared concern for the advantage of their union existing between the dockers and the defenders.[3] On the question of what would count as a 'just cause' Lord Maugham stressed that it was not sufficient to show that the predominant or true motive had not been injury. There was no authority to show that combinations causing damage would be justified if the object was 'dislike of the religious views or the politics or the race or the

[1] (1942) A.C. 435.
[2] See below, p. 215, for an account of the judicial interpretation of the 1906 Act.
[3] Whether the identity would be 'sufficient' if those combining had merely been members of the same bargaining confederation, or members of unions affiliated to the T.U.C. was not said. Lord Thankerton did say that the defenders would not be justified in availing themselves of the service of *any* other group—for example those whose only connection with the union was a payment for services rendered.

colour of the plaintiff, or a mere demonstration of power by busy-bodies. Again, the persons joining in the combination may have been induced so to act by payment of money, or by some other consideration'.[1] On the other hand, Lord Wright regarded the trading interest defence itself as merely one of a series of legitimate justifications, though he was not prepared to say what the others were, remarking that this 'must be left for the future to decide'. The Lord Chancellor agreed. He said,

It may well be that in this corner of the law it is not possible to lay down with precision an exact and exhaustive proposition like an algebraic formula which will provide an automatic answer in every case.[2]

Rookes v. Barnard

This review of the changing attitude of the courts would be in-complete without an account of the very recent decision in the case of Rookes v. Barnard.[3]

Rookes, an ex-member of the Draughtsmen's union, was dis-charged as the result of a strike threat made to enforce the closed shop in the design office of the British Overseas Airways Corpora-tion. It was admitted that if the strike had taken place it would have involved a breach of the strikers' contract of employment, for which they would presumably have been liable if the employer had decided to bring an action.[4] However, this action was not brought by B.O.A.C. but by the injured third party—Rookes. He sued the two leading lay officials of the union employed in the design office, and the local full-time official, for damages.

Sachs J. found for the plaintiff[5] by ruling that the defendants had combined to *threaten to break contracts*, which he regarded as an unlawful act constituting the tort of intimidation. Since it was admitted that the acts complained of were done in furtherance of a trade dispute it was also necessary to decide that they were un-protected by sections one and three of the 1906 Trades Disputes Act.

It will be remembered that Section one protects acts done in furtherance of trade disputes unless they would be actionable if done by one person. Sachs J. ruled that the tort of intimidation was such an act. Section three says acts furthering a trade dispute are not

---

[1] A.C., p. 451.   [2] A.C. (1942), p. 446.
[3] (1962) 2 All E.R. 579. At the moment of writing this case is the subject of an appeal to the House of Lords.
[4] See p. 208 above.   [5] (1961) 2 All E.R. 825.

actionable 'only' on the grounds that they constitute inducement to breach of contract, 'or' because they are an interference with the trade, business or employment of another person.[1] Sachs J. decided that, since the acts complained of were unlawful on the additional grounds that they amounted to intimidation, section three afforded no protection.[2]

By unanimously reversing this decision on the grounds that they did, the Court of Appeal have strikingly reaffirmed the protection which both the 1906 Act and the common law has granted to trade unionists pursuing the closed shop since the days of Quinn *v.* Leathem. In doing so they relied mainly on the fact that, as the plaintiffs argued, and as was widely accepted before the judgment of Sachs J. in the lower court,[3] the mere issuing of a threat to strike, which if carried out involves a breach of contract, cannot constitute what Pearson L.J. called the 'obscure, unfamiliar and peculiar' tort of intimidation.[4]

Indeed, they went on to rule that threats to break contracts, and even breaches of contract, cannot form the basis of any action in tort by an injured third party. In fact, the acts complained of, according to Sellers L.J., were all subject to the trading interest defence, since 'The defendants were pursuing trade union interests and not merely seeking to injure the plaintiff'.[5] Moreover, even if this were not so, and an unlawful act had taken place, the protection of the 1906 Act was still available. It protected the full-time official because if the strike had occurred it would have amounted to breach of contract, and this was specifically covered by the first part of section three. Since 'there can be no liability for threats where there would be no liability for doing that which is threatened' there could be no grounds for action.[6] Finally, both Sellers L.J. and Donnovan

---

[1] See p. 208 above for the actual text of the 1906 Act.

[2] It is arguable that the effect of this judgment, if it had been upheld, would be to create the paradoxical situation in which workers, and their officials, were more free to *threaten* strikes that never took place, than they were to strike without warning, and without issuing threats. K. W. Wedderburn, in *The Right to Threaten Strikes* (24 M.L.R., 1961 at p. 578) states: 'If the defendants had struck in breach of contract, and had done no more, presumably they could not have been liable to Rookes, whatever their liabilities to B.O.A.C.' On the other hand, he argues that if it was to be accepted that a threat to break a contract constituted grounds for action by an injured third party, it would be logical (though not desirable) to extend such liability to cover actual breaches, which would conflict with the fundamental doctrine of privity of contract.

[3] See *Wedderburn, op. cit.*

[4] *Op. cit.*, p. 608. He added it 'has its roots in cases of physical violence and threats of violence'.

[5] *Op. cit.*, p. 583.

[6] *Op. cit.*, p. 603. (See also K. W. Wedderburn's second article on this case, which discusses the judgment in the 1962 Court of Appeal—25 M.L.R., 513, (1962).)

P

L.J. maintained that quite apart from the common law position the lay officials were protected by the second part of section three, which covers interference with trade, business and employment.

But perhaps the most significant quotation from this most recent of closed shop cases comes from Sellers L.J. Before announcing that the defendants were all clearly motivated throughout by the desire to defend their legitimate trading interests, he said:

It can be said in justification of the defendants' and the unions' conduct that the plaintiff whilst retaining his employment, and whilst outside the union and avoiding its obligations, would enjoy such benefits as the union could achieve from the employer for its members. This might well not be acceptable to his colleagues.[1]

The argument behind that most deeply felt and instinctive trade union defence for the closed shop—the common obligation argument —could not be put more succinctly by any member of the Genera Council of the T.U.C.

(3) THE PRESENT POSITION AND ITS RATIONALE

(a) The Limits of Existing Immunity

As a result of the series of cases and statutes described in the previous section, it can be said that to-day the closed shop objective may be pursued by customary trade union methods without giving rise to actionable consequences. The reaching of a closed shop agreement, excluding non-members of specified unions, either on a post-entry or pre-entry basis, is neither a statutory or common law crime, nor a ground for action under statute or common law. Any man may refuse to work with another who is not a member of a specified trade union, and may persuade others to do likewise. Any man, or group of men, may threaten to strike if non-members are not removed. Such acts are legal, and would be so if the Act of 1906 were repealed. To obtain a closed shop men may peacefully picket and take part in other customary activities associated with a strike—so long as they do not commit an offence such as trespass, obstruction, violence, disorderly following, watching and besetting, and so on.[2] If they, or their leaders, induce or threaten to cause a

---

[1] Op. cit., p. 583.
[2] It now seems established that the Act of 1875 does not add to the liabilities of unions, as it has been interpreted. In the words of Fletcher Moulton L.J., section 7 (1) & (4) '. . . legalizes nothing, and it renders nothing wrongful that was not so before' (Ward Lock v. O.P.A.S. (1906), 22 T.L.R., p. 329). Furthermore, the common law view of the various forms of crime or tort involved nowadays does not seem to effectively restrict trade union activities such as picketing, etc.

breach of contract, then, as the law now stands, they will be protected against any action in tort, so long as they can show that the
acts complained of are instrumental to the advancing of the closed
shop objective.[1] If no contract is broken or threatened, or if it is but
the defendants do not know of it, they will not be liable even if they
cannot show that they are promoting or furthering a trade dispute
within the interpretation of the Act.

Yet it must be stressed that the progressive extension of common
law immunity granted in recent years has been accompanied by a
narrowing of the general immunity provided under the 1906 Act.
Judicial interpretation has established that before the courts will
accept that the acts apply a number of conditions must be met.
These conditions relate to two main issues: the character of the
dispute and the connection between the dispute and the acts done in
contemplation or furtherance of it. The subject matter of the
dispute must be related to a contract of employment, it must concern
some industrial condition and not relate to a political difference or
personal quarrel.[2] It must be definite and have substance,[3] and the
onus of proving its existence rests on the person alleging it.[4] Acts
done in contemplation or furtherance of the dispute must have a
particular connection with it. Those which aid or encourage one
of the disputants are covered, if done when the dispute is impending
or likely to occur.[5] On the other hand, and most importantly, if the
paramount object is to injure one of the disputants for malicious
reasons then none of the acts done in contemplation or furtherance
of the dispute will be protected by the Act.[6]

By interpreting the Act in this way the courts have managed to
re-assert a measure of their former jurisdiction over the boundaries
of legally justifiable union action. For it is no longer possible to
assert that considerations of motive are irrelevant; the motives in

[1] The continued liability of strikers for a breach of their own contract of employment is
not, in practice, an important liability. An employer who decides to punish, say, the leaders
of repeated lightning strikes to enforce the closed shop does not have to go to law to accomplish
this. Within the factory he has a range of far more effective and immediate sanctions at his
disposal, culminating in the most effective sanction of all: dismissal. The employer who
decides it is not worth his while to set in motion any of these sanctions is hardly likely to
turn to the slow and cumbersome machinery of a civil action for breach of contract.

[2] Conway v. Wade (1909) A.C. 506; Larkin v. Long (1915), A.C. 814 and Huntley v.
Thornton (1957), 1 All E.R. 234. (This last case is discussed further at p. 714.)

[3] Conway v. Wade, op. cit.

[4] Larkin v. Long, op. cit.

[5] Larkin v. Long, op. cit., and Bent's Brewery v. Hogan (1945), 2 All E.R. 570.

[6] Huntley v. Thornton, op. cit. See also Trade Union Law and Practice, by H. Vester and
A. H. Gardner (Sweet and Maxwell, 1958), Chap. 15, for an account of the present degree
of immunity granted by the 1906 Act.

question are now a matter for the courts to decide. It is arguable that this is a violation of the intentions of those who passed the Act of 1906, and that it carries with it potential dangers from the union point of view. However, because it has occurred at a time when the common law was taking a more tolerant view of such practices as the closed shop it has gone largely unobserved.

(b) The Rationale of the Present Position

The central issue facing those whose job it was to determine the attitude of the law towards union activities in general, and the closed shop in particular, was easy to state—if not to settle. As individuals, workers cannot compete on equal terms with employers. This justifies combination. Nevertheless, in advancing their interests collectively, workers indulge in a range of coercive devices, which affect employers and employees and sometimes inflict damage on others who are not party to their disputes. It is arguable, also, that sometimes the settlements arrived at have generally disadvantageous economic effects. The question therefore arose: should workers be allowed freedom to pursue the advancement of their collective interests in any way they wish, irrespective of the methods they use and the consequences which follow? If not, on what principles should a line be drawn between justifiable and unjustifiable action, and what sanctions ought to be imposed on the former?

If this is the general problem the issue of justifying the closed shop is a sub-species of it. Given the answer to this question the problem arises of whether or not, on the principles determined, action against non-members is justified.

By 1875, with minor exceptions, it had been decided that the need to match employer power justified the removal of most criminal sanctions. This decision appears logical enough. No clear distinction can be drawn between the activities of unions which would have justified the proposals of the majority report. In practice the legislation suggested, if effective, would probably have crippled union growth, and in the case of the closed shop it would have been disproportionately restrictive on a number of groups.

With criminal liability removed, the courts, after a period, turned to issues of civil liability. In the case of the right to exclude non-members the problem turned on three points. First, what were the *civil* rights of the parties involved. Did a man have a right to employ his labour as he wished—or did others have the right to decide with whom they should work? Was it a transgression of rights if combination to exclude non-members resulted in inducing or procuring a breach of contract, or in coercing others not to enter into contracts? It is clear that if certain views were to be accepted on these issues the exclusion of non-members would not be legally justifiable. The effective use of the exclusion sanction involved the threat of inducing a cancellation of contracts, for example, and it is incompatible with the acceptance of the individual's right to employ his labour as he wishes where he likes. Some judges took a view of individual rights in these matters which contradicted what others were saying about the right to refuse to work, except on certain conditions, etc. Indeed, it is difficult to see how there could be any reconciliation of the conflicting rights put forward at the time. As was stressed, an absolute right to work, at the trade of one's choosing, unhampered by the interference of others, is incompatible with the right to strike to impose working conditions on employers and employees alike. Whenever conflicting demands of this sort are clothed in the language of absolute right there can be no solution. In an effort to find one, the courts tended to fall back on the second of their points of reference—the question of motive.

The argument advanced was that acts which would be actionable if done for a bad motive might be legal if done for a just cause. In effect the principle adopted was that it was actionable to combine to cause damage for malicious reasons but justifiable to do so to advance 'legitimate' trading interests. The assumption appeared to be that it was not for the courts to set the boundaries between justifiable and unjustifiable competition of this sort. In practice this apparently neutral test was applied so as to discriminate against trade unions. Given the judicial prejudices of the period, this was perhaps bound to happen, for the motive test is only formally neutral. It is always open to any court to decide that in its opinion the defendants are motivated by malice. In the last analysis this is an argument about what is going on inside somebody's head at a certain point in time, and this is, in a sense, essentially unprovable.[1] Opponents of a particular decision may, as many did, point to what appears to be analogous circumstances involving employers where the action was dismissed. But no case is quite like another and the issue is, at base, a matter of subjective evaluation. In practice, malice is apt to act as

[1] Naturally, difficulties of this sort are not confined to cases that turn on the presence or absence of malice. Whenever a court has to take into account the *intentions* of defendants, or accused, it may be up against similar problems.

a residual in cases of this sort. It is more likely to be found where there is no other explanation, in terms of a defence of 'legitimate' interests, which the court is willing to recognize. It is worth remembering that before the First World War the notion that trade unions could be said to advance and protect 'legitimate' interests was by no means universally accepted.

The third point at issue concerned the justifiability of retaining the motive test in conspiracy cases, after it had been eliminated from cases involving individuals. To the non-lawyer this must appear an illogical development. As a result of Allen *v.* Flood, liability appeared to be confined to questions of inducement or procurement of a breach of contract. Allowed to stand this would have resulted in a considerable withdrawal of jurisdiction, and it seems impossible not to conclude that the courts felt that some way round this highly contested judgment must be found. It is worth recalling that in the case of McGuire *v.* Andrews,[1] decided in 1904, action to enforce a closed shop was justified by reference to Allen *v.* Flood and the judge replied that this was a case in which the House of Lords had given a decision 'which they have been getting round ever since'.[2]

Of course, it is arguable that those who combine to damage another thereby increase their power to inflict damage; but it is not tenable to argue that the degree of damage caused is invariably related to the existence or otherwise of combination. As the Lord Chancellor remarked in the Crofter case, such a contention is open to the 'obvious answer that this depends on the personality and influence of the individual' for 'the action of a single tyrant may be more potent to inflict suffering on the continent of Europe than a combination of less powerful persons'.[3] Significantly enough, after a consideration of various other possible arguments in favour of retaining additional liability in the case of combination the Lord Chancellor concluded that though the principle was well established, 'the legal reason for it may not be so easy to state'.[4]

But this is not all. Even if there were a difference between the degree of damage inflicted by combination, as against that inflicted by an individual, so that proof of combination could be accepted as a justification for additional liability, why should it follow that the question of whether liability should lie or not depends on the

---

[1] *The Times*, March 8, 1904.
[2] *Op. cit.* See also Askwith's evidence, *op. cit.*, p. 23.
[3] Crofter, *op. cit.*, p. 443.
[4] *Ibid.*

intentions of the combiners? And why should the motive of malice be penalized, and the motive of the trading interest defence waive liability? If it is unjustifiable to inflict damage maliciously in concert why should it be legal to damage maliciously when conspiracy cannot be proved? Conversely, if one is allowed to inflict damage as an individual, provided one avoids breaking contracts or inducing a breach of them, why should there be a particular liability for malicious damage when combination can be shown? It is hard to resist the conclusion of Askwith at this point. Because the courts were determined to get round Allen *v*. Flood they 'fell back' upon the ancient doctrine of conspiracy as a source of additional liability. In effect they used it as an excuse to reintroduce the flexible, subjective, traditional doctrine of motive.

The inevitable consequence was another Act to remove the effects of such a decision. But if the courts failed to provide satisfactory and consistent principles to govern the civil liabilities of unions did the 1903 Commission fare any better? The intention of the Act was to reinstate the law as it had been understood to exist in 1875. The outcome was an Act which defined the extent of union immunity in a way that appeared to cover virtually all forms of action on the part of trade unionists. In fact, the interpretation given by the courts to the Act since 1906 has narrowed the actual immunity granted, while it is arguable that in some ways the closed shop itself is afforded a wider degree of immunity by virtue of developments within the common law. What is to be said of this development?

It should surely be granted that in general terms the factual basis on which it is grounded is accurate enough. The closed shop advances the power of unions that obtain it, and in certain circumstances effective job regulation is not possible without its functions. Despite the tendency of trade unionists to justify action to obtain the closed shop simply on grounds of a moral objection to workmen refusing to accept their common obligations, there seems no reason to doubt that those who lead closed shop drives are aware of the advances which accrue from the practice, and that the persistence with which the practice is demanded is largely determined by its use in overcoming particular problems. In other words, trade unions are usually motivated predominantly by the desire to advance their trading interests when they take action to exclude non-members. Moreover, once the doctrine of the 'predominant motive' is accepted it is not necessary to deny that there may be, on occasion, other considerations involved. Malice there may be, personal animosity and a desire to demonstrate the strength of collective power there clearly often is. But for the most part, as we have seen, when no advantages appear to follow from the exclusion of non-unionists these *tend* to be tolerated, even where union strength is such that action against them would probably be successful.

Thus it may be argued that most of the objections raised earlier to grounding liability in motive are no longer of practical importance. Since equity has been achieved, as well as consistency, does it matter if the logic of the distinction between individual and conspiracy is open to doubt, so long as the trading interest defence is always allowed? What if the test adopted seems arbitrary, so long as it is consistently applied? In short, even if the present degree of immunity is grounded on unsatisfactory premises, does this matter so long as the immunity remains?

One can argue that it does. Not only have the courts been unable to develop a satisfactory and consistent set of principles by which to judge the justifiable limits of union action in the civil field. The principles they have developed are only intelligible on the assumption that one accepts the general arguments first advanced by the minority report. Questions of contract apart, the single important liability remaining is that of unjustifiable damage by conspiracy. It is assumed that the exclusion of non-members, along with other coercive acts of trade unionists, are justified when used to advance group interests (rather than maliciously). If it is asked why this is so, the answer must surely be that workers must be free to combine to advance their interests if they are to match employer power. But this does not so much explain the problem as explain it away. As was noted, the central issue to be considered when discussing the justifiability of action to obtain the closed shop is this; given that combination is justified to match employer power, how far should unions be allowed to go in pursuing their objectives to this end irrespective of the consequences to others? It is no real answer to reply—as far as they like so long as they are not motivated by malice. Nobody, except perhaps a few judges and their juries, ever thought trade unionists habitually inflict damage mainly out of malice. Indeed, one may doubt how far the doctrine of malice was ever believed. It seems more plausible to regard the assumption of malicious intention as a convenient, flexible device, which enabled courts to grant a remedy when no clearly defined wrong had taken place. The difficulty was that when applied to trade interference it led to charges of prejudice and partiality. Once the courts were willing to accept that workers used their collective sanctions to defend their legitimate collective interests, plausibility and impartiality triumphed—but at the cost of flexibility. Nowadays, so long as they can show that they are motivated by their own interpretation of their own interests there would appear to be *no* effective barrier placed on the extent to which collective coercion may be used against non-members.

In recent years, as Chapter 10 will show, this has led to growing criticisms of the present legal position. What these criticisms amount to, in fact, is a re-emergence of one of the basic arguments advanced in the majority report. What is doubted is not the need for combination to attain strength, but the need for the degree of strength attained as a result of the immunities granted. What is questioned (as the degree of union power is presumed to rise partly as a result of legal immunities) is the continued relevance of the matching power argument when used to justify all that is done under cover of the existing degree of legal immunity.

At the end of Chapter 7 it was argued that the justification of a practice like the closed shop raises three questions: approval of the purposes for which it was used, acceptance of its necessity for the furtherance of these purposes, and the conviction that, on balance, it does not result in various secondary consequences which reduce its overall justifiability. Most contemporary criticism of the legal position of trade unions, and the position accorded the right to exclude non-members, concerns the second and third of these questions.

The need to match employer power by combination continues to be accepted. What is questioned is whether it is necessary, or justifiable, to allow unions to retain *all* the sanctions they now enjoy, and whether their use does not lead to consequences which constitute a case for a further attempt to circumscribe the limits of legal immunity.

In a sense this was bound to happen. It is one of the weaknesses of the matching power argument that it can be used to justify *any* given amount of legal immunity, although those who regard the immunity as excessive can always argue that in their opinion the need to match employer power no longer justifies the full extent of the immunity which exists. In recent years there has been a growing feeling that union power has increased, and a number of highly publicized court cases have appeared to indicate that the powers granted as a result of existing immunities have been abused or used unnecessarily.[1] These developments have increased the number of critics of the present position, and given point to their proposals for reform. As in 1867, the issues raised involve questions of public interest, civil liberty and economic policy, and are not confined to the right to exclude non-members. Indeed, many of the more far-reaching reforms are concerned with the right to exclude ex-members, an issue not considered by the 1867 Royal Commission, and not raised in this chapter. The justification of this right raises analogous issues to those considered above, but legal principles which govern its lawful limits are somewhat different. For this reason it has been made the subject of a separate chapter.

[1] See Chap. 10.

CHAPTER 9

THE RIGHT TO EXCLUDE EX-MEMBERS FROM THE JOB

(1) THE AUTHORIZATION PRINCIPLE

IN defining the right of unions to exclude non-members the main
basis of the law's jurisdiction was the common law doctrine of
conspiracy. One of the main objectives of the Acts of 1871, 1875
and 1906 was to remove the effects of this doctrine in the realms of
criminal and civil law. The basis of the law's jurisdiction over the
right of trade unionists to exclude ex-members is founded on
grounds of status and contract.

The union rule book is regarded by the courts as a legally binding
contract. It follows that in cases where it can be shown that expulsion
is contrary to the rules, the courts will grant a remedy. The remedies
available are a declaration, an injunction and an award of damages.[1]

Courts insist that unions respect both procedural and substantive
rules, although the degree of jurisdiction they have established over
the different kinds of substantive rule varies.[2] Essentially two principles have been developed which allow them to mitigate and to
some extent to control the powers of unions to expel existing members. These may be termed the *authorization* principle and the
principle of *natural justice*. What the first involves is that a court
will decide that a member has been wrongfully, and thus illegally
expelled, unless the expulsion has been:

(a) expressly authorized by the rule book;
(b) pronounced on grounds specifically mentioned therein;
(c) decided by the body authorized under the rules, and
(d) strictly in accordance with the forms and procedures laid down in the rule
book.

What the second principle involves is that the court will decide that
a member has been wrongfully expelled if there is any violation of
what is termed 'natural justice'.[3]

---

[1] Bonsor *v.* the Musicians' Union (1956), A.C. 104 decided that a trade union (in Bonsor's
case a registered one) was liable for damages in cases of wrongful expulsion. The position of
an unregistered union is unclear.
[2] See p. 99 above for the different types involved.
[3] See below for an elaboration of this term.

Since an action for wrongful expulsion is technically an action for breach of contract the 'meaning' of the rules remain in the last resort a question of law which the court may decide. In general the courts have tended to interpret rules strictly. For example, a right to inflict more severe penalties does not carry with it a right to inflict less severe ones,[1] and the provisions of an agreement signed by authorized union officials cannot be added to the list of acts for which a member can be expelled.[2] On the other hand, the courts do not claim to sit in appellate jurisdiction on the bodies which expel members,[3] and they have disclaimed the right to review proceedings.[4] Moreover, as Grunfeld writes:

Where the ground for expulsion in the rule is specific and unambiguous, the prior question of interpretation is automatically resolved and the question of whether a breach of contract was committed will generally be a simple question of fact.[5]

Where a member has been expelled for violating a specific rule the function of the court is simply to determine whether the union acted without malice, according to its rules, and whether the procedure was in accord with natural justice.[6] In the case of Maclean v. The Workers' Union,[7] for example, the plaintiff participated in a political campaign for the office of general secretary, in an attempt to rid the union of allegedly corrupt leaders. The rules specifically provided that he could not distribute circulars without the approval of the very officials he was attempting to defeat. When he disobeyed, the rules stated that the same officers could remove him from his newly-won office and expel him. Maugham J. held that Maclean was bound by this disciplinary procedure.

If, on the other hand, the stated grounds for expulsion are ambiguously worded or, in the circumstances of a particular case, are capable of more than one interpretation, the courts will adopt 'that interpretation, that meaning, which is against the union relying on its rule but in favour of the weaker party to the contract, the individual member'.[8] In Kelly v. N.S.O.P.A., for example, a man was

---

[1] Burn v. National Amalgamated Labourers' Union, (1920) 2 Ch., 364.
[2] Andrews v. N.U.P.E., *The Times*, July 9, 1955; Spring v. N.A.S.D. (1956), 2 All E.R. 221.
[3] Young v. Ladies Imperial Club (1920), 2 K.B. 523; Dawkins v. Antrobus (1881), 17 Ch. D. 615.
[4] Lecson v. General Council, etc. (1890), 43 Ch. D. 366.
[5] *Op. cit.*, p. 10. The most obvious examples of specific and unambiguous expulsion rules refer to expulsion for arrears; most rules about trading offences probably admit of some interpretation, as do all general expulsion rules.
[6] Dawkins v. Antrobus, *op. cit.*, per Brett, L.J., p. 630.
[7] (1929) 1 Ch. D. 602.   [8] Grunfeld, *op. cit.*, p. 10.

expelled from the union for 'conduct detrimental to the interests of the society'.[1] As the union operated a closed shop he was also excluded from the job. It was claimed that by working part-time as a porter Kelly was a danger to his fellow members through fatigue. His overseer denied this, and on these facts it was held that the extra work was not 'detrimental' within the meaning of the rule. In another case the rules provided that members should not indulge in 'unfair competition' in renting, taking or letting of a ground or position.[2] One member, granted a site by the Bradford Corporation, refused to give it up in favour of another who had occupied the site before the war and to whom it was allotted by the union. On refusing to pay a fine he was expelled and the court decided that on the evidence it was 'unreasonable' to find him guilty of unfair competition.

But the courts have upheld expulsions based on general rules. In Wolstenholme v. the A.M.A.[3] the plaintiff wrote to head office alleging that fellow members were undercutting union rates. He repeatedly failed to give the branch committee details of his charges, eventually retracted them, promising to write to head office correcting the bad impression he had caused. Failing to do this, and after being given a number of chances to redeem himself, he denied both retraction and promise. He was thereupon expelled under a rule for conduct which 'brought the union into discredit'. The court decided that the plaintiff's action had discredited the branch in the eyes of head office, and the expulsion was justified. Finally, in a more recent case,[4] a casual jobbing hand in a printing firm absented himself without notice and in consequence a non-unionist was employed. He was summoned before the branch committee and, after a hearing, instructed to do the work. He refused and was expelled for having 'knowingly acted to the detriment of the interests of the union'. The court held that this was a justified expulsion.

Commenting on some of these cases Grunfeld has written:

in none of the reported decisions did the courts try to interpret the general expulsion rule against the union by averring that it was ambiguous because capable of many meanings. In each case they sought an effective meaning for the rule in relation to the critical events preceding the particular expulsion.[5]

[1] (1915) 84 L.J. K.B. 2236.   [2] Lee v. the Showmen's Guild (1952), 2 Q.B. 329.
[3] (1920) 2 Ch. O. 388.   [4] Evans v. N.U.P.B.P.W. (1938), 4 All E.R. 51.
[5] Op. cit., p. 13.

But, of course, this has meant that the precise construction likely to be put on any rule, in a given case, is difficult to determine and in no case 'was the attempt made to establish legal criteria to guide future courts in their interpretation of general expulsion rules'.[1]

(2) NATURAL JUSTICE

Judicial interpretations of the authorization principle mainly affect substantive rules. The principle of natural justice is directed at the procedures unions follow in deciding whether these rules have been broken. For many years the courts were reluctant to interfere in the internal arrangements of 'voluntary bodies' like trade unions, particularly in respect of their procedural rules.[2]

In recent cases, however, a distinction has tended to be drawn between the tribunals of purely social bodies, like cricket clubs and dramatic societies, and the powers entrusted to bodies like branch committees considering expulsion from unions operating a closed shop.[3] This change has expressed itself in a growing concern for what are termed the principles of natural justice. Grunfeld defines these as requiring that 'the alleged offender should know the charge against him and that the domestic tribunal should fairly listen to both sides and come to its decision in good faith'.[4]

Perhaps the best short account of the general principles involved is Professor Lloyd's.[5] His views may be summarized thus:

(1) The Society must serve a notice specifying the charge upon the member and such statement must contain the specific charge which is to be made.

(2) After notice has been served a proper hearing must be held at which the accused must be given an opportunity to defend himself. Strict procedures of the regular courts need not be adhered to but the tribunal is bound to deal only with the charges specified.

(3) The decision of the tribunal must be arrived at in good faith and without bias.

Sometimes the rule book contains procedural provisions of this sort. More often the rules do not expressly provide for each of the

---

[1] Ibid.
[2] Much of the law in relation to expulsion from a trade union has been arrived at as a result of the courts considering cases of alleged wrongful expulsion from other associations such as social clubs, sports societies and so on, all of whom have been regarded as 'voluntary associations'.
[3] See the remarks of Denning L.J. and Romer L.J. in the case of Lee v. the Showmen's Guild, op. cit.
[4] Op. cit., p. 15.
[5] The Law Relating to Unincorporated Associations, by Dennis Lloyd, Sweet and Maxwell, 1938, pp. 127–8.

requirements of natural justice, and in one instance at least a union rule book may be said to expressly exclude one of its principles.[1] But, Grunfeld writes:

. . . whether the rules of 'natural justice' are included in a union's rules wholly or partly or not at all, an expulsion which contravenes the 'natural justice' procedure in any way is, in law, a wrongful expulsion.[2]

Moreover, 'in the light of recent judicial *dicta* . . . a union rule purporting to exclude the need for observing the principles of "natural justice" would be held to be invalid as against public policy'.[3] To the extent that this is so, of course, the courts have established a degree of jurisdiction over procedural rules (via the natural justice principle) more fundamental than that over substantive rules (via the authorization principle). For, in the first case, they are not affected to the same extent by the actual content of the rules. They are able to 'read in' the principles of natural justice, as it were, and set them up as a standard to which the union must conform. Basically the authorization principle accepts the rules as they are and seeks to interpret them.[4]

Yet the principles of natural justice have not always been interpreted with equal strictness in cases of alleged wrongful expulsion. A court has upheld the punishment of an offence which only emerged in the course of an inquiry,[5] though in another more recent case the judge ruled that mere personal knowledge of the charge was no substitute for actual notification.[6] The need to notify all those concerned was upheld in a non-union case involving a ladies' club decided in 1920, when the judge held that all the members of the committee authorized to expel members should be informed of the

[1] I.e. the N.U.G.M.W. rule book which allows its executive to refuse to give any reason for an expulsion, and fails to provide for a notice of charges made and a right to a hearing. Of course it does not follow from this that expulsions take Place within the N.U.G.M.W. without regard for the principles of natural justice, it is merely that the rules do not stipulate that they must.

[2] *Op. cit.*, p. 15.

[3] Grunfeld, *op. cit.*, p. 15. See Dawkins *v.* Antrobus, *op. cit.*; Abbott *v.* Sullivan (1952), 1 Q.B. 189, Lee *op. cit.* at p. 342. On the other hand, on the basis of Maclean *v.* The Workers' Union, *op. cit.*, Citrine argued that 'either entirely or to a greater or lesser degree' unions may exclude natural justice through the rule book (Citrine, *op. cit.*, p. 219). The truth seems to be that of all the law pertaining to trade union discipline the area concerning natural justice is the most confused. The inconsistencies in the cases indicate that the law is still in a state of flux, although the general tendency is towards interpretation adopted by Grunfeld.

[4] The suggestion of Lord Denning that the courts are justified in going further in the case of all union rules is discussed below.

[5] Russell *v.* Norfolk (1949), 1 All E.R. 109. This was not a trade union case.

[6] Norman *v.* National Dock Labour Board (1957), 1. Lloyds Report, 455. This case was also not a trade union one, but it did involve exclusion from the job.

meeting at which the case was to be considered.[1] On the all-important issue of the right to a hearing doubt appears to arise as to whether the hearing must be oral, or whether or not the defendant has the right to be present throughout.[2] On the right to cross-examine the position is not entirely clear, but courts have tended to say that this is not always necessary in order to see that right is done. Finally, on freedom from bias or bad faith, the first of these is not construed as an absence of predispositions or prejudices of a general nature; nor is it interpreted in the strictly judicial sense which would result in the disqualification of any judge who was a member of an association maintaining an action before the court. Clearly the first interpretation would be impossible and the second impracticable. The sort of bias struck at tends to be that of a person manifestly sitting in his own cause, or that of one with a direct and special financial interest in the outcome of a case. Obviously it is difficult to draw a line between the presence and absence of bias, partly because the body whose order is disobeyed is often the one charged with the right to expel, partly because in a sense all members have a financial interest in the outcome of the case. The presence of bad faith is even more difficult to establish. In effect it must be shown that the finding arrived at is clearly absurd on the facts, and has been made by a wanton disregard of other principles of natural justice. But in this case, of course, redress can be obtained without the need to prove bad faith.

Two final points should be discussed. How far could a union go in writing its rule book so that the expelling body is given absolute power to expel at its discretion? This question has not been raised directly, but both Citrine, in his *Trade Union Law*, and Professor Dennis Lloyd, in *The Law Relating to Unincorporated Associations*, assume that it could be done.[3] However, as F. P. Graham maintains, analysis of the authorities cited for these statements shows that they are based on non-trade union cases.[4] He submits that, nowadays, courts would not allow the same freedom of expulsion to trade unions.[5] Finally, because of the contractual nature of union rule books, is the expelled member bound to make

---

[1] Young v. Ladies Imperial Club, *op. cit.*

[2] London Export Corporation v. Jubilee Coffee Roasting Co. (1958), 2 All E.R. 411. In this case, another non-union one, Diplock J. decided this last point in the negative.

[3] Citrine, *op. cit.*, p. 214. Lloyd, *op. cit.*, p. 129.

[4] I.e. Cassel v. Inglis (1916), 2 Ch. 211; Weinberger v. Inglis (1919), A.C. 606; Hayman v. Governors of Rugby School (1874), 18 Eq 28, Dawkins v. Antrobus, *op. cit.*

[5] This conclusion is explicit in the reasoning behind Denning L.J.'s opinion in Lee v. The Showmen's Guild, *op. cit.*

full use of all its appeals procedure before turning to the courts? There is no reported case which squarely accepts this doctrine, although Graham argues that there have been several cases where the parties concerned assumed that the law imposed such a requirement.[1]

This brief review of the main points at issue when the courts apply either the authorization or the natural justice principle is not meant to be comprehensive. It serves merely to illustrate the kind of considerations which determine whether or not the expulsion from a union operating a closed shop is likely to be regarded as lawful if challenged. What is obvious is how different these considerations are from those affecting the same union's right to exclude non-members from the job.

It is assumed that trade unionists are justified in combining to obtain the discharge of any worker who will not join a specified union, so long as they do not break their own contract of employment and are not motivated by malice. In any case such action is reckoned to be a trade dispute under the 1906 Act, and as a result of the passage of this Act no court will entertain an action in tort against the union as such. It is also accepted that trade unionists may take similar action against those they refuse to allow into the union. There is no right to entry into British unions, even when exclusion entails exclusion from the job.[2]

Yet once membership of a union has been obtained, the rights of the worker expand. It is no longer lawful to expel him from the union and exclude him from the job as a non-unionist, so long as the liabilities outlined above are avoided. It must be shown, in addition, that the ex-member in question has broken a rule of the union embodied in its rule book which justified expulsion. The courts will interpret the rules strictly in cases of this sort, and will also demand that the case against the member is considered in a way that does not violate natural justice.

---

[1] *Op. cit.*, p. 19. See also *Judicial Review of Expulsions by a Domestic Tribunal*, by D. Lloyd, 15 M.L.R. (1952).

[2] Upjohn J. in Clarke *v.* N.U.F.T.O. (1957), *The Times*, October 18, ruled it was an established fact that unions had absolute freedom to control admissions, though there is no trade union case where such a claim has been the substance of an action. The nearest case is Weinberger *v.* Inglis ((1919), A.C. 606), which concerned the refusal to re-admit a one-time member of the Stock Exchange. A majority of the House of Lords ruled it only had to be shown that the committee had acted for what it thought to be a good reason, and that they might be required to act in good faith. Moreover, it should be realized that the fact that the plaintiff in this case had once been a member established a property right, which might conceivably have been infringed. In most union cases what is required is not a right to re-admission, however, but a right to admission; this clearly cannot be grounded in a property right.

From the viewpoint of the functions of the closed shop the contrast may be put like this. In so far as unions seek to put into effect the entry control and recruitment functions of the closed shop they are bound by one set of liabilities; in so far as they seek to uphold its retention and discipline functions they are bound by another. It was argued, in the previous chapter, that in the case of action against non-members the rights accorded were basically to be justified by reference to the matching power argument; but this is not so obviously the case for existing members of the union. They are assumed to have a right to continue within the union unless they can be shown to have broken its rules, and even then the case against them must be fairly tried by those authorized to do so.

It is possible to argue, however, that there is a sense in which the matching power argument covers both cases. On the assumption that a union's rule book consists of those disciplinary provisions necessary to uphold union authority, and thus to maximize union power, it is only just that unions should be allowed to punish those who defy authority, if necessary by expulsion. If they are to be allowed to utilize the sanctions of the closed shop on non-members they must be allowed to use them on existing members, but only if they too can be shown to be a threat to the maximization of union power. Since the rule book consists of the offences which constitute such a threat it follows that only if the rules are broken is there any need to expel the member and to exclude him from the job. On this argument the need to observe natural justice may be justified as the best way to ensure that the truth about the offences of members, and thus the extent to which they constitute a source of weakness, is discovered.

In fact, the assumption behind the attitude of the law to the exclusion of non-members is that of the rights of contracting parties. The contents of the rule book are the terms of the contract and they only sanction expulsion in certain eventualities. Nevertheless, despite the fact that this results in unions being substantially less free to exclude ex-members than they are to exclude non-members, it is often argued that the degree of freedom they enjoy in this field is too wide. In the next chapter some of the more recent criticisms of this sort will be considered.

CHAPTER 10

CONTEMPORARY CRITICISM

CONTEMPORARY proposals for circumscribing the degree of immunity granted to the closed shop may be conveniently classified from the viewpoint of their effect on its three functions.

The more far-reaching suggestions affect and even undermine all three functions, whereas less extreme remedies are only aimed at correcting assumed abuses in the way in which individual functions are used. Unfortunately, it is not always clear how far critics take their stand on grounds of civil liberty, or how far they are criticizing the closed shop's economic effects, just as it is sometimes unclear to what extent they are advocating a reduction in union power. It will be argued that it is essential to clarify one's attitude to these questions, which are crucial to determining attitudes towards proposals for reform.

The more common suggestions may be classified under three broad heads. They are:

(1) Suggestions for a Restrictive Practices Court for Labour;
(2) Suggestions for Circumscribing the Right to Reject Applicants;
(3) Suggestions for Extending the Basis of Legal Control over Expulsion Rules.

(1) SUGGESTIONS FOR A RESTRICTIVE PRACTICES COURT FOR LABOUR

This suggestion arises out of recent restrictive practices legislation in the field of industry and commerce, and in particular from an appreciation of the working of the Restrictive Practices Court, set up by the Act of 1956.[1]

(a) The Existing Court

The existing court is made up of a combination of judges and lay members, and considers agreements between two or more parties which restrict prices, quantities, and other conditions of supply goods. Its terms of reference cover most types of restrictive agreement operating in trade or industry. Such agreements must be registered, as the Board of Trade appoints, and in due course considered by the court. The court may declare any particular practice

---

[1] Restrictive Trade Practices Act, 4 & 5 Eliz. 2, C. 68, 1956. Sections 7 and 8 of the Act stipulate agreements to be disregarded, and exceptions. These include, among others, those relating to workmen and affecting conditions of employment.

contrary to the 'public interest'. The agreement maintaining it will then be void, and on application the court will issue an order restraining those who continue to operate it. Applications may originate from the Registrar of Restrictive Trading Agreements, or by persons affected by the agreement in question. Refusals to confirm constitute contempt of court.

In considering the principles upon which the court works it is essential to realize that the Act does not define what constitutes the public interest; all the practices covered by the Act are assumed to be *against* the public interest, unless the contrary is established before the court. What the Act does is to define, in some detail, the circumstances in which the court may decide this is so. The onus of proof is therefore placed on those who wish to retain a practice. They are afforded seven 'gateways' and a 'tailpiece'. To satisfy the court a practice must 'get through' one or another of the gateways, and satisfy the conditions set out in the tail-piece. Since the nub of the argument for a Restrictive Practices Court for Labour consists of a suggestion that the present court, or one analogous to it, ought to be empowered to consider similar practices maintained by trade unionists, it is necessary to set out, in a summary form, but in some detail, the provisions of this part of the Act.

Broadly speaking, the gateways may be summarized thus. The court must be convinced of one or another of the following:

(1) that the restriction is 'reasonably necessary' to protect the public against injury;

(2) that its removal would deny them 'specific and substantial benefits or advantages';

(3) that it is 'reasonably necessary' to prevent others restricting or preventing competition;

(4) that it is 'reasonably necessary' to enable the parties to negotiate 'fair terms' from those who control a 'preponderant part' of the market or trade;

(5) that its removal would be likely to cause a 'serious and adverse effect on the general level of unemployment' in areas where a substantial proportion of the trade is carried;

(6) that its removal is likely to cause 'a reduction in the volume or earnings of the export business';

(7) that it is 'reasonably required' to maintain another restriction not found contrary to the public interest by the court.

If the agreement maintaining the restriction passes through one or more of these gateways, and is not 'unreasonable' having regard to the 'balance between those circumstances and any detriment to the public or persons not party to the agreement', it may be allowed to stand.[1]

The provisions of the Act, and the interpretation put on them by the Court, have given rise to a considerable literature. It is not my intention in this study to examine either the provisions or the literature. This over-simple account of the statute itself, and its more obvious implications, is introduced simply to consider, in general terms, how far provisions of an analogous sort would be suitable if applied to union activities in general and the closed shop in particular.

The establishment of a court of this kind is an attempt on the part of the law to define and circumscribe those issues which the House of Lords refused to delimit in the Mogul case—i.e. the extent to which it is in the interests of public policy that men should be allowed to combine to advance their interests by limiting competition. It is plausible to assume that in the interests of equity if a new attitude is taken by the law in respect of agreements between employers, analogous provisions ought to apply to the activities of their employees. As one writer has put it, 'many of these employees' practices and agreements are as suitable to the depression era of unemployment (i.e. they are as out-of-date) as are some of the practices of employers. A strong case certainly seems to have been made out for their consideration.[2]

It is important to stress, before considering possible objections to this proposal, that in the case of the closed shop if the Act were extended to cover trade union practices a defence of sorts could be made out. The unions would probably rely mainly on gateways three, four and five. On the issue of preventing others from restricting competition, and enabling the negotiation of 'fair terms', they could argue that the closed shop, by helping to maintain union power, prevents powerful employers from dominating the market and dictating their own terms. They could also maintain that present-day labour markets are still far from perfectly competitive, if only because the number of persons selling labour still far exceeds the number of persons buying it. There is thus no reason to believe

[1] Section 21, op. cit.
[2] 'The Control of Monopolies and Restrictive Trade Practices', by Valentine Latham Korgham, in *Current Legal Problems*, Vol. 9, Stevens, 1956, p. 153. See also *A Giant's Strength*, a Study by the Inns of Court Conservative and Unionist Society, Christopher Johnson, 1958, p. 31. Unfortunately these writers fail to specify in any detail how they think the provisions of the 1956 Act should be applied to trade union practices.

that a greater degree of perfection would be introduced simply by insisting that unions should compete for members.

On the question of entry control they might assert that while this circumscribed the employer's freedom to deploy the labour force as he wished, this must be set alongside the compensating advantages which result from the establishment of industry-wide pre-entry shops. It can be argued that these actually add to the degree of labour mobility. By functioning as the source of labour supply the union raises the degree of perfection in the market, via a rise in the degree of knowledge.[1] It also increases effective mobility through the establishment of security of employment for those with the union card.

On the wider question of the use of the closed shop in helping to enforce other so-called 'restrictive practices' the unions would no doubt seek to show that these, too, were either (a) accompanied by compensating advantages, (b) necessary to protect the public via a consequent deterioration in craftsmanship, quality, and so on, or (c) that their removal would cause widespread and persistent unemployment. They would stress that even within the pre-entry shop employers may object to individual workers, and retain the right to discharge on grounds of inefficiency.

It would be alleged in reply that unions like the boilermakers and shipwrights use entry control to limit the total supply of labour, to prevent the promotion of the semi-skilled, and to maintain notional skill gaps. In this way the expansion of the industry is prevented, or made more costly, while the most economical distribution of work is impossible. In the case of newsprint workers, on the basis of the Royal Commission's evidence, it could be argued that even among semi-skilled workers wasteful and costly unilateral regulations have been imposed on employers with the aid of the closed shop.

Whether, on balance, the court would accept one set of arguments or another, and how far as a result they would want to go in striking at the closed shop, in its various forms, it is difficult to say; but obviously much would depend on how the court interpreted its statutory instructions where union practices were concerned. As Wilberforce, Campbell and Elles wrote of the 1956 Act:

It is apparent on the face of it, and without reference to many of the debates which have taken place upon the Policy of it, that the section is dealing with matters

---

[1] E.g. the advertisements for vacancies in union journals, and the assistance which unions give to employers looking for workers in scarce supply.

involving considerations of social and economic policy. Very much will depend on the frame of mind in which the application of the section is undertaken, whether a liberal or narrow interpretation is given to the seven alternatives, whether the court adopts a role of arbiter between contending parties . . . whether the court is content to make a broad jury-finding of 'guilty' or 'not guilty', or whether it considers it its duty to follow out the implications of any practice under examination, and how far it does so.[1]

Such considerations, they continued, 'quite unavoidably' involve value judgements, which are dependent on disputable assessments of the evidence put before the court. They concluded:

What it is called on to do is to balance incommensurables and it is of little assistance to add that the result of the process is to be something reasonable.[2]

If anything this understates the case. It is not merely that, as has been argued, it is difficult to tell what would be the consequences of abolishing various trading practices, while allowing others to remain. It is that even if the court is reasonably sure how far a course of action will result in disadvantages, while another may result in advantages, how is it to balance one set of consequences against another? Much must depend, in practice, on the predilections and attitudes of the court. As it is, it seems generally agreed that the present court has interpreted the gateways relatively strictly, and, partly as a consequence, most of the parties it has threatened to investigate have abandoned their restrictive agreements before they could be brought before it. Thus, in the first two and a half years of the court's existence, although the parties to 490 agreements were advised of intention to start proceedings only nine cases were eventually defended, and of the seven cases reported in the Registrar's first report only one resulted in the restrictions being regarded as entirely in conformity with the public interest.[3] Some idea of the strictness of the court can be gained from the fate of the well-known Cotton Yarn Spinners Association Agreement.[4] The court ruled this to be against the public interest, although it accepted that the consequence might well be that local unemployment would rise to 7.8 per cent. Whether, in the face of developments of this sort, unions like the boilermakers and shipwrights, or the printers, would be able to 'squeeze' their pre-entry practices past the court is extremely doubtful.

[1] *The Law of Restrictive Trade Practices and Monopolies*, Sweet and Maxwell, 1957, p. 350.
[2] *Op. cit.*, p. 360.
[3] *Report of the Registrar for Restrictive Practices*, Cmnd. 1273, H.M.S.O., January 1961.
[4] Reports of Restrictive Practices Cases, Incorporated Council of Law Reporting for England and Wales, March 1959, pp. 118–19.

(b) Objections to the Proposal

What is certain is that whether they were able to do so or not the trade unions would undoubtedly object most strenuously to being made to defend themselves in this way, and with good reason. For the argument which must surely be assumed to lie behind the 1956 Act is that in the field of manufacturing industry 'as a general rule trade competition and a free market are more beneficial than stabilized prices'.[1] But this is just what unions exist to deny in the field of employment bargaining; it is, after all, the very crux of the matching power argument.

Unions could therefore argue that if this principle were to be accepted, and applied without discrimination to the labour market it would make nonsense of the assumptions upon which most existing labour law is based. It is, presumably, because they realized something of the sort, that Parliament excluded the activities of unions from the provisions of the 1956 Act.

This criticism could, of course, be partly met by the institution of a different act to govern trade union practices, setting up a separate court. Here the onus of proof could be shifted. This court could assume that union rules, agreements and customs were 'in the public interest' unless the contrary could be proved.

But once again everything would depend on the nature of the proof demanded, and the interpretation which the court placed upon its statutory provisions. Much would still turn on the predilections of the court. When one bears in mind the conflicting attitudes of contemporary economists to the problem of determining the economic effects of various forms of union action, it seems that it would be difficult to reach generally acceptable conclusions. Summarizing the state of this section of economic theory one of the most distinguished of labour economists, Professor J. T. Dunlop, has written:

The varied descriptions and explanations proffered by economists put one in mind of the conflicting impressions of the elephant, developed by a group of blind men, each of whom explored a different sector of its anatomy.[2]

[1] 'Restrictive Practices in the Cotton Industry', by J. A. G. Griffith, *The Listener*, July 9, 1959, B.B.C. London, p. 49. Many contemporary economists would deny this proposition —or at least maintain that it is oversimple.
[2] *The Theory of Wage Determination*, Macmillan, 1957, p. xi. See also the discussion of recent U.S.A. research into this subject by Paul Sultan, in *Right to Work Laws*, Institute of Industrial Relations, University of California, 1958, at p. 126. Also the critique of Barbara Wootton in *The Social Foundations of Wages Policy*, Allen and Unwin, 1955.

Moreover, however much the scales were weighted in favour of union agreements it is still possible to raise more fundamental objections to the notion of a restrictive practices court for labour, so long as the criteria by which it is judged remains a mainly economic one. As Professor Chamberlain has asked, is it correct to view the union-management struggle as a mere 'exchange relationship' in which unions seek to maximize power simply to effect a change in the terms of sale for labour?

This 'market' view of trade union activities, argues Chamberlain, ignores the way in which, as a result of the day-to-day process of union bargaining, there is an inevitable 'sharing of industrial sovereignty' which

proceeds along lines of establishing rules, regulations or 'laws' which are *mutually* acceptable—which carry the approval of the employees, through their representatives as well as the acceptance of the employer. . . . Government by discussion enters into industry (as it did in the state) when the ruler can no longer arbitrarily force obedience to his laws, and must get the consent of those who are to obey the regulations.[1]

Thus contemporary 'collective bargaining', by its very nature involves the union representatives in the managerial role.

By matching employer power, if need be via the closed shop, the union does not only force employers to pay higher wages and improve conditions; it participates in the formulation of those rules and regulations, formerly the exclusive prerogative of management, which affect the working lives of its members. Of course, even without unionization the collective power of workers may affect managerial prerogatives, just as even without formal recognition the pressures of unilateral regulation may circumscribe managerial freedom. What union organization and the development of formalized procedures of collective bargaining does, is to institutionalize and strengthen this development.

The more powerful the union, the more it can command a share in the formulation of works rules. The more the content of the bargaining process extends to cover new subjects of negotiation and new works rules, the more widespread the area over which sovereignty is shared; the more arbitrary managerial power is forced to accept an established and recognized procedure of consultation, negotiation, and collective agreement. In this way the worker comes to exchange a position of privilege for a position based on a pattern of industrial rights which the union has helped to determine.

[1] *Collective Bargaining*, by Neil W. Chamberlain, McGraw Hill, New York, 1951, p. 129.

If this argument is accepted it follows that union practices cannot be evaluated simply in economic terms; even in terms of their effect on the general economic interest, however evaluated. Trade unions can argue that they have important political as well as economic effects. That they assist in the redistribution of power as well as income. That they make possible a wider dispersal of authority at the place of work; it may be said in their favour that they make possible the development and maintenance of effective industrial democracy.

But this is not all. It is not merely that one of the objectives of union activity is to tame and control the arbitrary use of managerial authority; it is not only that the union-management struggle has non-economic effects; it can be argued in addition that one of the basic functions of trade unions has always been to champion non-economic and *uneconomic* demands, in direct opposition to those of an economic character. This is the view taken by Frank Tannenbaum, in his work *A Philosophy of Labour*. He argues that, in a sense, unions have never been primarily interested in economic growth at all, and their very existence can be construed to some extent as a 'denial of both the philosophy and the practice of a free economy'. He continues, 'We have here an unconscious reassertion that man must in some degree be identified with his work, must be attached to it, and must have an attachment for it.' He goes on to say that the unons' primary objective often is 'To make the job secure', and only secondarily to 'force it to yield a high monetary reward'. In certain circumstances, in fact, 'a high wage and job security may in any case prove destructive to each other'.[1] In such circumstances unions must choose, and more often than not they decide in favour of the latter. The most obvious example of this was described in Chapter 5, where an account was given of the high manning standards that the unions impose on newspaper proprietors in London.[2] Essentially the continued maintenance of these standards represent a preference on the part of the workers concerned for security for all, rather than higher wages for some. If they were prepared to accept the much lower manning standards which the Royal Commission on the Press thought adequate the employers would be quite willing to exchange higher wages for those remaining in exchange for a really substantial staff cut. In the meantime there

[1] Alfred K. Knopf, New York, 1952, p. 115.
[2] See p. 114 above.

can be no doubt that the workers' insistence on no redundancy is a real drag on their ability to raise earnings.[1]

Then, again, unions are directly concerned for the status of their members as much as for higher monetary rewards. The resistance of craft unions to piece-work, and attempts to de-skill the job, are examples of this. Just as many unilateral regulations, such as those aimed at limiting output, are evidence of a preference for a reduction of effort and bustle, even at the cost of higher wages. Why, it can be asked, are these considerations to be excluded in the name of a narrowly defined and questionable conception of the needs of economic efficiency?

The relevance of these arguments to proposals to set up a restrictive practices court for labour should be obvious. The argument is that in the matter of industrial relations it is not merely fallacious to assume that the public interest can be loosely equated with the break-up of collective agreements, it is equally wrong to take it for granted that in this field the public interest can be defined predominantly in economic terms.

It follows that it is not proved that a practice like the closed shop is contrary to the public interest *simply because it can be shown that it sometimes results in a maldistribution of economic resources.* Also to be weighed in the balance is the question of how useful and necessary the practice is to the group which uses it, in order to counterbalance arbitrary employer authority, and to add to the general security and status of the workers involved.

At this stage it is worth remembering two points made in Chapter 8.[2] First, it was argued that while there were reasons for believing that the closed shop might result in general economic disadvantages, it could not be assumed that there was a sphere of union regulation —e.g. wage bargaining—which was necessarily free from this defect. It could not even be assumed that on balance the closed shop causes more economic damage than excessive wage demands. Second, if this was so, one effective argument against a general ban on the closed shop is that this would strike disproportionately at particular industrial groups, who had greater need of the practice than others.

---

[1] Unfortunately the Royal Commission did not appreciate this. Their suggestions for reducing manpower fail to stress the opportunity this would give to raise earnings while lowering costs. Consequently they are less than fair to their own case—which, it should be noted, is construed in narrow economic terms. (Report of the Royal Commission, Chap. 4, *op. cit.*)

[2] See p. 194.

In the light of these two conclusions it follows that if a restrictive practices court were set up to deal with labour matters, it would need to determine both its principles and its priorities with considerable care.

If the court were to proceed on strictly economic lines it ought surely to concentrate, at least initially, on those union practices that can be argued to do the most harm—for example, it should investigate unions in a semi-monopolistic position that enforce so-called 'inflationary' wage demands. (After all, union wage regulations are almost precisely analogous to those adopted by bodies like the cotton spinners; i.e. agreements are made not to sell a commodity (labour) below a fixed price.) Moreover, even when it came to consider the closed shop it ought to proceed industry by industry, or even union by union, within an industry, if it were to make any attempt to allow for the differential importance of the practice to various groups.

If the court were expected to consider non-economic factors the problem would be far more complex. Having estimated the balance of economic advantage and disadvantage of a particular closed shop it would have to allow for the counterbalancing advantages presumed to flow from its role in upholding job security, craft status, and so on.

In the opinion of the writer the difficulties inherent in such a proposal when added to the difficulties of enforcement combine to make it less than worthwhile. The simple assumptions of the 1956 Act cannot be applied to the problem of determining the public interest in the field of industrial relations, where the issues involved are complex and the consequences of intervention very disputable. Of course an act could be drafted, and a court set up to operate it; what remains to be shown is whether it would be helpful and whether it is the best way of dealing with the problems involved.[1]

Naturally, this conclusion will fail to satisfy those who remain convinced of the necessary and invariable incompatibility between collective restrictions and the public interest. As in 1867 they will tend to support any move against what they regard as unjustifiable

[1] Presumably those who believe that the National Incomes Commission can exert some influence would argue that it represents a more practical attempt to prevent the worst sort of inflationary wage settlement.

'restrictive practices' in the name of competition. Such people, as Paul Sultan remarks, will naturally tend to

verbalize about the merit of competition and, more important, to retreat to competition as the regulator of economic activity when society faces the difficulty of establishing and implementing standards of public policy to serve in its place.[1]

Nor, he goes on, will it be any use telling those who take this view that we live in an imperfectly competitive world and labour has the right to draw its own conclusions from this. One might as well tell a Christian that 'the trouble with religion is that we live in an irreligious world'.[2] To those who do not share this absolutist view, yet continue to doubt whether the existing degree of immunity granted to the closed shop is fully necessary, it is possible to suggest less far-reaching and more precise proposals of a rather different sort. One such is that reformers should concentrate on the unjustifiable effects of the pre-entry shop. From the viewpoint of its effects on civil liberty, it is argued, it is this aspect of the closed shop which is nowadays indefensible. Suggestions of this sort are considered in the next section.

(2) SUGGESTIONS FOR CIRCUMSCRIBING THE RIGHT TO REJECT APPLICANTS

Potentially, at least, the idea of a Restrictive Practices Court for Labour threatens all three functions of the closed shop. Suggestions for circumscribing the union's right to reject applicants mainly affect the entry-control function, though some proposals would undermine the disciplinary function as well. It is necessary to draw a distinction here between those who totally reject all rights to control entry and those who merely wish to restrict its use.

On the second ground objection may be raised to a refusal to allow entry on particular grounds, such as personal animosity, or racial prejudice. In the case of British unions by far the most common complaint of this sort concerns nepotism.

Printers and dockers are the main offenders here. If challenged, they reply that when the number of would-be entrants acceptable on grounds of educational capacity, etc., exceeds, as it does, the number required, some principle of selection must be found. Nepotism, they claim, only enters at this point. Moreover, it has

---

[1] *Op. cit.*, p. 129.   [2] *Ibid.*

organizational advantages; it ensures that only those with a 'good trade union background' are chosen. This really means that the workers concerned are more likely to have a proper respect for the unilateral regulations and job demarcations of the craft unions. Similar arguments have been advanced in respect of the kinship claims of dockers, or Billingsgate fish porters. Here honesty is also mentioned. Good relations are said to depend on reliability and uprightness of labour supplied by the union. By 'keeping it in the family', one is told, this is ensured.

Presumably even nepotism is to be preferred to the sale of union tickets to the highest bidder, but clearly it offends the principle of equality of opportunity. Given unions *ought* to be allowed to exercise entry control, perhaps there is a case for compilation of a waiting list of suitable persons, or even a ballot. Pressed on this unionists usually assert that a man is entitled to 'look after his own', sometimes they go further and maintain that the queue for the job is the result of their efforts in the past, so that they have the right to dispose of any new places that arise.

Arguments like these fail to convince those concerned with the right of excluded workers, and usually result in further criticism of the use of the entry control function. In *A Giant's Strength*, for example, it is argued that within the closed shop no union should be allowed to exclude 'a duly qualified applicant of good character'.[1]

Presumably unions like the boilermakers and shipwrights could keep their entry qualifications but not their apprenticeship ratios. Dockers could refuse to admit those with anti-union records, but not on the ground that more entrants would lower overtime opportunities. In short, entry control to secure a job preference for existing members, or to uphold a skill gap would be justified, but not entry-control intended to limit *total* numbers available.

The unions reply to this argument partly by reference to the economic factors stressed earlier; they point to past variations in labour demand in the trades where entry control operates. But they also fall back on non-economic arguments, based on the assertion of the right of workers, in combination, to enjoy the same rights as employers. If employers can decide how many men it is in their interest to employ, they demand, why cannot workers do the same?

[1] *Op. cit.*, p. 41.

The same arguments are used to reject the suggestions of those who go still further and deny the unions *all* right to operate the entry control functions of the closed shop. This was the intention of the framers of the American Taft-Hartley Act.[1] Unions were allowed to use the recruitment and retention functions of the closed shop only if they gave up the use of the exclusion threat for all other purposes. This was termed the principle of the *open union*. What was involved was a choice between a closed union, with an open shop, and an open union, with a closed shop.[2] Unions can only demand the discharge of workers for a failure to pay entrance fees or subscriptions; so far as the act is effective the closed shop is thus denied both its entry control and its disciplinary functions. If unions wish to exclude workers on other grounds they must allow them to work on the job as non-unionists.

The customary reply of British unions which operate entry control to suggestions of this sort is that they are self-defeating. Abolish the right of workers to combine collectively to impose entry qualifications, it is said, and you seriously reduce the attractiveness of those jobs where entry control is effective and important. In this, it seems, unions like the Watermen and Lightermen, are compared with exclusive public schools. It is only because everybody cannot go that so many people want to; it is only because those responsible keep some people out that they are under pressure to let so many in. Far from the principle of the open union representing a victory for the right to work, to the extent that it is effective it reduces the attractiveness of enjoying such a right. This argument can be put with special force when, as in the case of newsprint, the labour supply shop is used to back union imposed manning standards and other restrictions that result in the employer being forced to retain a considerable part of a labour force that he would like to discharge. In cases of this sort the unions can justifiably argue that while they are undoubtedly regulating entrance they are also expanding, or at least maintaining, total employment opportunities. They can also argue that they are making the trade in question more

---

[1] June 23, *c.* 120, 61 STAT 140.
[2] Pre-entry shops, discriminatory hiring halls, and preferential treatment for unionists are banned by the Act. Unions operating post-entry shops cannot demand excessive or discriminatory fees or dues. Persons expelled for reasons other than non-payment of normal fees and dues are to be treated as members of the union for the purposes of the Act. Once again this study is not concerned with the detailed working of the Taft-Hartley Act, it is discussed merely as an instance of an attempt to impose the open union principle. The purpose is exemplary rather than comparative.

secure against a background of increasingly menacing technical change.

Of course, as the Royal Commission on the Press pointed out, this will only continue to be so if the unions do not exploit their position to the point where they affect the ability of particular papers to survive. If this does happen, then, as the Royal Commission warns, the unions might find that restrictions imposed in the name of job security, craft status, and so on, are helping 'to kill at least some of the geese which lay the reputedly golden eggs'.[1]

But once again arguments of this sort turn on disputable and largely unprovable assumptions. In such circumstances one can merely make one's own position clear. I feel that there is no essential difference between the granting of a right to control entry, collectively, and the right to combine to affect other aspects of the job. However, it obviously does not follow from this that *all* uses of the entry control function are justifiable. Indeed, it seems to me that exclusion on grounds entirely unconnected with the maintenance of union power *is* unjustifiable. The fact that occasionally employers may discriminate against applicants on grounds of personal animosity, or racial prejudice, and so on, does not justify unions doing so.

Difficulty arises when one comes to consider entry control for purposes connected with the maintenance of union power, which appears to be objectionable on other grounds. One then has to decide how far union power will be reduced if they are abandoned, and how far one is prepared to see this happen. Obviously in the past the entry control function has been a crucial weapon in the hands of several union groups; how far it continues to be crucial it is difficult to say, just as the disadvantageous effects which follow from it are extremely difficult to measure. In principle I for one would not be against a circumscription of union freedom in this field, mainly on grounds of civil liberty. If it can be shown that it is unlikely that the wages and conditions of a group like the newsprint workers would deteriorate markedly, if they gave up some of their entry control practices, then there seems to me to be a case for limiting their freedom in this field; with one proviso. Before embarking on a project of this sort it is necessary to be reasonably certain that the legal measures involved would produce the desired effect. This is a subject which will be referred to again in the next chapter.

[1] *Op. cit.*, p. 32.

(3) Suggestions for Extending the Basis of Legal Control over Expulsion Rules

(a) Common Law Jurisdiction

Although the freedom of unions to exclude ex-members is already more limited than its right to exclude non-members, suggestions have been made for extending the grounds of jurisdiction in this field. These affect the retention and discipline functions of the closed shop, though they may not be intended to cause an overall reduction in the general level of union power. In most cases emphasis has been put either on extensions of common law liability, or on possible changes in statute law.[1]

On the first grounds Lord Denning has argued[2] that the logical assumptions of the contract theory should not apply to expulsion from unions operating a closed shop. For the member, in making such a contract, is not free to negotiate the terms he wishes. The courts therefore have the right to ensure that the contract entered into is limited by the bounds of public policy. This involves intervention when 'unfair and unreasonable' terms have been imposed by the weaker party on the stronger.

In his *Road to Justice* Lord Denning develops this view with respect to imposed contracts generally, taking as examples the standard contracts of bodies such as insurance companies, laundries, etc. He suggests that while allowing the stronger parties in such cases to make 'what conditions they please', the courts have 'sought to mitigate their stringency by all sorts of ingenious devices'. This is unsatisfactory because the stronger parties still evade their proper responsibilities and 'If it should happen that the courts find a way round the wording of one condition, the companies promptly alter the wording so as to get their own way again'.[3]

The position adopted appears diametrically opposed to the arguments of both the minority and majority reports of 1867. It is not argued, with the majority, that *only* unions use unjustifiable social coercion. It is accepted that there is nothing specially coercive about the disciplinary functions of the closed shop. Yet it is not suggested, *pace* the minority report, that the universality and complexity of social pressures constitutes a case for removing limitations of union

---

[1] Given the extent of immunity granted under the 1906 Act extensions of common law liability may also involve a preliminary change in statute law.
[2] See Bonsor *v.* Musicians' Union (1954), 1 All E.R. 825, and Lee *v.* Showmen's Guild (1952), 1 All E.R. 1180.   [3] Stevens and Sons, 1955, p. 92.

R

activity; quite the reverse. It is suggested that wherever it can be argued that coercion is an important element in a formally free contractual relationship, agreements reached should be made to pass the veto of the courts.

How wide an area this would affect is unclear, and it is not evident how the notions of 'reasonableness and fairness' would be interpreted. So far as can be judged, the criteria of unjustified coercion are closely connected with the existence of monopoly or restrictive agreement. Union rules are like the by-laws of railways, or the terms insisted upon by football pools, when there is little or no alternative to accepting them. This is deceptively simple. What Denning really seems to be against is unequal bargaining power, however rooted, which enables the stronger party to force an unfair settlement. It would appear that he does not take into account the matching power argument. He seems to assume that the principles of fairness and reasonableness are the same for all species of contract. But it may be that the rules which Lord Denning would regard as unfair and unreasonable, so far as they affect the recalcitrant member, actually help to prevent the imposition of exceedingly unequal contracts of employment throughout an entire trade. In other words, Lord Denning fails to appreciate the extent to which the contract of employment is itself an act of submission to standard terms fixed in advance by the employer—unless there are unions which, partly through the imposition of coercive rules, are able to match employer power. Certainly it may be argued that this is a matter which should be considered by the courts.

It may be replied that if disallowance of union rules results in more unequal bargaining the unfair and unreasonable consequences can be corrected by the courts. Certainly, if judges are to be allowed to set aside unfair and unreasonable clauses in respect of other contracts it is difficult to see why they should not be allowed a similar jurisdiction over employment contracts. But, even if this were practical, it would replace the present system of industrial relations with that of Elizabeth the First, and not even Lord Denning has seemed to be in favour of such a development.

It seems obvious that the results of such proposals would be that it would be even more difficult to tell, in advance, what union expulsions were lawful and what were not. Perhaps only a few rules would be struck at; perhaps not. Perhaps the limits of justifiable expulsion would depend very much on who considered the case. Largely because of this it seems reasonable to look for other remedies.

One such is that the courts should be encouraged to hold that a claim for wrongful expulsion is allowable in tort. This view has been advanced by Professor Lloyd, in a recent article entitled 'The Right to Work'.[1] The fullest explanation of what is involved is provided by a Canadian writer, E. F. Whitmore.[2] Like Professor Lloyd, Whitmore criticizes the grounding of jurisdiction in contract, along similar lines to Denning. The development of a basis in tort, he says, would allow the courts to develop a greater degree of direct control over the content of substantive rules.[3]

The theoretical basis of this development is that membership of a union is conceived as a 'status relationship' which is 'consensual in origin but not contractual in all its elements'. Thus the rule book does not necessarily stand for all the intentions of the contractors. 'Some of the incidents arise from the nature of the relationship and from its function', i.e. from the fact that members of a union have consented to form an association to regulate employment, etc. The effect of this is made clear to the non-lawyer in the next sentence. It enables the law to escape the constrictions of the contract theory and 'to devise rights and duties which are not expressed in the constitution and which may run counter to them'.[4]

Professor Lloyd concurs, though he suggests a rather different theoretical basis for tortious liability. As he puts it:

treat the deprivation of a man's right to work by wrongful expulsion, or its equivalent, as an intentional wrong in the absence of lawful justification. What would constitute such justification would have to be worked out case by case, as with the tort of wrongfully procuring a breach of contract, e.g. proof of a bona fide mistake might be accepted as a valid defence.[5]

Fortunately, it is not necessary to choose between this theory of derivation and that of Whitmore; it is more important to estimate what would be involved if a basis in tort were accepted.

Once again much depends on the judges called on to set the precedents. In fact the development of a basis in tort, as envisaged by the writers quoted above, seems even more of an invitation to courts to write the union rule book than the suggestions of Lord

[1] *Current Legal Problems*, Vol. 10, Stevens, 1957, p. 41.
[2] *Can. Bar Review* (1956), 34, p. 188.
[3] See also A. R. W. Carruthers in *Can. Bar Review* (1956), 34, p. 70. This articled discusses the Canadian case of Tunney *v*. Orchard (1955) 15, W.W.R. (N.S.) 49 (M.C.A.), in which a basis in tort on similar lines was allowed.
[4] *Op. cit.*, p. 195.   [5] *Op. cit.*, p. 47.

Denning. On the status theory it is proposed, in effect, that courts should be free to invent whatever rights and duties they think fit between a union and its members. On Professor Lloyd's theory the fact of exclusion from the job on grounds of expulsion seems to be regarded as a *prima facie* wrong requiring justification. Presumably the trading interest defence will not be available, because this is not normally the case in instances of breach of contract, and the whole object of the development of a basis in tort is to narrow rather than widen liability. Unfortunately, we are not told what defence should be accepted. What can be said, however, is that once again the effective use of the disciplinary and retention functions of the closed shop may depend more on the judge who tries the case than the rule book of the union.

Yet it must be admitted that despite the fact that the right to exclude ex-members is more restricted than the right to exclude non-members there is some force in the criticisms made. Whatever the precise degree of existing jurisdiction, it is obvious from F. P. Graham's analysis of the rule books of eighty unions, representing 94 per cent of the T.U.C.'s total membership, which was quoted in Chapter 4, that many of them grant extremely widespread powers to those set in authority over individual union members. Indeed, it appears as though some rules almost invite injustice and abuse.

Important unions, like the Transport and General Workers and the General and Municipal Workers, may expel for reasons deemed 'expedient' or 'sufficient' by their national executives; one union allows for expulsion without any reason being given; in five unions, members may be expelled simply because they have been convicted of a criminal charge; sixteen unions operate restrictions on the circulation of election material, and the rule book of the General and Municipal Workers also states that candidates cannot stand for office (either nationally or regionally) unless they are approved of by the National Executive. In eleven unions there is no machinery for internal appeal against expulsion, and sixteen grant powers of expulsion to the branch committee.[1]

Moreover, it is not merely that some rule books give exceedingly wide powers to union leaders, while shielding them from the necessity of justifying the use of their powers. It is not only that some specific expulsion rules are open to objection, and in many cases appeals provisions are inadequate. It is not even that in the

[1] See F. P. Graham, *op. cit.*, pp. 22 and 47.

case of a few unions the rule book *reads* like an attempt to give more or less unlimited powers to a self-perpetuating oligarchy. It is that the average union rule book is obscure, ambiguous, and likely to result in unlawful expulsion. For example, there are at least ten unions where there are no provisions for expulsion at all. In many others there are rules which create offences without prescribing penalties. Quite frequently all the rule book says about an offence is that the executive may 'deal with' those who commit it. Thirty-six of the eighty-odd rule books studied by Graham fail to make clear who has the authority to expel members falling into arrears, and twenty-six contain the flaw that led to the Bonsor controversy —i.e. an expulsion clause that hints that the member may be expelled as an administrative act by a branch officer when the rule book as a whole reserves the power of expulsion in other instances to a higher body.[1]

Rules of this sort indicate that many union rule books are badly in need of reform, even if one cannot accept the proposals considered so far. Moreover, the fact that nowadays central leadership is increasingly reluctant to invoke the punitive powers of the rule book, is they fear they may be challenged in court, does not mean that those who have demanded punishment will agree that nothing further need be done. On the contrary, the danger, then, is that local groups or local leaders, refused what they regard as their rights on their inaccurate if plausible reading of the rule book, may decide to take the law into their own hands.

The recent case of Huntley *v.* Thornton[2] shows that this can result in a situation which is even more unsatisfactory from the viewpoint both of the union and the individual member. For this reason alone the decision in this case is crucial to an understanding of the case for a reform of the present position. Indeed it will be argued below that properly understood the Huntley Thornton case is a convincing argument for a statutory, as against a common law solution. It is therefore necessary, before considering proposals for statutory reform, to outline briefly the issues involved in this case.

Huntley, a member of the Amalgamated Engineering Union, refused to strike because he claimed, correctly, that the strike in question was not called in a way covered by the rule book. Defending his conduct before the Hartlepool District Committee he lost his temper, hurled his rule book across the room, 'shouting that we were only a shower',[3] and left. Asked to expel him the executive

---

[1] Graham, *op. cit.*, p. 39. [2] *Op. cit.* [3] *Op. cit.*, p. 239.

council refused. Huntley then gave a number of press interviews and the district committee wrote to the executive claiming that 'many shop stewards in the district have stated that in the event of this man being allowed to retain his membership they will immediately resign'.[1] They continued, '... (we) have the greatest difficulty in keeping our members in the same shop as Brother Huntley from taking this matter into their own hands'.[2] The executive still refused to expel him, however, although shortly afterwards local pressure got Huntley the sack.

After leaving the district for a fortnight he returned and gave his side of the story in another press interview. The district committee then wrote to all stewards in the area instructing them to 'inform your labour office should they give Huntley a job, it is our intention to withdraw all labour in protest'.[3] They also wrote to the neighbouring district committee, on Tees Side, asking them to do their best to prevent Huntley getting work. After being refused several jobs as a result, Huntley was taken on in Tees Side. When his fellow workers discovered who he was they refused to work with him. He was discharged and advised to make his peace with the union. He then asked to meet the Hartlepool District Committee, but they refused. On March 17, 1954, he issued a writ alleging a conspiracy to injure, citing the members of the district committee and others involved. Next day he applied for his union card and sent the 4s. he claimed was due for arrears. This was returned. Twice subsequently he applied for his card. On May 14 the branch secretary wrote to say he owed the union £3. 3s. 6d.—but no card was sent. On June 8 the branch secretary wrote saying he had been expelled, under rule 27, for arrears of twenty-six weeks.

Two and a half years later Harman J. awarded Huntley £500 damages against the members of the Hartlepool District Committee.

The defendants argued that they had been motivated throughout by the need to defend their trading interests, and that in any event the dispute in question was covered by the 1906 Act. The judge refused to accept this. He maintained that the issue of expulsion was settled by the executive at an early stage. Subsequent acts of the district committee sought to flout this decision and to produce, by other means 'all the effects of expulsion'. Thus, while pretending to punish the plaintiff for disloyalty, the defendants themselves were guilty of this offence. For 'by this time they had entirely lost sight of what the interests of the union demanded and thought only of

[1] *Op. cit.*, p. 241.　　[2] *Ibid.*　　[3] *Op. cit.*, p. 243.

their own ruffled dignity'.[1] To this end they grossly abused their powers, interfered with other districts that were none of their business, refused the plaintiff a chance to make his peace and engineered his expulsion.[2] Since the dispute was an 'internecine struggle' between members of the union no interests of the trade were involved. What was furthered was not a trade dispute, within the meaning of the 1906 Act, but a personal grudge.

As was seen in Chapter 8, while it is clear that the motive of those combining is the test in conspiracy, one may question whether it was intended to be the test of disputes covered by the 1906 Act.[3] If the view of Harman J. prevails, however, wherever it is possible to prove conspiracy it will be possible to avoid the limitations imposed by the Act, since a malicious motive will imply that those combining are not acting in contemplation or furtherance of a trade dispute. It is argued that this development is a potentially dangerous one for trade unions, which considerably strengthens the case for a reform of the existing legal position along statutory rather than common law lines.

If union rule books, in their present ambiguous and unsatisfactory state, are to be strictly interpreted, and natural justice is to be 'read into' the rules, the chances are that already many routine expulsions are unlawful. If unlawful expulsion carries with it the stigma of bad publicity, and the award of substantial damages, then the central authorities of unions, when asked to concur in particular expulsions, may often refuse to do so, particularly where complex and emotionally charged issues of discipline are concerned. But, if Huntley v. Thornton is any guide, this will not necessarily be the end of the affair. Baulked of their sanctions local leadership may seek to secure the same effect by other means; in fact, as in the Huntley case, they may be under strong rank and file pressure to take further action. In such circumstances it is likely that elements of personal animosity will be present, particularly in the minds of those who take the lead in initiating the substitute sanctions. If it were to be assumed that the guardians of what is in the interests of the local group are the body authorized under the rules to approve expulsion,

---

[1] *Op. cit.*, p. 249.
[2] The Tees Side District Committee were in effect granted the trading interest defence. They had acted, said the judge, without fully appreciating the motives of the Hartlepool D.C., believing Huntley to be a non-unionist.   [3] See p. 215 above.

then the trading interest defence is likely to be denied those who seek to get round their decisions and produce much the same result by other means. The way would then be open for an action for malicious conspiracy.

Moreover, the alleged 'offences' of those whose punishment is sought need not be anywhere near as precise as Huntley's was. Whenever there is a pattern of unilateral regulation, consisting of various informal group practices and customs, a member may break one of these without laying himself open to expulsion—at least this may be the view taken by the national executive of the union. Local militants may then demand that 'something be done' to get round a decision which they will naturally tend to regard as weak, or even motivated by animosity. Other things being equal the more tension and estrangement there is between the group and the national leadership, the more likely the group is to want to 'take the law into its own hands'.

Yet unsatisfactory as this may be from the union's point of view,[1] it is no more satisfactory from the standpoint of the unjustifiably expelled or excluded member. It will be remembered that it took two and a half years for Huntley to secure redress, and it is impossible to estimate how many more cases there are like his which never reach the courts. It is these factors which should be borne in mind when considering the proposals for some reform based on changes in statute law.

(b) Statutory Control

One suggestion which has been canvassed is put forward by the authors of *A Giant's Strength*. They suggest an act empowering the Registrar of Friendly Societies to de-register unions operating a closed shop, and to deny them the immunities of the Acts of 1871, 1876 and 1906 unless their rule books conform to the following provisions:

(a) a right of appeal from any branch to an independent body, with right of representation and respect for natural justice;
(b) expulsion only to be allowed in cases of 'serious misconduct';
(c) matters of fact in dispute in expulsion charges to be decided by an 'objective' inquiry;
(d) unions denied the protection of the trade union acts mentioned above, on the

---

[1] Quite apart from the effect of the bad publicity unions are generally forced to find the costs in actions of this sort. Whatever the law may say their funds are in practice liable to be called upon to defray the expenses of cases of this kind.

grounds that their rules do not meet tests (a), (b) and (c), to be granted the right to appeal to the High Court.[1]

It is submitted that the idea of instituting such a 'screening' procedure is more important than the precise way in which the writers propose it shall be done, and does not depend on the satisfactoriness or otherwise of the actual tests they put forward.[2]

Naturally, whether the task is given to the registrar's department, or to some other body, or whether Parliament lays down the principles to be adopted in detail or not, the problem of interpreting such principles will always remain. Moreover, when this has been done, and the rule book authorized, there is still the problem of interpreting the actual meaning of individual rule books, and the task of deciding whether or not, in any individual case, expulsion was justified or not. This would remain the province of the courts, as now. It might therefore be argued that what began as an alternative to judicial review comes to much the same thing in the end; but this is not correct.

If such a suggestion were adopted a number of advantages would follow. First, it would be easy to eliminate, in advance, those specific expulsion rules that were thought objectionable without subjecting the entire contents of the rule book to the consequences of a series of judicial decisions based on the attempts of various judges to interpret vague notions like 'fairness' or 'reasonability'. Second, it would be possible to influence much more directly, and purposefully, the general conduct of expulsions in the great majority of cases where no appeal to the courts is made. Thirdly, standards of clarity and preciseness could be enforced, and ambiguous rules of the sort which tend to result in unlawful expulsion could be eliminated. In short, by forcing unions to revise their rules in order to conform to certain principles, it would be possible to secure a greater degree of control over the conduct of expulsions without

[1] *Op. cit.*, pp. 54–55. The list actually contains two other provisions. One is relatively unimportant and relates to the issue of incorporating the Bridlington Agreement in union rules. The other is more important, but consists of a modified right of entry to a union operating a closed shop. This affects the right to exclude non-members, rather than ex-members, and it is discussed further at p. 271 below.

[2] In fact the threat of deregistration might well turn out to be an insufficiently powerful sanction to force unions to submit their rules to the Registrar, and accept his decisions about their justifiability. The more important immunities granted under the Trade Union Acts are not confined to registered unions, and nowadays the changed attitude of the common law means that the acts themselves are not so important. Unions could survive, and many do, without the benefits of registration. In the next chapter a more effective sanction is suggested, which would compel unions to submit their rule books to the Registrar.

undermining still further the reliability of rule books and the lawful-
ness of existing expulsion procedures. The result might well be that
with their rule books overhauled and duly 'authorized' unions
operating a closed shop would gain more confidence in applying the
sanctions that remained to them. As a consequence there would be
less likelihood of local attempts to circumnavigate central decisions
in expulsion cases.

For all these reasons it is maintained that if the case for a reform
of the existing situation is accepted there is much to be said for
action along these lines. Certainly it would appear to the layman
to be preferable to the development of further categories of common
law liability, resulting in more uncertainty, and a greater likelihood
of action similar to that of the Hartlepool District Committee of the
Engineers.

But many complex issues remain to be settled, even if this proposition is accepted. What precisely should be the limits of justifiable
expulsion, under the terms of the authorized rule book? How far is
it intended to strike at union power generally, or merely to correct
certain abuses?

The authors of *A Giant's Strength* do not attempt to settle these
issues. They would limit expulsion from a closed shop union to
instances of 'serious misconduct', but this notion is as vague and
ambiguous as that of 'reasonableness' and 'fairness'. They sometimes
write as though they believe that the unions have more power than
they need, but it is unclear how far they desire to reduce union power
generally and the functions of the closed shop in particular. Yet it is
essential to decide these issues before attempting to compile a model
rule book. If, for example, one's main concern is to correct abuses,
then the primary objective will be to ensure that natural justice is
observed and victimization avoided. On this ground objection will
be raised to such things as branch discretion over fines, the compilation of local by-laws which carry the penalty of expulsion, absence
of adequate hearings, etc. For these are the sort of rules that lay
themselves open to abuse at local level, and permit disproportionately severe treatment of certain individuals on personal grounds.
By far the most important rule, in this respect, is one which authorizes expulsion without the right of appeal. If, on the other hand,
the intention is to reduce the total extent of the disciplinary powers
of the closed shop, then, presumably, the rules which most offend
are the general or 'blanket' expulsion rules, and after them the more
extreme specific ones. As has been argued, proposals of this sort

may be justified by reference to one or two arguments; either it is said that such rules are no longer necessary, in order to enable unions to match employer power, or that even if they are they cannot be allowed to stand in the name of public policy, or civil liberty, etc. But this is to raise once again all the largely unresolvable and highly disputable issues raised first by the Royal Commission of 1867.

It should be clear by now that each one of the suggestions made in this chapter presupposes a particular attitude towards these questions, albeit unavowed. Proposals for a Restrictive Practices Court for Labour arise, basically, out of respect for competition and a belief that there is much to be said for applying the same sort of principles to labour bargaining. Proposals for enforcing the open union are rooted in certain assumptions about the 'rights' of individual workers, and employers to be freed from certain forms of collective coercion. Proposals for extending the basis of legal control over expulsion rules cannot be evaluated unless and until one decides how far one wishes to reduce the range and force of collective coercion.

So far as possible it has been the intention of this chapter in considering these suggestions to strike a relatively objective note, reviewing each of the criticisms and suggestions in turn while stressing throughout the extent to which one's attitude towards them turned on the largely unresolved and still disputable issues first raised by the Royal Commission of 1867. Nevertheless, a number of preferences were expressed, and it seemed worthwhile, in a final chapter, drawing together what has been written in this section of the book in order to introduce a number of suggestions for possible reform.

This involves a statement of the writer's own attitude towards the continued justifiability of the closed shop, in the light of what has been discovered about its purposes and effects. The next chapter begins with this statement.

CHAPTER 11

CONCLUSIONS AND SUGGESTIONS

(1) THE CONTINUED JUSTIFIABILITY OF THE CLOSED SHOP

IN Chapter 7 it was maintained that before one could approve of the closed shop it was necessary to show that:

(a) the purposes for which it was used were justifiable;
(b) it was necessary to fulfil those purposes;
(c) it did not result in disadvantages sufficient to outweigh the benefits it made possible.

The first object of this chapter is to define the writer's attitude to these questions.

It seems to me that, in general terms, the closed shop is justifiable —although it is sometimes used unnecessarily and is liable to abuse. It is usually demanded where unions face problems of organization and control which are insoluble without its aid. Unless such problems can be solved three things may happen:

(1) It may be impossible to develop enough collective strength either to secure recognition, and the right to participate in bilateral job regulation, or to impose any sort of unilateral regulation;
(2) even if recognition can be secured the union may still be too weak to take effective action if individual employers refuse to observe agreements;
(3) even if this is possible, it may still not be strong enough to secure any 'improvements' in wages and conditions.[1]

Where either of the first two situations are likely, the justification of the closed shop can be based on the argument that unless workers are free to demand and obtain it they will be unable to sustain a system of visible job regulation. In Chamberlain's words the employer will be free to 'force obedience to his laws' and the system of 'self-government' which trade union participation in job regulation represents will no longer be possible. In such a situation the only alternative to surrendering to the arbitrary rules of the employer is an extension of state intervention.

It is submitted that this would be very much against the spirit and tradition of the British system of industrial relations, and a retrograde step. As Professor Kahn-Freund has argued:

[1] See p. 95 above for an analysis of union objectives in job regulation, and the relationship with the closed shop.

there exists something like an inverse correlation between the practical significance of legal sanctions and the degree to which industrial relations have reached a state of maturity.[1]

This doctrine has always been generally accepted in Britain. As a result, government intervention has been designed 'to stimulate collective bargaining and the application of collective agreements by indirect inducements in preference to direct compulsion'. It is only when these methods fail that the state provides, in Kahn-Freund's words:

substitute standards enforceable by legal sanctions. The principles and procedures which govern the establishment of these standards are intended to assist the industries concerned in developing voluntary bargaining habits. All statutory methods of wage fixing and other conditions of employment are by the law itself considered as second best.[2]

It is not easy to list all the groups in which the closed shop is essential, if the choice between state regulation and the arbitrary rule of the employer is to be avoided. However, it seems reasonable to suppose that comprehensively closed groups like merchant seamen and musicians would find it impossible to maintain effective organization without its aid, and several less organized groups, such as builders' labourers and distributive workers, depend on it for the limited degree of organization which they have achieved. Nor is this all. It is not too much to argue that the only hope which most of the more weakly-organized groups have of dispensing with the 'prop' of minimum wage legislation, and the 'Wages Council System' is the attainment of the closed shop. The fact that at the moment there are no closed shops among groups like laundry workers or agricultural labourers, does not mean that they would not benefit if there were. Nor does it mean that if the level of unionization rises in these groups demands for the practice will not be made; the reverse is probably the case. I would regard this as a welcome development, and would consider the growth of actual closed shops in these industries as a sign that their industrial relations were advancing to what Professor Kahn-Freund has termed a more 'mature' stage.

But such arguments can only be used to justify the closed shop where the conditions set out in (1) and (2) above apply. This is not always the case. A few printers, and many engineers, sustain a viable system of job regulation without the aid of the closed shop, although they would be in a better position to defend and improve their

---

[1] Flanders and Clegg, *op. cit.*, p. 43.   [2] *Op. cit.*, p. 66.

position if they could obtain it.[1] To maintain a *general* justification of the practice it must be assumed that it can be justified in these instances as well, by reference to the benefits it ensures. It must also be assumed that it does not result in disadvantages to others, or to the general interest, which outweigh these advantages.

Any decision on questions of this sort must be very much a matter of personal judgment, but I would maintain that a general justification for the closed shop can be made in this way. Despite the extra bargaining position which individual workers now enjoy as a result of a high level of employment; despite the extension of social security provisions (despite, in short, all that has happened since 1867), I believe that workers still need to combine to match the power of employers. I do not agree that under cover of existing legal immunities, including the right to demand and obtain the closed shop, unions have developed a 'Giant's Strength' which threatens to overwhelm those who resist their demands. Undoubtedly there are those who would agree with the authors of *A Giant's Strength*, who are 'apprehensive that the great powers the unions have been given may be used tyrannically or in a manner contrary to the best interests of the country as a whole'.[2] It seems to me that there is at least as much truth in the view of V. L. Allen, who recently wrote, in his *Trade Unions and the Government*, of the 'Legend of Power', which unions now enjoy, arguing that 'much misinformed opinion about unions (has) . . . diverted attention from those who have held real power in the community; from industrialists, the Church, the Press, the Establishment and the Aristocracy'.[3] In fact, all statements of this sort must be asserted, rather than proved, but it is important to remember how much the attitude one adopts towards the closed shop depends, in the last analysis, on such personal assessments. To me it seems that despite the very considerable powers which unions now enjoy, the power from which most workers still need to be protected is that of the employers. Despite union participation in job regulation the initiative in decision taking remains with employers. Generally, unions can do no more than try to influence those managerial decisions which vitally affect their members. If

---

[1] Of course it is often argued, by trade unionists, that groups of this sort depend on, and even batten off, the more highly organized groups in their industry who usually have obtained the closed shop. In other words, that the wages and conditions which have been established in the industry are largely the result of the efforts of the better organized sections. To the extent that this is admitted it may be argued that *all* workers in the industry are benefiting from the closed shop.   [2] *Op. cit.*, p. 26.

[3] Longmans Green, 1960, p. 313.

they feel that to do this more effectively they need the extra strength and discipline which only the closed shop can provide, I do not feel that the existing balance of power in industry justifies the law in trying to prevent them.

Nor do I accept that there is any essential difference between allowing unions to use collective sanctions in an attempt to regulate wages and conditions, and permitting the enforcement of entry control via the closed shop. The scope of union interest in entry control is, in any case, largely determined by the extent to which it is felt to be necessary to maintain effective job regulation. Whether entry control is more justifiable when enforced unilaterally, via a union imposed closed shop, or bilaterally, via a collective agreement, seems to me impossible to say. But there would appear to be no good reason why, in itself, the attempt to control entry should be regarded as especially unjustifiable—although entry control for certain purposes might be objectionable.

Similarly, with the so-called economic disadvantages of entry control. I can see no case for drawing a hard and fast line. It is not merely that other union practices may be even more economically disadvantageous; it is that it is far from clear what would be the eventual economic effect of legislating against any particular range of union activities. It is worth noting here that Peter Wiles, after roundly condemning all union 'restrictive practices', in his *Are Trade Unions' Necessary*, wisely concluded that there was no practical case for declaring them illegal, since the result would be that something similar or just as bad would soon thrust 'its ugly head through the loopholes of the law'.[1] Similarly, shipbuilding employers, though vociferous in condemning the boilermakers' union for various restrictive practices, including entry control and the maintenance of the skill gap, do not seek a legislative solution. What they hope is that the union will eventually be weaned away from the worst of these practices.

Finally, there is no convincing evidence that at present there are any industries or trades where the power of the unions, derived partly from the closed shop, is a *crucial* factor in limiting efficiency. Even the Royal Commission on the Press did not claim this. They believed that union ruthlessness and managerial weakness had combined to drive up labour costs in four national dailies to a point which was 12 per cent above optimum efficiency level,[2] but they

[1] *Encounter*, September 1956, p. 11.   [2] *Op. cit.*, p. 215.

admitted that such comparatively marginal factors were in no way responsible for the economic collapse of papers like the *News Chronicle* and *Star*. Summarizing the contribution which reduced labour costs could make to struggling newspapers the Commissioners were forced to conclude that 'the key to the solution of the economic difficulties of competitive newspapers, if it is to be found anywhere, is hardly to be found here'.[1]

Similarly, J. R. Parkinson, in his full-length study, *The Economics of Shipbuilding*, decided that the rigid job demarcations imposed by the unions in commercial shipbuilding were not of vital economic importance. He continued:

. . . irrespective of demarcation troubles a few shipyards in the country have achieved a standard of productivity comparable with the best in the world, and it would be as wrong to assume that demarcation was the main reason for the failure of the others to attain comparable standards as it would be to assume that other shipyards in other countries untroubled by demarcation issues invariably achieve higher standards of productivity than British yards. The cost of demarcation to the British industry should not be exaggerated.[2]

Quoting a pre-war survey of the industry, which concluded that 'in a well managed yard inefficiency due to rigid demarcation might be of the order of less than 5 per cent of the wages bill', Parkinson commented: 'This estimate, while it can scarcely have been founded on a detailed investigation, probably puts the cost in its right perspective.'

It should therefore be clear that what follows is written from the viewpoint of one who accepts the general justifiability of both the pre- and post-entry shop. Undoubtedly the practice sometimes results in a restriction of individual liberty, and probably it sometimes has disadvantageous economic effects. Non-unionists and employers are often coerced, and existing members are forced to obey union rules and orders by means of the threat of exclusion from the job. In its pre-entry form the practice is sometimes used to deny whole classes of workers the right to compete for particular jobs. But, in the great majority of cases, these things are done in order to assist in the maintenance and improvement of the unions' powers of job regulation, and in order to make possible greater opportunities for group protection and advancement. The inevitable restrictions on personal liberty they involve, and even the possible maldistribution of economic resources which result, seem to me to be the price which must be paid if the unions are to be

---

[1] *Op. cit.*, p. 31. [2] Cambridge University Press, 1960, p. 166.

allowed the freedom they require in order to pursue such objectives in the most effective way.

But I would seek to draw a line between acceptance of the general justifiability of the closed shop and approval of the use of the exclusion sanction in any particular instance. A general case must be made out against the closed shop before one can support legislation the intention of which is to suppress it by law. A general case must also be made out against the use of any one of the functions of the practice—say entry control—before one can approve of legislation aimed at striking at this function alone. I do not think such general arguments can be sustained.

But it does not follow from this that the powers which the closed shop confers are never abused. Nor does it mean that nothing ought to be done to try to prevent this. One may distinguish between the acceptance of a general right and approval of the way in which it is used in exceptional cases. One may say that men ought to be allowed to campaign for and obtain the closed shop and yet want to bring its use under public control. I would argue that while the closed shop should continue to be recognized as a lawful and 'legitimate' trade union objective, the actual imposition of the exclusion sanction requires some degree of justification in each specific case. In short, I think it ought to be plausible to argue that it was *functionally necessary*. This implies:

(a) that the enforcement of the closed shop results in certain benefits to those who combine to impose it;
(b) that its enforcement was necessary in order to secure this result;
(c) that the benefits resulting outweigh the losses suffered by those who are damaged as a result of its enforcement.

Benefits and losses may be measured either in economic terms, or in terms of individual liberty, but it must be stressed that to feel that the benefits, on balance, 'outweigh' the losses, it is not necessary to believe that those who impose the closed shop gain more *in toto* than those who lose. This need only be the case where one approves of the existing distribution of advantage and disadvantage. One might feel that the group who gains is more in need, or deserves to gain more, than the group which loses. One would then want to approve of the attainment of a closed shop which produced such a result even if it could not be shown that it produced a net gain. What is meant by saying that benefits 'outweigh' disadvantages is merely that on balance this results in a redistribution of advantage and disadvantage, however measured or judged, which is preferable

S

to that existing before. Unless the enforcement of the closed shop sanctions could be so justified in a particular instance then I, for one, would not approve of their employment.

Yet it is not suggested that the *legal* right to employ such sanctions should be made dependent upon advance proof, in each instance, of *functional justification*. Quite apart from the practical difficulties this would involve, in strict logical terms, as was argued throughout Chapter 10, a detailed weighing of advantage and disadvantage which is not possible in matters of this sort. It is difficult to determine what constitutes a given degree of advantage, and impossible to measure this against other advantages and disadvantages in any objective way.[1] Any attempt to enforce such a principle would constitute, in effect, a surrender to the judgements of those empowered to interpret the principle. The consequences, from the union point of view, would be as uncertain, and therefore as unacceptable, as proposals to extend the scope of judicial control by developing new forms of common law liability. But this does not mean that nothing can be done to narrow the existing degree of immunity along lines suggested by the principle of functional justification. The next section contains a number of proposals for doing this.

(2) Proposals for Reform

(a) Restrictions on the Right to Exclude Non-Members

Let us consider the position of the elderly worker who refuses to join a union when his factory is affected by a closed shop drive. If he is an isolated case, and does not seek to persuade others to follow his example, many trade unionists would agree not to insist on what they would regard as their 'right' to demand his exclusion. This will be more likely to be their attitude if the employer concerned is willing to agree that all future labour recruited will be regarded as entering a closed shop. By acting in this way the workers concerned are themselves recognizing the principle of functional justification. If the employer is willing to make such a concession then clearly the temporary presence of the odd non-unionist is no real threat to the union's position, just as his replacement by a union member will not add substantially to its bargaining power. But not all union groups are as tolerant as this. One has heard of small groups or isolated individuals being forced to leave their jobs in circumstances

[1] Nevertheless, all social activity, and social policy, involves attempts to make such judgements. The matching power argument itself is dependent on just such a judgement. The trouble with it is that it is too general, and so it can be used to justify almost limitless immunity.

in which it appeared to be obvious that the penalties inflicted on the individual, as a result, were out of all proportion to the potential threat to the group.

It will, of course, be argued that the men concerned could avoid such a penalty by agreeing to conform, so that in a sense they 'chose' to suffer. But the question at issue is whether any group has the right to restrict the liberty of another and to inflict substantial damage upon them, unless they fulfil certain conditions. When there is no necessity to act in this way, and no interest of the first group is involved, I would say no.

Can anything be done about this? I think so. It could be made illegal to discharge, or demand the discharge of, any workers on grounds of non-unionism, where the employer concerned was prepared to agree to sign an agreement the terms of which might be broadly as follows:

(1) All future labour engaged on certain types of work in certain areas must become and remain members of specified unions;

(2) Existing members in those areas would not be permitted to lapse from the union, and if expelled lawfully would be liable to be discharged;

(3) Existing non-unionists in these areas would be 'encouraged' to join the union, and if they refused 'reasonable' efforts would be made to employ them in areas not covered by the registration shop.[1]

Once such an agreement was accepted it would be illegal to obtain the discharge of any workers employed in an area which it covered. A law of this sort might be enforced much in the way that under the Taft-Hartley and Wagner Acts 'unfair labour practices' were made illegal in the United States; i.e. by lodging a complaint of an unfair labour practice with the National Labour Relations Board any person may set the machinery of the Act in operation. Complaints are investigated by the Board, and if well founded a hearing is arranged before one of their trial examiners. Afterwards review agents go over the trial examiners' report and present summary records and proposed findings and rulings to the Board itself for final action. Final appeal to the ordinary courts is retained since the Board must bring an action in court to enforce its own orders.[2] It might not be necessary to set up a body of the size or composition of the N.L.R.B., which has a number of other functions as well, but this point is discussed further below.

[1] It will be remembered that such an arrangement, described as a 'registration shop', was reached in the case of a large motor firm. See p. 120 above.
[2] See Sultan, *op. cit.*, for further details of the working of the Act and decisions in recent cases.

S*

This suggested procedure is advanced more as an example of what might be done than as a definitive solution, but if enforced it would, I feel, go far to protect the relatively few workers who have developed genuine 'conscientious objections' to joining trade unions. These men are often elderly workers, employed for many years in an open shop. They are the main group who suffer as a result of the present position. The proposal would also offer reasonable protection to the unions, and a positive organizational advantage in exchange for a not very important surrender of what they would no doubt regard as their rights.

It might be doubted, however, how far such a commonsense solution can be imposed by statute in circumstances in which the parties cannot agree to it without the aid of the law. It would always be open to the union concerned to reject the registration shop proposal.[1] Moreover, even if they accepted and workers were discharged in circumstances which were clearly illegal, how many of them would take legal action to enforce their rights?

The average worker is unfamiliar with the law, and views litigation as a slow and expensive process. Moreover, even if these problems were overcome and enforcement powers were given to some official authority, ways might still be found of avoiding the effects of such an Act. Unions might sign such an agreement, and subsequently demand the discharge of individuals they objected to on grounds other than non-unionism. Faced with a stoppage over such an issue many employers would be only too willing to find plausible reasons for ceasing to employ those who 'failed to get on' with their fellow workers.

On this question of enforcement it is worth looking at what has happened recently in the United States. In particular the example of the 1946 Taft-Hartley Act, and the various 'Right to Work' laws passed by individual states are worthy of study. Reviewing the first four years of the former Act, which outlawed the pre-entry shop, Sumner H. Slichter concluded that the practice could not be eliminated by law in industries where it was already well established.[2] Writing on the same theme in 1960 Seymour Martin Lipset concluded that the Act 'has had no effect in promoting individual workers rights. There have been few individuals who took advantage

---

[1] To impose it on them would, I feel, encourage circumvention of its provisions—see below.

[2] Revision of the Taft-Hartley Act, *Quarterly Journal of Economics*, Vol. 67, Harvard, U.S.A., 1953, p. 63.

of rights under the Act to keep their jobs.'[1] In the case of 'Right to Work' laws, which usually go further than Taft-Hartley, and seek to ban the post-entry shop, Frederick W. Meyers has shown that in Texas, and within the traditionally closed areas 'the old practices remain in force and violate not simply state law but federal legislation as well'.[2]

But, in reviewing these and other findings in the field, Lipset asserts that the trouble has been that the framers of such acts have been ignorant of the working of unions and hostile to their intentions. Consequently both members and union leaders have regarded their acts as 'punitive legislation. The consequence was the unenforceability and inadequacy described.' Lipset concludes that if it is to succeed legislation of this sort ought to encourage self-regulation by unions themselves, and ought not to be obviously intended to 'impair the collective bargaining strength of the unions'. It should also be concerned with the more moderate task of laying down certain 'minimum preconditions' within which the unions can work.[3]

These are wise words, too often overlooked by those who suggest new laws to deal with old abuses in the field of industrial relations. It is contended that the proposals put forward in this chapter, broadly speaking, fulfil such stipulations.

Moreover, it is not a sufficient argument against trying to correct an abuse to show that one may not *always* succeed. Indeed, so long as the consequences of partial failure would not be worse than the existing situation it is no argument at all. It is more reasonable to suggest, as Seymour Martin Lipset has done, that in the field of labour legislation, at least,

the significance of law does not necessarily lie in the extent to which it is obeyed. One of its major functions is to set a moral code or standard which society considers proper but whose parts can be violated within certain limits. If most people commit adultery occasionally—as Kinsey has demonstrated—this does not have much effect on family stability, but if everyone feels free to commit adultery whenever he wishes, the family system as we know it would not exist. . . . People

[1] *The Law and Trade Union Democracy*, a report to The Fund for the Republic, New York, U.S.A., 1960, p. 35.
[2] *Right to Work in Practice*, The Fund for the Republic, New York, U.S.A., 1959, p. 4. On the other hand, it would not be correct to imply that all these acts have had absolutely no effect. Sultan (*op. cit.*, p. 89) says since Taft-Hartley it has been more difficult for unions to secure the discharge of employees for reasons *other* than failure to tender dues, and Meyers himself maintains that Right to Work statutes can have an indirect effect on the 'climate of organization' so that 'campaigns that might otherwise have been won have been lost'. (*Ibid.*) The significance of this last point is referred to again below [3] *Ibid.*

may engage in illegal or immoral actions, but the fact that they know these actions are illegal reduces the extent to which they occur, even if violators are rarely prosecuted.

It is important to recognize, therefore, that the function of labour legislation may not be as much to create viable laws that can be used 'against' unions, as to set moral standards in an area of institutional behaviour that previously was outside the realm of *explicit* moral standards.[1]

It is because I believe that the principle of functional justification is one that ought to be made explicit whenever possible that I believe that there is a case for trying to use it in this way to limit the right of unions to exclude non-members. It is because it is not intended to undermine union power, but merely to correct its abuse, that I believe that there may be a chance that many trade unionists, and their leaders, might come to accept it as a justifiable norm to apply.

It must be admitted that at the moment most of them would probably maintain that the solution proposed is an unwarrantable intrusion into the internal affairs of the unions, of an unusual and dangerous kind.[2] British unions have always been particularly anxious to minimize the interference of the law in their affairs, with such success that there is certainly less legal intervention in British unions than in the unions of any other industrialized country. Any proposal to increase legal intervention will, therefore, be bound to be rigorously scrutinized, and rightly so, for British unions have drawn a number of important advantages from the existing tradition. Two cogent reasons can, however, be given for serious consideration of further legislation on the question of the closed shop. The first is that the courts, as has been seen, are already extending the area of their intervention in this field, and as we have seen there are very weighty precedents for trade union support for legislation to provide clear rules when the courts try to take over control of trade union affairs by 'judge made law'.[3] Secondly, as has been shown, there is already a strong demand for legislation in this field coming from other quarters. This may increase and ultimately lead to parliamentary action whether the trade unions wish it or not.

---

[1] *Op. cit.*, p. 59.

[2] In this connection a comparison might justly be made with the United States. The 'unfair labour practices' device, which was introduced into the Wagner Act as a weapon for the unions to use, was easily turned against them in the Taft-Hartley Act some twelve years later. Unions might argue that by setting up an organization like the N.L.R.B. Britain was inviting a similar development.

[3] In this connection the judgment of Sachs J. in Rookes *v.* Barnard, and Harman J. in Huntley *v.* Thornton were both symptomatic and highly significant.

In these circumstances it would surely be wise for the trade unions at least to think about what would be the most satisfactory form of legislation if legislation there has to be.

(b) Restrictions on the Right to Exclude Ex-Members

It is easier to discover a simple and effective way of applying the principle of functional justification to the right to exclude ex-members, although this too requires an extension of 'outside interference'. This can be done by developing the suggestion of *A Giant's Strength* for empowering the Registrar of Friendly Societies, or some such person, to enforce prescribed rule book standards on all unions. In this way clarity, and certainty, can be combined with the protection of the individual from the more common abuses of the closed shop. This would be done in two distinct ways. Firstly, any rule which permits the use of the exclusion sanction in a way considered unnecessary would be disallowed; secondly, model rules embodying safeguards would be insisted upon. Unions would be compelled to submit their rule books for authorization to the requisite authority. After a specified period no union would be allowed to issue a rule book unless it had been authorized. Since the principles to be enforced would have general utility there would be need to make a distinction between unions operating closed shops and those confined to open shop areas. *All* unions ought to be forced to comply with the principles laid down. There would also be no need to interfere with the ultimate powers of the courts to interpret union rule books and consider actions for wrongful expulsion. Indeed, by clarifying and simplifying union rule books, this proposal should make the task of the courts much simpler.

The reformer of union rule books may be concerned with four types of union rule: procedural, substantive, admissive, and electoral. What would be required if each type were required to pass the tests suggested?

(i) PROCEDURAL RULES

In procedural rules what is required is that the principles of natural justice should be observed. The principles are designed to prevent victimization, personal bias and other abuses, and to assist in the discovery of the facts. There is no good reason why any member should be expelled from a union in a way which violates natural justice, and every reason for insisting that rule books show respect for the principle. Since courts now 'read' natural justice into the rules there is a positive advantage, from the union point of view, in writing its demands into the rule book in advance. This should reduce the number of unintentionally and unnecessarily unlawful expulsions. Yet observance of natural justice would not undermine the necessary disciplinary functions of the closed shop. Those it was necessary to expel could still be dealt with.

It is neither possible nor desirable to set out in any detail the kind of procedural rules required to observe the needs of natural justice, but in the light of what has been discovered about union expulsion procedures there are a number of things to be ensured. First, in all cases other than a failure to pay dues, members charged with offences under the rules should be sent a copy of the charge together with a reference to the appropriate rule.[1] Secondly, there should be provisions for a hearing, before the branch or branch committee, with an opportunity to give evidence in defence and, if need be, call witnesses, etc. Thirdly, there should be a right of appeal to a national body, and the final appeal ought to lie with some body other than the supreme governing authority. Ample precedents exist for this. The Engineers, Health Service Employees, and Bisakta, all have such provisions in their rules. Perhaps the best are those of Bisakta where the final court consists of:

Twelve persons, being trade unionists and members of any organization affiliated to the Trades Union Congress or to the Scottish Trades Union Congress, or to the Labour Party and not being beneficially interested directly or indirectly in the funds of the Association.[2]

Fourthly, and not normally considered by would-be reformers, the procedure relating to charges should be rigidly phased. There seems no reason why the unions' final appeal court should not sit at least twice a year, and any member charged with an offence carrying the extreme penalty of expulsion ought to be able to obtain a decision from the court within twelve months of lodging the charge. It could also be insisted that no member, or group of members, had the right to demand the discharge of another member charged with an offence under the rules while that person was still using the procedure. If this were done unions could be allowed, as at the moment, to insist on the payment of fines before access to appeals procedure is admitted.

---

[1] The provisions required in cases of expulsion for a failure to pay dues are dealt with below.
[2] Bisakta Rule Book, *op. cit.*, Rule 43. The intention is to ensure an independent and fair hearing where expulsion proceedings are commenced and prosecuted by the national leadership itself. If such provisions are insisted upon it might not be necessary to insist that the branch should always act as a 'court of first instance'.

(2) Substantive Rules

The standards needed for substantive rules are more complex and disputable. I cannot see why unions should be allowed to expel members without giving any reason, under exceedingly vague or comprehensive blanket expulsion rules. The number of occasions when the union would be damaged by being made to give a reason is exceedingly small. In view of the impracticability of defining, in advance, a comprehensive list of offences, there is a functional case for a general expulsion rule, so long as it is framed in terms of causing wilful damage to the union or its trading interest. In specific expulsion rules most of the more common examples listed in Chapter 4 would be justifiable on functional grounds. For example, persistent blacklegging, other serious trading offences, and attempts to defraud, ought to be punishable under the rules. But, once again, one must ensure that such rules do not provide vindictive groups with the opportunity to impose severe penalties on those they dislike where less draconic sanctions are all that are necessary to uphold union discipline. Special regard should be paid to rules sanctioning expulsion for disobedience to the orders of one authority. If written in a certain way they can be used to deprive a man of his trade for the slightest offence. There should also be an attempt to see that penalties for particular offences are rigidly graduated. A fine of up to £5 for failure to come out on strike is a relatively minor penalty, which may be nonetheless effective. Unless it can be shown that, in a particular individual's case it has been ineffective in the past, there is no reason why he should be expelled from the union. The damage caused, if the union operates a widespread closed shop, is out of all proportion to the offence.

It would do no harm to force unions to err on the side of leniency in these matters. If they are concerned about the maintenance of union discipline, what they need are not crushing penalties, which they are afraid to use and which invite attempts to get round them, but easily understood and reliable graduated sanctions. The final weapon of expulsion should be kept in reserve. It might be made compulsory to include a rule stipulating that no member could be expelled in any circumstances for a first offence against the union's disciplinary code. Certainly more use should be made of fines for first and second offences. It is also doubtful if offences against branch by-laws should remain grounds for expulsion. There should be no expulsion rule unconnected with the defence of union interests —i.e. rules which provide for the expulsion of convicted persons should be disallowed. Automatic lapsing should be allowed, but with safeguards. A rule like that of the boilermakers, which sanctioned a termination of membership for being a mere 20s. in arrears is too severe. Automatic lapsing should only be authorized after a period of six months, and then a written notification should be sent at least a month before the member is struck off from the district office.[1]

Lapsed members who wish to pay up, or workers re-entering the union required to pay an entrance fee, should not be expected to furnish exaggerated and arbitrary payments, though nothing should be done to put a premium on the non-payment of subscriptions. Every union should be forced to embody a resignation rule, allowing members to resign on leaving the trade. Re-entrance fees should be nominal, and figures like £50 should be disallowed.[2] On the other hand, the needs of union discipline make it inadvisable to insist on a general right to resign and join another union, while working within a closed shop. This would undoubtedly encourage poaching, and secessions from the union. For similar reasons there seems no point in objecting to unions including a rule which binds their members to accept the terms of the Bridlington Agreement.

These suggestions are not supposed to be comprehensive, and are introduced in such detail largely in order to serve as illustrations of the way in which the principle of functional justification can be applied. It might be that the authority set up to screen such rules should be allowed a wide discretion in interpreting the principle, and the act empowering them to do this ought to do no more than enunciate, in general terms, the implications of the principle itself.

---

[1] This may appear a small detail, but it is important. Trade unionists with whom this has been discussed have stressed that general unions and others, like the M.U., with a large turnover would find it difficult to insist that branch secretaries sent out warnings of this sort. In fact it is preferable that higher levels of the hierarchy should do this. It is sometimes suggested that local groups who wish to rid themselves of troublemakers have in the past allowed these characters to get into arrears deliberately, and have then demanded that they be expelled under automatic lapsing rules. If a notice had to be sent out first by the district secretary this would be less likely to happen. Local officials could strike lapsed members off their register and send their names to the district office. The district office would send out a standard letter and, if nothing was heard from the member in four weeks, expulsion would be formally confirmed. A procedure of this sort should reconcile the demands of collective discipline and efficient administration with the need to protect the individual from possible victimization. It is thus a good example of the kind of approach that is being recommended.

[2] See the case of Harkness v. the E.T.U. (1956), The Times, June 26–30.

(3) ADMISSION RULES

If one accepts the right of unions to control entry via the closed shop there is no case for insisting that unions embody in their rules a stipulation that no worker, who is willing to join, shall be denied a right to entry; but there is a case for certain modified rights of re-entry, and for vetoing rules which stipulate that entrance shall be refused on particular grounds. For example, the first time a man is excluded from the union for non-payment of dues the rules could insist that he should be given the right to re-enter the union within a specified time, so long as he pays a fine which represents the dues he would have paid had he been a member. The rules would state that the man should be regarded as a 'suspended', and not an expelled member.

If the man were expelled for a disciplinary offence, then, provided the provisions relating to disciplinary offences are overhauled as suggested, there is no case for allowing a right of re-entry. Where men are persistent lapsers, or evaders, the chances are that they will have been excluded more than once for the non-payment of dues.

The position is more difficult in the case of applicants for entry who have never been members. One could insist that no union should be allowed to operate racial, religious or political barriers by reference to the rules, and I would like to use the rule book to try to prevent entry-control being exercised on grounds other than those directly related to trading interests. The difficulties here are practical ones. Almost all refusals to admit can be justified to some extent by reference to trading interests, and so even if one could ensure that the terms of the rule book were being observed such provisions might have little effect.

(4) ELECTORAL RULES

Finally, we come to the standards to be applied to rules governing the way in which various levels of union leadership are selected. The need to subject such rules to the authorization process is not so obvious as in the case of the other types of rule considered. A word of explanation is therefore necessary. Writers like Allen and Goldstein,[1] make much of the low degree of democratic participation which they claim exists in many British unions. As Allen puts it: 'A meagre number of rank and file members are active in trade union government and they, along with officials, appear to have

---

[1] See Allen, *Power in Trade Unions, op. cit.*, and Goldstein, *op. cit.*

disproportionate power and responsibility.'[1] Allen sees in this an argument against the closed shop. For only within the open shop, he argues, are the inactive majority free to resign if dissatisfied and thus check the minority's 'temptation to exploit their power (which is often too great to be resisted)'.[2] On the other hand, says Allen, 'A trade union leader who is in continual fear of losing his members will inevitably take steps to satisfy their wants; he will use his authority warily and "canalize" the activities of his officials in the fear of losing members; the size of his union determines the status of his union and its strength, and therefore its ability to fulfil its functions effectively. A falling membership is a much greater stimulant than a strongly worded resolution.'[3]

In my opinion this judgment is oversimple. It suggests that the more a union recruits within the closed sections of industry the more likely it is that its leaders will become irresponsible oligarchs unconcerned with the satisfaction of their members' demands. There is little evidence that this is so. Are the leaders of the boilermakers and shipwrights less responsive to membership demands than, say, the leaders of the General and Municipal Workers? Are Amalgamated Engineering Union officials less concerned with rank and file pressure than, for example, leaders of the Transport and Salaried Staffs Association? Obviously the degree to which any union leadership is subject to membership pressure depends on numerous factors quite unconnected with the presence or absence of the closed shop. Factors of history, tradition, leadership attitude and so on, all enter into this equation. Other things being equal, unions organizing cohesive and highly stable groups are more likely to exhibit strong rank and file pressure than those recruiting disparate, scattered and mobile groups. Groups where local bargaining is important find it easier to influence and control leaders who negotiate on their behalf than those who rely on the outcome of national negotiations. These and many other influences help to determine the extent to which individual leadership groups are subjected to so-called 'democratic control' by their members. Nor is it necessarily the case that undemocratic or oligarchic leadership groups relax their concern for membership demands, and become less 'militant' as a result.

Certainly there does not appear to be anything about the closed shop, as such, which makes it more likely that the longer it lasts and

---

[1] *Power in Trade Unions, op. cit.,* p. 62.   [2] *Op. cit.,* p. 63.   [3] *Ibid.*

the more it spreads the more union leaders will feel safe in ignoring the basic needs of their members. As has been seen, although the practice strengthens the leadership's position it can usually only be imposed, and in the end maintained, while the great majority feel it is worth their while to support the leadership without the use of its sanctions. Outside the sphere of the employer initiated closed shop it is a weapon used, and usable, against a minority not a majority. Moreover, as has been argued, the practice has a habit-forming effect; if anything it increases solidarity, and an awareness of the opportunities made possible by effective action. Inside a closed shop, as often as not, the majority come to make more demands of their leaders—at least at local level.[1] What is true, and what involves a special concern for the electoral rules of unions operating a closed shop, is that if, for reasons largely unconnected with the practice, a closed shop union develops an oligarchic, irresponsible and in other ways unsatisfactory leadership, the powers at its disposal are much stronger. Therefore the consequences of it abusing these powers are more serious. It is for this reason that it is not enough to review the procedural, substantive and admissive rules of unions to protect the individual worker from the arbitrary and unnecessary use of the closed shop sanctions. One should also try to ensure that the leaders who have to administer these rules emerge, at least in the most important instances, as a result of an elective process which is itself fair and not open to obvious abuse.

It would be inadvisable to consider in any detail what this would require in individual cases. The methods by which the leaders of British unions are selected are exceedingly complex. Each union constitution provides for its own individual mixture of elected and appointed officers, responsible in various ways to full-time or lay committees, working under the general supervision of annual or biennial conferences or committees. Nominees are selected, and candidates elected and re-elected, by different methods and with

---

[1] On the other hand, Meyers (*op. cit.*) concluded that in Texas the passage of 'Right to Work Laws' banning the closed shop had the effect of making the unions 'more responsive to the demands of a tiny vocal minority of the membership. It has consequently caused issues to be pressed through grievance machinery which, under conditions of union security (i.e. the closed shop) would not and should not be taken up. The union leader without security is often most responsive not to the majority of loyal union members who will remain, but to the small minority, often irresponsible, whose continued membership is doubtful.' (p. 41). This evidence tends to underscore the view taken above that the effect of the closed shop in this field is essentially one that affects *minorities*. Without the closed shop to fall back on, leadership, according to Meyers, was forced to adopt positions 'conditioned by minorities'. When they were allowed to use it the practice might have been used to discipline, or threaten, these minorities.

varying results. It would probably be admitted that it is advisable for the more important national posts to be subject to election, and probably the supreme policy-making body of the union should be an elected one. But beyond this it would require an exhaustive factual study to determine whether, for example, elected officials were generally more honest and efficient than appointed officials, whether lay executives are better able to control general secretaries than those composed of full-time members. All that the body set up to authorize union rules should be asked to ensure would be that the electoral and appointment provisions contained in any rule book had no obviously unfair rules or provisions which would lay themselves open to abuse. Thus, for example, they might disallow rules such as those which permit restrictions on the circulation of election material. Finally, with the recent E.T.U. case in mind, it might insist that all unions above a certain size should be compelled to appoint one or more independent returning officers drawn from a panel compiled by the Registrar, much as they are now compelled to appoint auditors. It would be the duty of these returning officers to supervise and oversee national elections.

One final question must be disposed of before leaving the subject of proposed restrictions on the right to exclude ex-members from the job. It has been suggested to the writer[1] that, while the case for an overhaul of existing rule books is overwhelming, it does not necessarily follow that this must be done via an increase in legal intervention. Why not leave such a task to the unions themselves; why not propose that the T.U.C. should draw up a model rule book along the lines outlined above? It should be obvious that, if this were to happen, the present writer would regard it as a most welcome development, indeed, if any important union decided to reform its own rule book in the direction suggested I would consider this a significant advance. Nevertheless, it must be admitted that the chances of the T.U.C. being able to push through such a comprehensive change in union rules is extremely slim.[2] It is invariably difficult to secure consent for widespread changes in union rule books, and I do not believe that the sort of uniformity and standardization presupposed in the section above is obtainable without the aid of some external sanction. The sanctions suggested are

---

[1] By K. W. Wedderburn.

[2] There is, in fact, an uninspiring precedent here. For several years the T.U.C. has tried to get member unions to adopt a simple rule which would enable them to expel members recruited in violation of the Bridlington Agreement. But rules of this sort are still very far from universal.

merely those thought to be the least objectionable and most effective for the purpose in hand.

(c) Possible Restrictions on the Right to Exclude Existing Members

The restrictions on the right to exclude both non-members and ex-members advanced above are not foolproof; they are put forward as ways of eliminating the most flagrant abuses of the closed shop, and confining its uses to situations in which it is functionally justifiable. Their aim is not to undermine the practice, but to civilize its use. Since they would preserve and clarify the circumstances in which unions could justifiably use the closed shop sanction, they might reduce the chances that local groups, denied the right to expel members who they considered deserved such punishment, would seek as in the Huntley-Thornton case, to produce all the effects of expulsion by other means.

But since one must assume that there will continue to be occasions when local groups will want to punish individuals in ways not sanctioned by the higher levels of union authority, it is necessary to consider, finally, whether anything can or should be done about this. What is involved here is the right of trade unionists to use the exclusion sanction against *existing members* of the union. There are a number of issues involved here. First, can any group of workers, who are members of a union, justifiably punish one of their number other than by virtue of procedures and penalties prescribed in the rule book? Second, if they can, is what they do committed 'in the name of the union' for offences against it? These are highly contentious questions, and all that can be done is to set down the writer's own opinion.

The answer to the first question is surely yes. As was seen in Chapters 8 and 9, those who developed the present framework of immunity were not primarily concerned with the legalization of authorized trade union action alone. What was legitimized was the use of collective action in a much more general sense. In order to be better able to match employer power workers combined in formalized associations and formulated rules to govern them. But it does not follow that they ought to be refused the right to act collectively outside the scope of their chosen institutions. This may be expressed by saying that the right to defend their trading interests must be presumed to belong to workers as workers, rather than workers as trade unionists. Unions are not the repositories of workers' 'rights', they are the agents of collective action. They may demand loyalty and require punitive sanctions, but the fundamental right to combine should not be handed to unions as an absolute monopoly, As the majority report of the 1867 Commission made clear it is the right of the worker to combine to match employer power which justifies the existence of unions and not *vice versa*.

Moreover, as unions grow in power and effectiveness the retention of such a right is more necessary than ever. Much of the search for ways of narrowing the existing degree of immunity granted to unions stems from the fear that nowadays union majorities may be able to abuse their powers, or neglect the interests of minorities. As Hugh Clegg argues, it may be 'as well for the liberties of trade union members that expulsion cannot put an end to unofficial strikes, for this type of strike has become one of the main weapons of union members against official decisions contrary to their desires'.[1]

But if one grants union members the right to act 'independently' of the union; if one allows them to interpret their own trading interests and act collectively to defend them, a number of difficulties arise. To begin with, this cannot be done without the existence of collective sanctions imposed on those who do not comply with group decisions. One of the most common contemporary workshop customs is the shop-floor meeting. Under the leadership of stewards whose position and powers are very ill-defined in many union rule-books, they take decisions on matters of immediate trading interest, which are regarded as binding. Similarly, in many workplace groups patterns of unilateral regulation have developed which appear in no union rule book. As Clegg points out, when local unions were first formed 'the working customs and union rules might be the same. But this could not last.'[2] Some unions have attempted to deal with this problem by empowering local branches to pass by-laws which have the force of rules, but not all have done this, and in any case it is doubtful whether even in those unions branch by-laws adequately reflect the complexity and scope of individual workshop regulations. Nevertheless, working groups regard their 'unofficial' customs as binding on all who work in the group. If, like the decisions of the shop floor meeting, they cannot be enforced via the rule-book, they must be enforced in some other way. In the last analysis this involves refusing to work alongside

---

[1] Clegg goes on to add, however, 'this is a weapon which can be, and frequently is, mis-used'. (The Rights of British Trade Union Members, in *Labor in a Free Society*, Univ. of California Press, 1959, p. 128.)   [2] *Op. cit.*, p. 124.

another member of the union who will not conform, i.e. the operation of the exclusion sanction, not on the grounds of non-unionism,
but directed against those who have committed no offence against
the union. It follows from this, I think, that action of this sort must
be justified by reference to the members' rights as workers rather
than as trade unionists. But this is not the end of the problem.

It is one thing to agree that where the rule-book is silent members
may supplement its provisions. It is one thing to agree that members
have the right to take collective action to protect their own trading
interests irrespective of, and if necessary in defiance of, their properly
constituted leaders under the rule book. It is another thing to accept
that in order to be able to do this they are justified in securing the
discharge of a fellow member who has committed no offence against
the union as such. Action of this sort is doubly questionable where
it involves breaking specific union rules—for example those related
to the authorization of strikes. For it can be argued that to punish a
member who has committed no offence against the union, members
are committing an offence themselves. In other words, it is they
who should be punished and not the member.

It seems to me that there is no generally valid answer as to whether
or not action of this sort is justified. Two incompatible sets of rights
are being advanced and it is difficult to choose between them. The
union member can claim that his right of employment should be
protected, not infringed, so long as he has committed no offence
against the union. The workers can argue that they have the right,
as workers, to decide who they will work with; if a man will not
accept collective decisions, or customs, then they must be allowed
to take collective action against him. If this involves a breach of
union rules, they may argue, this only goes to show that their
trading interests cannot be adequately defended by remaining within
the confines of the rules.

In matters of this sort one can do no more than express personal
preferences. With the principle of functional justification in mind
it seems to me that the exclusion of an existing member can only be
justified if two conditions are met. First, the offence in question
must be a serious and vital one, undermining an unofficial practice
or decision of great importance to group trading interests. Secondly,
it ought to be clear that only the exclusion sanction will uphold
the practice or decision in this particular case.

For example, in Huntley *v.* Thornton it was decided that in
attempting to punish Huntley more severely than the executive

council agreed the district committee were motivated by malice; this need not necessarily be the case in every incident of this sort. If a man refuses to obey his shop steward, as Huntley did, his workmates may decide at a shop-floor meeting that he merits expulsion. Informed that the rule book will not justify this, they may decide to refuse to work with him. Malice need not enter into their decision —though, as in Huntley *v*. Thornton, it may do so. If, subsequently, other members visit still more punishment on the man in question, they too need not necessarily be motivated by malice. It may seem to them that by acting in this way the trading interests of the district, or simply the trading interests of the working group, will be better protected. But this does not mean that they will be justified on the principles above.

It may be that the trading interests involved were sufficiently protected because, as in the Huntley case, the union was prepared to sanction a minor penalty. One may disagree with this, accepting the justifiability of the man's workmates using the exclusion sanction, yet want to deny the need for the more drastic action which followed —even if it was not predominantly motivated by malice. As has been argued above, it is the weaknesses of the present legal position that it assumes that almost any act is justified so long as it is done with the *intention* of defending trading interests. This is denied by the principle of functional justification. What needs to be shown, on this principle, is not merely the existence of a just or proper intention, but the *need* to employ the weapon used.

There is one further ground on which one may object to action similar to that of the district committee in the Huntley case. As Harman J. said, they 'sought to flout the executive committee's decision and to produce by other means . . . all the effects of expulsion'.[1] It is arguable that the ultimate sanction of expulsion from a union operating closed shops is properly regarded as belonging to the union as such.[2] It ought to be reserved for offences against the union, and not offences against particular groups of workers who may also be trade unionists. By trying to produce all the effects of expulsion, by using their positions as union officers, the district committee were, I would submit, quite unjustified. It is, moreover, in accordance with the principle of functional justification that the more far-reaching punishment of expulsion from unions operating a closed shop should be restricted in its use. The sanction represents

[1] *Op. cit.*, p. 249.
[2] I.e. to workers as trade unionists rather than to workers as workers.

the most severe penalty workers can impose by collective action; it ought to be reserved for offences of a general character. The rule book is the place to specify such offences, and prescribe their penalties.

If it were practical to do so I would like to confine the lawful use of the exclusion sanction against *existing* members of the union to situations where it was functionally justifiable—in the way that it was suggested above that its use against non-members should be restricted. Unfortunately, I am not convinced that a satisfactory formula can be found for ensuring just this. The problem is that in respect of the use of the exclusion sanction against existing members there is no equivalent of a registration shop agreement.[1] The assumption, in the case of such an agreement, is that once it is accepted, along the lines specified above, the legitimate trading interests of the group are all taken care of; thus further action is unnecessary and may be made unlawful.[2]

On balance it seems advisable to leave the legal position as it is. Already, as the Huntley case shows, the worst attempts to 'get round' the rule book may not be beyond the reach of the law—even if it is necessary to decide that those involved were motivated by malice. The position is not wholly satisfactory, partly because it is not possible to tell how far the courts may go in deciding that local groups were motivated by malice rather than the desire to defend group interests, and partly because many of the worst cases of a functionally unjustifiable use of the exclusion sanction may not come before the courts. Nevertheless, one cannot always discover satisfactory remedies in matters of this sort, and it is necessary to decide on the least unsatisfactory course.

(3) CONCLUSIONS

The proposals in this chapter derive from accepting the closed shop as a growing and justifiable feature of British industrial relations which needs to be subjected to a greater measure of public control to eliminate its abuses and unnecessary use. It is suggested that this can best be done by a change in statute law, because an extension of common law liability would increase uncertainty and fail to deal with incidents of minor injustice which never come before the courts. Yet it is not suggested that judicial review should be ousted altogether;

[1] See p. 263 above.
[2] It would be possible to make it illegal to exclude existing members unless they committed 'serious' breaches of 'vital group customs', and so on; but this would give rise to difficulties of interpretation, and probably of enforcement as well.

merely that its impact should be directed towards ends that have been statutorily prescribed. What is needed in the field of labour law is certainty, precision, easy redress, and, if possible, relative privacy. It is suggested that in respect of the closed shop these can best be promoted by statutory reform along the lines suggested.

Two suggestions are made. It could be made illegal to discharge or demand the discharge of non-members where a 'registration shop' agreement has been negotiated. It should also be made compulsory to submit union rule books to an authorization process aimed at enforcing the standards of functional necessity and natural justice. To operate these reforms it might be advisable to create a public authority which could, if necessary, take over the existing functions of the Registrar of Friendly Societies in regard to trade unions. The authority would have the duty of administering what, in effect, would be another trade union act; this would involve interpreting and applying the rule book standards and, if need be, investigating alleged infringements of the limits set for the exclusion sanction as defined in the act.

Those with a greater knowledge of the law than the present writer may say that one or another of these suggestions is impractical, or inadvisable, for various reasons. They may be right. The suggestions are those of a layman, advanced in order to indicate the kind of action which might be feasible. They are exemplary, not definitive. They are also advanced on the understanding that no set of legal provisions, however carefully drafted, can ensure that a practice like the closed shop is only used in ways that are functionally justifiable. Despite the actions of any public authority in the future, men will probably continue to be expelled and excluded in ways which are contrary to natural justice and in circumstances where such action is unnecessary. For this reason it is advisable, finally, to stress that a satisfactory legal framework does not involve acceptance of the fact that no injustice can take place. Because of this one may still want to condemn a particular act of expulsion, or exclusion, without desiring to change the law to make it illegal. One may still want to say to trade unionists, 'Of course, you are legally entitled to do this, and you should be so entitled, but I still feel that in this particular instance it ought not to be done'.

Yet this qualification needs to be stated with care lest it gives rise to the wrong impression. For what it is worth, the writer does not believe that British trade unionists, on the whole, habitually use the sanctions of the closed shop in an unnecessarily illiberal way. They may justify their right to impose exclusion 'in all circumstances', by reference to the common obligation argument, but very often, in practice, they admit the relevance of the principle of functional justification. This seems to me to be quite admissable. So long as, when enforcing the closed shop, one has regard to the needs of functional justification, it does not matter if one argues 'in principle' that workers have no 'right' to refuse to support the union from whose activities they derive benefits.

In effect this comes to mean no more than that every worker 'ought to join his appropriate trade union'. This I believe.

APPENDIX

A NOTE ON THE ESTIMATES CONTAINED IN CHAPTER TWO

I. SOURCES

Three sorts of information were required: (a) information concerning the distribution of the labour force, broken down into the required occupations; (b) information concerning the unions organizing such groups, and their level of organization; (c) information about the prevalence of the closed shop, the forms it takes and attitudes towards it in each industry.

(a) The Distribution of the Labour Force

The basic source was the Ministry of Labour Gazette, supplemented by information supplied by the Ministry and other Government Departments. Also of use was the Annual Abstract of Statistics, the Census of Production, the Census of Distribution, the Reports of the Traffic Commissioners, the Central Register Office's Classification of Occupations, the Digest of Civil Service Staff Statistics, the Reports of nationalized industries, and various detailed figures concerning the distribution of the labour force in their industry collected by particular employers' associations.

(b) Union Organization

Information was collected from 107 unions and employees' associations. Virtually all important unions with a membership affected by the closed shop were contacted. In the case of many of the larger unions it was necessary to interview a considerable number of officials, with a knowledge of the position in different sections of industry.

Unionization figures were based on affiliations to the T.U.C. and various federations, where unions were members of such bodies, and returns to the Registrar of Friendly Societies where this was not the case. In a minority of cases it was necessary to obtain the membership of unaffiliated and unregistered unions, and these were requested from the union concerned. Use was also made of confidential censuses conducted by individual unions. In case of the Woodworkers and the Engineers it was possible to conduct a specially designed sample survey of branches containing questions concerning the industrial distribution of the union's membership.

(c) The Prevalence of the Closed Shop, its forms and attitudes adopted towards it

Information for use under this heading was obtained from each of the 107 unions contacted, and similar inquiries were made of 54 employers'

and employees' associations, and representatives of the employers' side of
33 joint negotiating bodies. It was possible to supplement this information
by means of six additional sources. These were:

1. Statistics and records supplied by the Ministry of Labour relating to recorded
   closed shop strikes for the years 1945–57.[1]
2. A confidential study of the closed shop in British industry, undertaken by the
   personnel department of a large engineering firm.[2]
3. A survey of A.S.W. Branch Secretaries.[3]
4. A survey of A.E.U. Branch Secretaries.[4]
5. A survey of engineering firms.[5]
6. A survey of shop stewards, employed mainly in engineering.[6]

2. RELATIVE RELIABILITY OF THE ESTIMATES

Five features contribute towards the reliability of the estimates. First,
and most important, reliable estimates are much easier to obtain when the
group in question is commonly accepted to be either *comprehensively*
open or closed. As soon as it is admitted that there remains a substantial
proportion of non-unionists surrounding a closed shop section, the problem of measurement arises.

Secondly, reliable information is more readily available when the
practice is *accepted* by both sides. Estimates of the number of workers in
formal closed shops are especially reliable, but even where the practice has
been accorded informal recognition for some time, there is usually little
doubt as to its extensiveness, the form it takes, or the number of workers
covered. On the other hand, when the practice is to some extent imposed
on an unwilling management by means of local union strength, there is
often some disagreement between union and management representative
as to the extent of the practice, and the observer may have to decide for
himself between them.

Thirdly, reliable estimates are much more easy to obtain when the
industry is *centralized*, either under the control of one owner, or if organized by one or a small number of unions.

Fourthly, in a small minority of cases, failure to persuade those in a
position to know to reveal their *knowledge*, may result in inadequate
information, or the degree of frankness shown by union and employer
may result in the observer doubting the general usefulness of what he
has been told.

Finally, in some cases it was clear that the information gathered could
have been made more complete if additional *research* had been undertaken,
but pressure of time, and the relative unimportance of the group involved,
combined to force the writer to decide against this.

[1] See p. 64 above. [2] See p. 89 above.
[3] See p. viii above. [4] See p. viii above.
[5] See p. 70 above. [6] See p. 286 below.

These five factors may be referred to respectively as the degrees of *comprehensiveness, recognition, centralization, co-operation* and *research*. They are present in varying degrees in varying cases and because of this the important thing to determine is whether or not the information about a particular group is *on balance* more or less reliable. When this is done it is possible to compile a list of groups the information about which can be ranged roughly in order of possible margins of error. Three broad categories may be noted, and the types of groups they cover are set out below.

(a) Groups where the margin of error is insignificant

This category includes all the comprehensively closed groups and mixed groups covered by the formal closed shop such as co-operative workers, i.e. about 47 per cent of all workers affected. The closed shop position in all these groups is well known, and subject to little dispute. Similarly clear is the position in the comprehensively open groups, such as the non-industrial civil service, education, agriculture, and so on.

(b) Groups where the margin of error may be more significant

Most 'mixed' groups come in this category, which contains just over 46 per cent of all workers in closed shops. It is dominated by the engineering and building and civil engineering trades, which between them account for approximately 71 per cent of workers in this category.

The remaining 29 per cent are drawn from a variety of trades—e.g. semi-skilled and unskilled workers in iron and steel, clothing workers, fishermen, skilled maintenance workers in the closed shop dominated trades, and other textile and transport workers. It was necessary to make an estimate of the size of the closed shop area in each case, but it is thought that there was sufficient information available to enable this to be done with reasonable accuracy. In most of these trades there is no dispute of substance between employers and unions concerning the prevalence of the practice, and in many of them the closed shop, where it exists, is generally recognized.

In the case of engineering and building and civil engineering, it was necessary to undertake additional inquiries before a similar degree of accuracy could be achieved. In engineering, by far the largest industry, three separate surveys were undertaken. First, a cross-section of ninety engineering firms with a labour force of over 200,000 were contacted, and details of the closed shop position were collected from management and union representatives. Second, advantage was taken of a survey of local union representatives being undertaken by three members of Nuffield College—Mr. H. A. Clegg, Mr. Rex Adams, and Mr. A. J. Killick, in connection with their book *Trade Union Officers*.[1] They asked

---

[1] *Op. cit.*, see p. 29 for details concerning this questionnaire.

students of Ruskin College to handle a questionnaire addressed to shop stewards in their home districts containing a number of questions about the closed shop. 226 respondents replied, drawn from every important industrial district. Eighty-eight of these were employed in a cross-section of engineering firms.

Thirdly, a questionnaire containing a number of closed shop questions was circulated to a representative cross-section of A.E.U. branch secretaries. Returns covered approximately 15 per cent of A.E.U. branches.

Each one of these surveys supported very similar estimates of the extent of the closed shop, and they all confirmed the views of union officers and others who maintained that engineering was a mainly closed trade. This conclusion was also reinforced by the results of the confidential survey undertaken by the personnel department of a large engineering firm which the writer was allowed to see.[1] This was largely concentrated on the engineering industry, and was based on extensive inquiries made in a further twenty-six firms.

In building and civil engineering the difficulties to be overcome before a reasonably accurate estimate could be made of the extent of the closed shop were less complex. The numbers involved were smaller, central information was more reliable, and it was accepted that there were few closed shops outside craftsmen. It was clear that the major source of further information was the craft unions, and ideally a survey of the position in all the major organizations should have been undertaken. Eventually it was decided that only one survey was practicable, and the largest union was chosen—i.e. the Woodworkers. This union recruits among 30 per cent of the craftsmen in building and civil engineering. A questionnaire was distributed to a structured sample of 25 per cent of branches. It was returned by 75 per cent of those contacted, representing 19 per cent of the union's total membership.

Assuming that the other craft unions have managed to impose the closed shop on the same proportion of their members as the A.S.W. there would seem to be just over 100,000 craftsmen affected. Bearing in mind what is known about the position in other unions, this seems a reasonable assumption. Groups like the bricklayers are reckoned to have relatively few closed groups, whereas the painters are thought to have more than their proportionate share. Probably the safest course was to accept the figure of 100,000 as a rough total for the whole industry, that is to say *inclusive* of labourers affected by the closed shop. The probability is that this underestimates the spread of the practice.

(c) Groups in which the margin of error is most significant

This category consists mostly of mainly open groups which are closed shop prone—e.g. the paper-box and carton trade, other mining and quarrying, small-scale metal using, chemicals, non-metalliferous mining products,

See p. 89 above.

and so on. Also included are some groups that are not closed shop prone, such as local government employees and gas and electricity supply workers. In most cases a series of circumstances combine to result in the presence of a margin of error which it is difficult to eliminate. In some cases the problem arises from the disputed nature of attempts to impose the closed shop, and the absence of compatible accounts of its prevalence coming from both sides of industry. In other instances, both the lack of centralized knowledge, insufficient co-operation or inadequate research, resulted in not enough being found out to justify making a precise estimate. Whatever the reason, it is among these trades that one has most doubts about the estimates made, though even here the total effect of all the possible errors involved should not be exaggerated.

First, the total number of workers covered by the closed shop in any one group in this category is small, often extremely small. It follows that although the actual margin of error in any one case may be large, the total effect of all possible errors cannot be very substantial. In any case, only about 7 per cent of the total number of workers estimated to be in closed shops are employed in groups of this kind.

In the second place, and even if this were not the case, it has been decided throughout to err on the cautious side. That is to say, where there was a serious doubt as to which one of a series of figures was the right one, a figure was decided well on the low side of the estimates. The reason for this was that one of the main contentions drawn from the estimates and developed in subsequent chapters, was the widespread nature of the closed shop and the conclusion that follows from this; that it should be regarded as a normal industrial practice demands for which are the rule rather than the exception as the level of unionization rises. To establish this it was essential to show that the closed shop covered a substantial proportion of trade unionists, and an even larger section of those with a high level of unionization. It is submitted that this contention has been established, using estimates that err—to the extent that they do—on the conservative side.

It follows that even if the overall estimates were inaccurate by as much as 20 per cent, which is extremely unlikely, the *actual* figures would probably only tend to confirm still more the basic proposition they are used to support.

TABLE OF STATUTES AND CASES CITED

Statutes

1871, Trade Union Act, 34 & 35 Vict., c. 31 . . . . 198f.
1871, Criminal Law Amendment Act, 34 & 35 Vict., c. 32   199, 252
1875, Conspiracy and Protection of Property Act, 38 & 39 Vict.,
  c. 86 . . . . . . 199, 207, 214, 250, 252
1906, Trade Disputes Act, 6 Edw. 7, c. 47 . . 199n, 207–13
1927, Trade Dispute & Trade Unions Act, 17 & 18, Geo. 5, c. 22   57
1946, Trade Disputes & Trade Union Act, 9 & 10 Geo. VI, c. 51   57
1956, Restrictive Trade Practices Act, 4 & 5 Eliz. 2, c. 68 . .231–41

Cases

Abbot v. Sullivan, (1952) 1 Q.B. 189 . . . . . 227n.
Allen v. Flood, (1898) A.C. 1 . . . . 200–4, 206, 218f.
Andrews v. National Union of Public Employees (1955) *The
  Times*, July 9 . . . . 224n.
Bent's Brewery v. Hogan, (1945) 2 All E.R. 570 . . . 215n.
Bonsor v. Musicians' Union, (1956) A.C. 104. . 223n., 245n., 249
Bowen v. Hall, (1881) 6 Q.B.D. 333 . . . . . 207n.
Bradford Corpn. v. Pickles, (1895) A.C. 587 . . . . 201n.
Burn v. Nat. Amalgamated Labourers Union, 2 Ch. 364 . 224n.
Cassel v. Inglis, (1916) 2 Ch. 211 . . . . . 228n.
Conway v. Wade, (1900) A.C. 506 . . . . . 215n.
Clarke v. National Union of Furniture Trade Operatives, (1957)
  The Times, Oct. 18 . . . . 229n.
Crofter Hand Woven Harris Tweed v. Veitch, (1942) A.C.
  435 . . . . 210, 218
Dawkins v. Antrobus, (1881) 17 Ch. D. 615 . . 224n., 227n., f.
Evans v. National Union of Printing Book-binding & Paper
  Workers, (1938) 4 All E.R. 51 . . . . . 225n.
Gaskell v. Lancashire & Cheshire Miners Federation, (1912)
  28 T.L.R. 518 208
Harkness v. Electrical Trades Union, (1956) *The Times*, June
  26–30 . . . . 270n.
Hayman v. Governors of Rugby School, (1874) 18 Eq. 28 . 228n.
Hodges v. Webb, (1920) 2 Ch. 70 209
Huntley v. Thornton, (1957) 1 All E.R. 234 . 215n., 228, 249–52,
  266n., 275–7
Huttley v. Simmons, (1897) 14 T.L.R. 150 . . . 203
Kearney v. Lloyd, (1890) L.R. Ir. 286 . . . . 203n.

Cases—continued

Kelly *v.* National Society of Operative Printers and Assistants,
(1915) 84 L.J. K.B. 2236 224
Larkin *v.* Long, (1915) A.C. 814 . . . . . . 215n.
Lee *v.* Showman's Guild, (1952) 1 All E.R. 1180 . 225–8, 245n.
Leeson *v.* General Council etc., (1890) 43 Ch. D. 366 . . 224n.
London Export Corporation *v.* Jubilee Coffee Roasting Co.,
(1958) 2 All E.R. 411 . . . . 228n.
Maclean *v.* The Workers' Union, (1929) 1 Ch. D. 602 . 224–7n.
McGuire *v.* Andrews and Others, (1904) *The Times*, March 8 . 218
Mogul S.S. Co. *v.* McGregor, Gow & Co., (1892) A.C. 25
186n., 200–2, 206, 210
Norman *v.* National Dock Labour Board, (1957) 1 Lloyds
Report 455 . . . . 227n.
Quinn *v.* Leathem, (1901) A.C. 495 . . 200, 203–7, 209–10, 213
R. *v.* Bunn, (1872) 12 Cox 316 . . . . . . 199n.
R. *v.* Stainer, (1870) L.R. 1 C.C.R. 230 . . . . 186n.
R. *v.* Starling, (1665) 1 Sid. 174 . . . . . . 186n.
Reynolds *v.* Shipping Federation, (1924) 1 Ch. D. 28 . 130, 209f.
Rookes *v.* Barnard, (1961) 2 All E.R. 825 (1962) 2 All E.R.
579 . . . . 212, 261, 266n.
Russell *v.* Norfolk, (1949) 1 All E.R. 109 . . . . 227n
Spring *v.* National Association of Stevedores and Dockers, (1956)
2 All E.R. 221 . . . . 73n.
Taff Vale *v.* Amalgamated Society of Railway Servants, (1901)
A.C. 426 206
Temperton *v.* Russell, (1893) 1 Q.B. 435 . . . 207n., 210n.
Tunney *v.* Orchard, (1955) 15 W.W.R. (N.S.) 49 (M.C.A.) . 247n.
Valentine *v.* Hyde, (1919) 2 Ch. 129 . . . . . 209n.
Ward Lock & Co. Ltd. *v.* Operative Printers' Assistants' Socy.
(1906) 22 T.L.R. 327 . . . . 214n.
Weinberger *v.* Inglis, (1919) A.C. 606 . . . . 228f., n.
White *v.* Riley, (1921) 1 Ch. 1 . . . . . . 209n.
Wolstenholme *v.* the Amal. Musicians' Union, (1920) 2 Ch. D.
388 225
Young *v.* Ladies Imperial Club, (1920) 2 K.B. 523 . . 224n., 228n.
Reports of the Restrictive Practices Cases, Vol. 1, March 1957–
December 1959, Incorporated Council of Law Reporting for
England and Wales, London, 1960 235

INDEX

Individual trade unions and professional associations will be found indexed under the general heading Trade Unions and Professional Associations. Items which are treated in the text specifically in their relation to the closed shop will be found indexed under Closed Shop.

Adams, Rex, 153, 284
Allen, V. L., 5–7, 59, 80, 84, 87–90, 104, 258, 271f.
Apprenticeship Ratios, 18, 38, 46, 136–8, 140
Askwith, G. R., 205n., 206f., 218n., 219
Authorization Principle, 223–6

Barou, N., 4, 6
Bevin, Ernest, 42
Bilateral Regulation, 98
Blacklegs, 6 (*see also* Scabs)
Booth, James, 188f., 191
Brewer, A. A., 166
Bridlington Agreement, 13, 253n., 274n.
Briggs Motor Bodies, 1, 97
British Broadcasting Corporation, 41, 69
British Motor Corporation, 15n.
British Overseas Airways Corporation, 212

Campbell, Alan, 234f.
Carr-Saunders, A. M., 75, 247n.
Chamberlain, N. W., 237, 256
Check Off, 23f., 54, 60, 74, 154
Citrine, N. A., 199n., 204, 227n., 228
Civil Service Arbitration Tribunal, 163
Clegg, H. A., vii, 145, 153, 201n., 276, 284
Closed Shop:
    and group morality, 143–5, 155f., 159, 166
    and solidarity, 80–88
    definition of, 3
    economic effects of, 188–96, 259f.
    employers' role and attitudes towards, 88–93, 167f., 171
    extent of the practice, 28–37, 78f.
Closed Shop Functions:
    entry control function, 17, 51, 56, 97, 132–43, 158, 161, 183, 194–7, 259
    discipline function, 97, 99–104
    membership function, 96–9
Closed Shop Position in Various Trades and Groups:
    actors, 57
    Admiralty workers, 47, 67, 79, 110
    American workers, 80
    bakers, 30, 53, 69, 92n., 125, 149
    boot and shoe workers, 36, 172–5
    builders and civil engineering workers, 28f., 32, 36, 65, 68, 71, 74, 109f., 148f., 157 161–8
    chemical and oil-refinery workers, 29, 31, 61, 65, 70, 90, 109, 118
    civil servants, 36, 63, 90, 162–8
    clerical and administrative workers, 34–6, 159
    clothing workers, 29, 35, 60, 70, 118, 149, 153
    comprehensively closed trades, 30, 63
    comprehensively open trades, 30
    coal miners, 29f., 32, 53f., 63, 65, 69, 80f., 115–18, 152f.
    cotton workers, 35, 67

Closed Shop Position in Various Trades and Groups—*continued*
  co-operative workers, 32, 33n., 53, 58–62
  craftsmen, 67f., 72
  distribution workers, 29, 32, 65, 74, 161, 196, 257
  dockers, 17, 29f., 37, 42, 53, 55f., 63, 69, 73f., 80f., 109, 112, 132f., 150, 155
  draughtsmen, 31, 71, 155
  electricians, 36, 58, 148, 169f., 288
  engineering workers, 28f., 31f., 48, 60, 63–7, 69f., 90, 109, 118, 149, 153, 166, 257, 286
  entertainment workers, 29, 53, 57f., 158f.
  exhibition trade workers, 125
  film and television workers, 31, 37, 41, 58, 150f., 158
  firemen, 36, 168
  fishermen, 29, 35, 37, 65, 133, 150
  food, drink and tobacco workers, 29, 118, 153
  gas workers, 35, 222
  hatters, 30, 37, 41, 63
  iron and steel workers, 29, 31, 38, 47, 49, 63, 65, 67, 156–8
  iron foundry workers, 65, 74
  journalists, 38
  Labour Party staff, 31
  local government workers, 29, 160, 288
  London Transport workers, 53, 56f.
  mainly closed trades, 30, 34, 90
  mainly open trades, 30
  maintenance workers, 68
  manufacturing workers, not elsewhere specified, 29
  motor-car workers, 199
  musicians, 31, 57f., 63, 71, 112, 149, 158f., 161, 196, 257
  newsprint workers, 17, 38
  non-manual workers, 32
  paper, box and carton workers, 29, 63, 65
  passenger transport and car hire workers, 29, 35
  pottery workers, 153
  printers, 19, 29f., 32, 37f., 45, 47, 65, 67, 81, 113f., 132, 136–9, 150–2, 155, 257, 259
  public utility workers, 29
  railwaymen, 29, 31, 36, 65, 74, 169–72
  road transport workers, 29, 47, 61, 65, 69, 110, 152, 154f., 161
  seamen, 29f., 36f., 43–5, 63, 65, 69, 109, 126–32, 158, 161, 196, 257
  service trades, 29
  shipbuilding workers, 29f., 38, 47, 63, 65, 67, 69, 71, 74, 81, 139–41, 150, 155f., 161, 259
  shop assistants, 160
  small-scale metal manufacturing workers, 29, 48
  teachers, 36, 75
  textile workers, 29, 37f., 50, 65, 153
  timber and furniture workers, 29, 35, 74
  trade union officers and staff, 31, 90
  veterinary surgeons, 32n.
  wholesale market workers, 31, 37, 39f., 63, 114, 132, 150f.
Closed Shop, Problems giving rise to demands for:
  enforcing unilateral regulations, 111–14, 151, 158, 169, 172
  inter-union competition, 110f., 166f., 172
  organizing and controlling the alternative labour force, 125–43, 150, 156–9, 166, 169, 172
  strike control, 122–5, 157f., 174
  strike solidarity, 114–22, 150, 152, 157, 169, 174
  turnover and contact, 108–10, 150, 152–7, 165, 169, 172
  worker indifference, 111
Closed Shop Prone Trades, 33–6, 78f., 89, 118, 149, 155
Closed Shop Strikes, 54, 64–6, 79, 88–92
Closed Shop, Trade Union Attitudes and Justifications for, 145f., 179–82

Closed Shop, Variations within the Practice:
 enforcement variations, 52
  formal recognition, 20, 52–64
  informal recognition, 21f., 53f., 58, 62–4
  union enforcement, 21f., 53–6, 58, 62–4
  employer initiated closed shops, 59f., 159f.
 form variations, 37
  craft qualification shop, 19, 38, 45–9
  labour pool shop, 17f., 37, 42–5
  labour supply shop, 37f., 39, 41
  post-entry shop, 16, 37, 52, 152–7, 183
  pre-entry shop, 16
  promotion veto shop, 20, 38, 49–51
 minor variations, 23f., 74f.
 regional variations, 72–4, 79
 scope variations, 22f., 67–74
Cole, G. D. H., 5f.
Common Obligation Argument, 179–84
Compulsory Trade Unionism, 7–9
Conservative Party, 40n., 61
Conspiracy:
 civil conspiracy, 199f., 202f., 203–7, 211, 222, 251
 criminal conspiracy, 198f.
Co-operative Movement, 29

Deakin, Arthur, 180
Denning, Lord Alfred, 226, 227f., n., 245–8
Drage, Geoffrey, 4
Dunlop, J. T., 236
Durham County Council, 61

Elles, P. M., 234f.
Evans, Sir Lincoln, 124n.

Federation of Master Printers, 138
Flanders, Allan, vii, 18n., 20n., 201n., 257n.
Fox, Alan, vii, 173–5
Functional Justification, 261–81

Gallup Poll on Trade Unions, 3n., 82f.
Gardner, A. H., 215n.
Goldstein, J., 108, 271n.
Graham, F. P., viii, 100, 228f., 248n., 249
Grunfeld, Cyril, vii, 100n., 224n., 225–7

Hedges, R. W., 186n.
Hobsbawm, E. J., 132
Hodge, John, 123
Hopkins, Father, 127–9n.
Houghton, Douglas, 163n.
Howell, George, 4
Humphreys, R. V., 163n.

Inns of Court Conservative and Unionist Society, 233n., 242, 252, 254, 258, 267

Jeffrys, J. B., 142f., n.

Kahn-Freund, Otto, vii, 181n., 201n., 210, 256f.
Killick, A. J., 153, 284
Knowles, K. G. J. C., vii, 64, 91n., 115n.
Korgham, V. L., 233n.

Labour, Ministry of, 27f., 61, 64–6, 91n., 132n., 284f.
Labour Party, 61f., 90, 159
Leiserson, W. M., 80
Lerner, S. W., 12, 167n.
Lipset, S. M., 264–6
Lloyd, Dennis, 226n., 228, 229n., 247f.
London Passenger Transport Board, 57

Marsh, A. I., viii
McKelvey, J. T., 56–8
Membership Choice, 74
Meyers, F. W., 265, 273n.
Miller, G. W., 86n.
Milne-Bailey, W., 6f., 79
Ministry of Labour (*see* Labour, Ministry of)

National Arbitration Tribunal, 174n.
National Coal Board, 53f.
National Dock Labour Board, 42, 52, 132
National Incomes Commission, 240n.
National Labor Relations Board (U.S.A.), 263, 266
National Maritime Board, 44, 131
Natural Justice, 226–30, 267–9

'100 per cent Trade Unionism', 10f., 16
Open Union Principle, 243, 255
Open Shop Trades, 26, 32, 34, 89
Order 1376, 61
Oxford University Press, 63n.

Page-Arnot, R., 116f.
Parkinson J. R., 141n., 196n., 260
Pay Pause (1961), 164
Plymouth Brethren, 182n.
Professional Associations, 75–8
Pugh, Sir Arthur, 124

Registrar of Friendly Societies, 28n., 252f., 280, 284
Registration Shop, 120, 263–7, 279f.
Restrictive Practices Court, 231–4, 255
Rideout, R. W., viii
Right to Entry to a Union, 229
Right to Work Laws (U.S.A.), 264–6
Roberts, B. C., 7n.
Rosen, N., 86n.
Rottenburg, Simon, 40f., n., 114
Ruskin College, 287
Royal Commissions:
    on the Press (1961–2), 114, 196n., 239n., 244, 259
    on Trade Disputes and Trade Combinations (1903–5), 205n., 206f.
    on Trade Unions and other Associations (1867–9), 4, 186–99, 208–12, 255.
    on Labour (1894), 113
    on Civil Service Pay (1930–1 and 1953–5), 163n.

Scabs, 177 (*see also* Blacklegs)
Scottish Association of Master Bakers, 56
Screening, 20–22
Semi-closed shop, 24–6, 34, 36, 47, 53, 79, 153, 170f., 174
Shipping Federation, 44f., 126–30, 209
Skill gap, 134–43
Slessor, Henry, 6f.
Slichter, Sumner H., 264
Smith, George, 85

Smithfield Market, Report of the Court of Inquiry into Industrial Unrest in, 40
Society of West-End Theatre Managers, 57f.
Stone, Julius, 205n.
Sultan, Paul, 87n., 236n., 241, 263n., 265

Taft-Hartley Act (U.S.A.), 243n., 263, 264–6n.
Tannenbaum, Frank, 238
Thorne, Will, 133
Tillyard, Sir Frank, 23n.
Trade Dispute, definition of, 208f., 215f., 250–3
Trading Interest Defence, 201–5, 207, 209–13, 217–20, 250–2, 276f.
Trades Union Congress:
    annual reports, 11
    attitude towards closed shop, 180–2
    Disputes Committee, 12, 73, 75
    Interim Report on Structure and Closer Unity, 12–16
Trade Union Rule Books, 99–103, 248f., 253–75, 267–75, 280
Trade Unions and Professional Associations:
    Amalgamated Engineering Union, viii, 14, 46–8, 100n., 101, 111, 142f., 166, 249, 268, 272, 284f., 287
    Amalgamated Society of Journeymen Felt-Hatters, 41n.
    Amalgamated Society of Woodworkers, viii, 46, 68, 284f., 287
    Amalgamated Union of Building Trade Workers, 47, 143
    Amalgamated Union of Foundry Workers, 48
    Association of Broadcasting Staffs, 41
    Association of Cinematograph and Allied Technicians, 41, 58, 69
    Association of Locomotive Engineers and Firemen, 169
    British Iron, Steel and Kindred Trades Association, 49, 101, 104, 122–5, 131n., 268
    British Medical Association, 61, 77n.
    Civil Service Clerical Association, 154, 165
    Confederation of Heath Service Employees, 100n., 268
    Draughtsmen and Allied Technicians' Association, 212–14
    Electrical Trades Union, 170
    Equity, 57f.
    Fire Brigades Union, 168
    Musicians' Union, 112, 270n.
    National Association of Local Government Officers, 33n.
    National Association of Stevedores and Dockers, 42, 73f.
    National Passenger Workers' Union, 57, 110
    National Society of Operative Printers and Assistants, 38f., 114
    National Union of Blastfurnacemen, 49
    National Union of Boot and Shoe Operatives, 172–5
    National Union of Dyers, Bleachers and Textile Workers, 39
    National Union of General and Municipal Workers, 14, 15n., 39, 42, 110, 153, 170, 227n., 248, 272
    National Union of Labour Organizers and Election Agents, 160
    National Union of Mineworkers (including Miners' Federation of Great Britain), 53f., 116–18, 181n.
    National Union of Printing Bookbinding and Paper Workers, 38, 45, 102, 108n.
    National Union of Public Employees, 110
    National Union of Railwaymen, 169–71, 172n.
    National Union of Seamen, 43, 69
    National Union of Sheet Metal Workers, Braziers and Coppersmiths, 48
    National Union of Tailor and Garment Workers, 35
    National Union of Teachers, 61
    National Union of Vehicle Builders, 14, 48, 111, 143
    Post Office Engineering Union, 164–6, 167n.
    Scottish Union of Bakers and Allied Workers, 56, 92
    Scottish Transport and General Workers' Union, 42
    Tobacco Workers' Union, 35
    Transport and General Workers' Union, 14, 15n., 39f., 42, 45, 57f., 73f., 86, 104, 108, 110f., 153f., 211, 248

Trade Unions and Professional Associations—*continued*
  Typographical Association, 136–9
  Union of Post Office Workers, 164
  Union of Shop, Distributive and Allied Workers, 58, 99n.
  United Society of Boilermakers, Blacksmiths, Shipbuilders and Structural Workers, 46–8
    100, 114, 139, 259, 270, 272
  Watermen, Lighter, Tugmen and Bargemen's Union, 42
Trade Unionists in Closed Shops, 28, 33, 34, 37
Truck Acts, 23
Tupper, Captain Edward, 129f., 177
Turner, H. A., 51n.

Unilateral Regulation, 95, 111–14

Vester, H., 215n.

Wallis, George, 59f., n.
Webb, Beatrice and Sydney, 8, 112, 134, 179, 185, 189, 193–5, 198
Wedderburn, K. W., vii, 213n., 274n.
Whitmore, E. F., 247
Wilberforce, R. O., 234f.
Wiles, Peter, 259
Williams, Gertrude, 49, 140f.
Wilson, P. A., 75
Wilson, Havelock, 126, 129
Wooton, Barbara, 236n.

Zweig, F., 196n.